Transforming
Citizenship

Transforming Citizenship

DEMOCRACY, MEMBERSHIP, AND BELONGING IN LATINO COMMUNITIES

RAYMOND A. ROCCO

Michigan State University Press • East Lansing

♾ The paper used in this publication meets the minimum requirements of
ANSI/NISO Z39.48-1992 (R 1997) (Permanence of Paper).

 Michigan State University Press
East Lansing, Michigan 48823-5245

Printed and bound in the United States of America.

20 19 18 17 16 15 14   1 2 3 4 5 6 7 8 9 10

LIBRARY OF CONGRESS CATALOGING-IN-PUBLICATION DATA
Rocco, Raymond A.
Transforming citizenship : democracy, membership, and belonging in
Latino communities / Raymond A. Rocco.
pages cm.—(Latinos in the United States series)
Includes bibliographical references and index.
ISBN 978-1-61186-133-4 (pbk. : alk. paper)—ISBN 978-1-60917-418-7 (pdf)—
ISBN 978-1-62895-001-4 (epub)—ISBN 978-1-62896-001-3 (mobi) 1. Hispanic
Americans—Politics and government. 2. Hispanic Americans—Ethnic
identity. 3. Citizenship—United States. 4. Political participation—United
States. I. Title.
E184.S75635 2014
305.868'073—dc23
2013046122

Cover and book design by Charlie Sharp, Sharp Des!gns, Lansing, Michigan

g green Michigan State University Press is a member of the Green Press
  press Initiative and is committed to developing and encouraging
  INITIATIVE
ecologically responsible publishing practices. For more information about
the Green Press Initiative and the use of recycled paper in book publishing,
please visit *www.greenpressinitiative.org*.

Visit Michigan State University Press at *www.msupress.org*

Contents

RUBÉN O. MARTINEZ

Transnational Workers and the Politics of Citizenship

THE LIBERALIZATION OF ECONOMIC MARKETS ACROSS THE GLOBE HAS INTENSI-fied the growth of a global economy and increased the migration of workers across national boundaries. The phenomenon of runaway plants, that is, plants closing in industrialized nations and opening in countries with lower operating structures, was part of the processes of globalization. Also central to the globalization processes was the imposition of structural adjustment policies on developing countries by the International Monetary Fund and the World Bank. To receive loans and/or low interest rates on loans, the borrowing nation had to adopt free-market practices of Western industrialized nations, including the elimination of trade barriers, deregulation of the economy, and the transfer of public-sector services to the private sector. These neoliberal policies and practices framed the rise of the global economy, and promoted the displacement of millions of people throughout the globe. Here in the United States, middle-class jobs declined while job growth was limited to low- and high-wage sectors. The growth of low-wage jobs was met by displaced workers from south of the border who came seeking opportunities to make a living, often not thinking of themselves as immigrants, but rather as transnational workers.

Transnational workers parallel the growth of the transnational capitalist class and its attendant "service class fraction," in the sense that where capital demands labor, workers will show up. Capital demands for low-wage labor in the United States are reflected in the rapid growth in numbers over the past three decades of foreign-born Latinos, many of whom are undocumented. Once here, these workers continue to maintain strong kinship and network ties to their communities of origin, giving their lives a truly transnational dimension, though perhaps not as flamboyant as that of their capitalist counterparts. These experiences as transnational workers and as undocumented immigrants have engendered widespread sensitivity among them regarding their rights both as workers and as human beings, and have brought into sharp focus issues surrounding citizenship. The influx of transnational workers engendered nativistic movements that challenged their presence here and demanded their exclusion and deportation. At the same time, at least one view of the concept of cultural citizenship was used to promote the normative view that there ought to be dialogue about the complexity that arises when national cultures become increasingly fragmented. This includes listening to the voices of the excluded; that is, those living outside the mainstream of American society.

On another level, however, life on a transnational plane gives rise to critical questions about citizenship and global citizenship. For example, does displacement from one's homeland and exclusion from the core institutions of the receiving society mean that, de facto, one has no human rights, no platform from which to voice one's concerns, and no society to which to belong? The nativists would respond with a vehement yes to this question. But what does their denial of rights to others produce in the lives of the excluded? What is the experience of non-citizenship, and how does one cope when one is in such a situation? How does one connect to or create a sense of community and build bonds of solidarity while occupying the status of non-citizen? How does one become part of society in an informal way that goes beyond the private realm and integrates one into the public realm? How does a family with citizen and non-citizen children cope with the glaring inequalities in opportunities and protections that distinguish their lives? All of these are questions about the experiential aspects of transnational workers and their families. Moreover, the experiences that attend these dimensions of transnational workers' lives are those that will frame and shape the future of citizenship both at national and global levels. Theoretical, empirical, and normative studies will surely be published as we move into the global future.

I am pleased to present Raymond Rocco's *Transforming Citizenship* as a pioneering work on associative citizenship and Latinos within the series on Latinos in the United States. His study focuses on the political conditions and issues produced by the rise of globalization and transnational workers. His work makes a significant contribution to the systematic study of the experiential aspects of the rights of Latino immigrants and transnational workers and the political challenges that have arisen in this country through their presence. Moreover, he makes it clear that associational networks serve as the basis upon which Latino immigrants have been able to generate movements that have given voice to their rights claims.

I am grateful to our mutual and good friend John Bretting for bringing Ray's work to my attention. It was he who called me early one Saturday morning a couple of years ago talking excitedly about the manuscript that Ray was producing. It was that call that led me to communicate with Ray and to reconnect with him on this project after the passage of many years since we had last seen each other. It has been both quite illuminating and gratifying to work with him over the past several months. Indeed, editing the series has been enormously fulfilling in this way for me. It is because of these intrinsic rewards that I look forward to new volumes in the series on Latinos in the United States, for I know that they will lead to the renewal of lapsed professional ties and the creation of new ones.

SUZANNE OBOLER

Foreword

WHAT DOES CITIZENSHIP MEAN IN THE CURRENT CONTEXT OF GLOBALIZATION and the consequent changing nature of the state? And insofar as citizenship signals membership in a society, what does it really mean to "belong" to a community of citizens? Who belongs, and how do people experience that belonging today? How do we even "know" that we belong?

Questions such as these long been a challenge for both scholars and activists concerned with the vicissitudes of membership and its meanings in national communities. In the U.S. context, their complexity has been reinforced as much by the mutability of race, of exclusion, as by the limitations of traditional liberal political theories that both contribute to and detract from our understanding of their impact on our society's daily life.

Certainly, the current era of globalization has contributed to exacerbating the grounds for inclusion and exclusion, bringing the role of diversity in social dynamics to the fore, increasing its significance and its centrality as much for public policies as for political theories and practice. Thus, in approaching issues of inclusion and exclusion, of who belongs in a given society, it is no longer sufficient to theorize political citizenship without fully incorporating the realities of racialization and difference that so thoroughly permeate and mark the political and social arenas of every society. Indeed, as Raymond Rocco's *Transforming Citizenship* impressively argues, their inherent relationship must be brought to light and better understood such that their interaction, and the multiple ways they are experienced in daily life are made central to any theorization of membership and its political expression in citizenship.

In this brilliantly argued book, Rocco transports us into the very core assumptions of earlier contributions by political theorists and thinkers whose efforts have focused largely on building on past liberal theories of inclusion that neglect to consider the lived experience of the millions of people whose race has long relegated them to social invisibility. In so doing, he shows how their consequent social exclusion and marginality is inextricably linked with the institutional frameworks and contexts within and through which citizenship finds its expression. Taking his readers through a step-by-step assessment of the ways that traditional liberal theorization of citizenship has long failed to fully address issues of diversity, Rocco then goes on to develop an alternative model for approaching citizenship—one that, as his case-study example suggests, is fully grounded in the inclusive concept of "associative citizenship"—to thus account for the millions who have long been excluded from full membership in the nation. Indeed, the import of this book's masterful theoretical contributions to our understanding of citizenship should not be underestimated. For, if it is true that the measure of a just society is how it treats its least fortunate, it is essential that any understanding of citizenship must also incorporate the lived experience of all its members, including those who have been relegated to what Partha Chatterjee once deemed the "fragments" of the nation.

Two singular events can serve here to briefly exemplify the multiple particularities of the lived experiences of citizenship as it is expressed on the ground. Despite their differences, they serve to point to the kinds of participatory experiences that must be included in any effort to construct an inclusive theory of citizenship. As Rocco's text emphasizes, it must both account for the diversity of the national community and simultaneously acknowledge the changing nature of the global context that is unambiguously contributing to the expansion of both the boundaries and the definition of the national community today.

The first is Barack Obama's long campaign in 2007–2008, prior to his first presidency—a campaign grounded in the "belief in the American people," as he so often insisted. This was a campaign that urged, and led, millions of Americans, regardless of race, class, ethnicity—and, as it turned out, also regardless of formal U.S. citizenship—to believe that they could indeed transform their discourse on hope, on "change we can believe in," into action by participating in the building of the largest social movement in the history of this country. The dramatic victory—the announcement that Barack Hussein Obama, an African American, would indeed become "the next President of the United States"—gave credence to the claim that "*Yes we can*," and brought those same millions together, whether on the streets of their cities and towns, in Chicago's Grant Park, through shared televised images, conscious as they all were of the historical and symbolic implications of this unprecedented gathering. A powerful current of achievement spread across the country, a singular moment that brought a sense of (re)empowerment to the people of the United States as citizens all, an experience of belonging born out of participation in what for many months had seemed more like a national social movement than an electoral campaign.

A similar current of hope—and yes, a moment of belonging, of citizenship irrespective of legal status—had been experienced two years before, in 2006, by millions of Latino/as as they, along with other immigrant nationals, also took to the streets with their chants of "*Sí se puede*" also resonating across the country, again regardless of race, of ethnicity, of class—and of political status. The main cause of their mobilization was not specifically labor or related material issues, such as wages, or better working conditions, housing, or health. Instead, the momentum came explicitly from the fact that the dignity of all Latino/as had been directly attacked by the passage of HR 4437 in December 2005, a congressional bill aimed at the criminalization of all immigrants, and implicitly aimed particularly at Latino/as, simply because they are—and/or are perceived to be—immigrants. As one Latina explained on a local Spanish radio program before the marches in Chicago, "We are going to march because we are going to show them that we are not criminals." In this case, the movement participants set aside their legal status as Latino/a citizens, residents, unauthorized immigrants, or refugees, and joined together to collectively affirm their belonging to the nation.

The two events show, unequivocally, that as the political expression of membership, the meaning of citizenship is best defined as a collectively lived sense of belonging—a sense of being "home," a sense of one's place, born primarily from daily life participation in the public sphere.

At one level, moments such as these shed light once again on the intent of such historical iconic phrases as "*We the people of the United States in order to form a more perfect union . . .*" that have for so long marked the way that U.S. citizens first learn to theorize their experience of membership in the nation. For, more than merely assuming the very existence of all who live in the United States as "a people," or imagining themselves as a community, these moments allow them to actually experience their belonging, and to affirm themselves as active participants in their nation.

Given that individuals' daily lives are marked and differentiated by the distinctive and diverse experiences created by race, by gender, class, sexuality, or generation, in approaching the study of citizenship in the United States, it thus seems important to ask: Is it even possible in this context to theorize citizenship and to understand its specificities in the messy complexity lived by the "American people"? Is it possible to fully acknowledge how they might impact traditional political theories of citizenship that have long abstracted the complexity of race from the debates on citizenship and belonging to the nation?

Certainly, as the nation's foundational documents and the tumultuous history of racism in U.S. society both attest, racial minorities have long been excluded from the understanding of who actually constitute "the people" of the United States. Indeed, from its very beginnings, the multiple struggles for citizenship and belonging in the nation have been indelibly marked as much by this exclusion as by the consequent nebulous terms of a legal inclusion gained largely through political and social struggles that have dominated the many debates, and movements, marches, and protests on the ground. It thus begs the question that in many ways ultimately seems to motivate Rocco's scholarship: what would happen if instead of paying mere lip service to, or overlooking, the issue of race and racial minorities' experiences, and their constant struggle for inclusion, we were instead to set race and discrimination at the core of theorizing citizenship? After all, even today the "people's" sense of belonging, like the policies and practices across the country—including New York's "Stop and Frisk" racial profiling, the lack of societal accountability or concern for the indiscriminate murders of African American and Latino youth, the unfair sentencing and disproportionate incarceration of racial minorities—clearly belies the official mantra of national commonality, the realized "*Yes, we can*" elation of both Obama's first electoral victory, and of the massive Latino/a marches of 2006–2007.

Again, it is perhaps not surprising that the meaning of citizenship and belonging has become a key issue of our times. The current era of global neoliberalism, marked by the fall of the Berlin Wall in the late 1980s, has been fed by the consolidation of a rampant capitalism with its skewed emphasis on the global expansion of financial institutions and markets, to the detriment of the social and political gains of organized labor and the practical opportunities for young people the world over. Globalization has thus visibly destabilized traditional social and economic structures of society, deepening existing political and racial differences and undermining democratic notions of justice and equality for all. Indeed, the manner in which globalization unfolded has hindered a much-needed general debate nationally, as well as within or among the older democracies, about *how* to define the very notion of a collectivity, of a national citizenry in the new techno-political context. Instead, countries became immersed in a dual process of expanding the scope of liberal democratic institutions at the state level, while simultaneously putting into question both historically inherited structures of citizenship rights and the very political reality of citizenship itself. The impact on the ground of these changes is increasingly visible today, and has manifested itself in different ways around the world, most notably through immigration and displacement, raising the dilemma of membership and the terms of belonging in yet new ways.

In the U.S. context, for example, this took the form of the "culture wars" waged in institutions and on the streets of urban areas across the country in the aftermath of the civil rights movements of the 1960s and 1970s. Throughout the 1990s, and largely spawned by the neoliberal economic policies first implemented during the Reagan years (1980–1988), these cultural struggles brought to light the extent of the societal resistance to the recognition, not of "diversity," but rather of the very real social, economic, and cultural differences created by the society's ongoing racism as experienced in minorities' daily lives. Emphasizing their right to have rights—including the right to their difference, African Americans and Latino/as in particular, along with other racial minorities, found new political and cultural forms of expression for their demands for justice, equality, and dignity. The "culture wars" of the 1990s undoubtedly contributed to affirming the very existence of difference in society. But today, as the national community increasingly accepts the decline of minorities' voting rights and access to education, their skyrocketing unemployment, their ongoing lack of adequate health care, their growing poverty and homelessness, these "wars" can also be seen to have served to justify the demise of the political and social gains of the 1960s, and most recently, to reinforce the indiscriminate and unwarranted criminalization of people of color.

In this context, Raymond Rocco's nuanced assessment of the scholarship on diversity published during this period merits close attention. Indeed, his book makes clear that while legal and societal institutions continue to grapple with the need to address inclusion, any theoretical framework proposed for the study of citizenship must account for the distinctive modes of experience in practice. As such, any effort to understand the meaning of citizenship today, as Rocco cogently argues, requires an alternative approach to its theorization—one that can simultaneously acknowledge the structural macro-realities of neoliberal globalization, and account for the changing nature of the political, economic, and demographic forces that impact the social and cultural realities of contemporary daily life in U.S. society.

This is precisely the purpose and achievement of *Transforming Citizenship*, which thus makes multiple and substantial theoretical and empirical contributions to our understanding of the challenges that the postmodern politics of belonging in U.S. society entail. Raymond Rocco's lucid discussion of Latina/os' activism and motivations is highly original and goes a long way to help change traditional ways of approaching citizenship. Focusing on the role of racialization and its impact in shaping Latino/as' exclusion, Rocco's careful and thoughtful critique of traditional liberal theorizations of citizenship, followed by his assessment of the foundational works that shaped the debates on difference and political inclusion during the 1990s culture wars era, results in an innovative framework that theoretically, empirically—and unequivocally—challenges mainstream theorists' abstract understanding of how citizenship is appropriated in society.

Grounded in empirical research on the political and social realities of Latino/as' lives and complex forms of exclusion from full participation in the U.S. polity, Rocco develops a new conceptual and empirically verifiable model of citizenship—one that can fully account for the lived experience of full membership, the constantly changing nature of political and institutional practices, and the politically limited and limiting experience of racialized minorities, particularly of Latino/as, in the United States.

He positions the analysis of rights claims within institutional spheres in the local contexts in which they occur, incorporating the "spaces of marginality" within which the excluded live their lives. In so doing, Rocco develops and exemplifies a new model of analysis, based on the concept of "associative citizenship," that is able to capture the multifaceted interaction between societal and political membership, as seen in the struggles and practical negotiations of politically underprivileged and disempowered racial minorities, to gain access to, and be able to intervene in, institutional spaces.

In developing his argument, Rocco thus eloquently demonstrates the extent to which the key theoretical and philosophical underpinnings of mainstream arguments and debates on what he calls "the current regime of citizenship" are inadequate to account for what he defines as a "complex relationship between civil society, public sphere, and rights claims." Indeed, he argues that traditional emphases on abstract definitions of citizenship have contributed to discourses that in fact obscure the historical presence, political experiences, and practices of Latino/as in daily life. As a result, they are denied being social protagonists in their own right, which reinforces their long-standing marginalization by hegemonic society.

Rocco points to four key dimensions that political theorists have for the most part failed either to take into account and/or to fully link and integrate; these serve to perpetuate the ongoing "exclusionary inclusion" of racial minorities, and specifically shape the experience of Latino/as as "perpetual foreigners." These are: membership, exclusion, belonging, and racialization. Arguing that these dimensions are apparent in the institutional and participatory forms of Latino/as' political involvement with U.S. mainstream society, Rocco rejects static and normative definitions of citizenship that cannot account for the changing dynamics of political and social relations and practices, contrasting these with his model of "associative citizenship," which captures the local and more global structural conditions impacting Latino/as' realities.

As this book brilliantly suggests, far from being unidimensional, citizenship is instead "ultimately a set of practices" that are both specific to and contingent on the concrete institutional sites in which societal membership and political membership interact. These affect identity formations and (re)define social relations, ensuring the need for continuous construction and affirmation of mutualities, trust, and solidarities necessary for the development of collective mobilization.

Moreover, as Rocco's proposed model makes abundantly clear, "associative citizenship" is *itself* a political strategy. For it allows Latinos to address—albeit often in ways that are nontraditional and that circumvent the boundaries of societal processes of exclusion—the complex political and social realities of racialized marginalization in which they negotiate their daily lives. By practicing this form of citizenship, marginalized groups develop political awareness, alliances, and interactions in institutional spaces, promoting thus a form of active participation in the life of the nation. In so doing, Latino/as both mark their presence and build political alliances, rooted in networks of trust, mutuality, and solidarity, enabling them both to challenge their location in the public sphere and, more broadly, to help redefine the meaning and practice of citizenship in the United States.

Ultimately, then, "associative citizenship" is an effective approach to postmodern political realities that is not limited solely to minorities, for it allows belonging to be formulated in a dynamic way—one that "neither sees an antagonism in every difference, nor mere differences in real antagonisms," to use B. Adamczak's thoughtful reflection in a different context.[1]

Today's political reality, immersed as it is in the cutthroat economic context of our times, needs not only to be better understood, but also transformed and overcome. Scholarship on, by, and about Latino/as is undoubtedly key to this process, engaged as it is in defining, analyzing, and debating the issues in thought-provoking and meaningful ways, while simultaneously pointing to their practical implications. *Transforming Citizenship: Democracy, Membership, and Belonging in Latino Communities* is a brilliant and rigorously argued book that is certain to make multiple and substantial contributions to our understanding of the role of racialization, its impact in shaping exclusion, and the changing meanings of citizenship and belonging in postmodern U.S. society.

Preface

FOR OVER TWO DECADES, MOST OF MY RESEARCH AND WRITING, AND A GOOD deal of my teaching, has focused on trying to understand the dynamic processes that have led to the transformation of Latino communities in the United States since the 1970s. When I was a youth growing up in a neighborhood bordering the barrios of Belvedere and El Hoyo in East Los Angeles, the contours of what it meant to be a Mexican in this country were part of the lived experience of daily life in segregated communities. For many youth of that generation who spoke virtually no English before attending grammar school, the initial encounter with white teachers who prohibited the use of Spanish while on school grounds was often a painful, tricky path that we had to travel. We were aware that there were other, segregated, older Mexican neighborhoods in Los Angeles, such as San Fernando, San Gabriel, and Wilmington. Most of us visited family, relatives, or family friends in these areas, and knew that Mexicans lived primarily in these neighborhoods and that white folks lived in the in-between spaces we saw on those family outings. We did not know why, just that that was the way it was. Fast-forward to the early 1980s when I began to notice the rapid change in the boundaries of Mexican communities throughout Los Angeles. Areas that had always been predominantly white or African American now had large concentrations of Mexicans, complete with panaderías, carnicerías, iglesias Pentecostales, and taco stands that came to life at night. The research that led to this book is rooted in that personal experience of the city's transformation that shaped the questions, perspectives, and theoretical development of the scholarly work that I have engaged in since then.

I was fortunate to explore some of these concerns with a small study group of Latino colleagues, including Rudy Torres, Francisco Vasquez, Richard Chabran, Luis Rubalcava, who met for several years in the mid to late 1980s to try to make sense of the new theoretical currents—deconstruction, cultural studies, the work of Raymond Williams, Foucault's alternative epistemology, various forms of revised Marxisms, and works by Latina feminists—all of which we looked to for direction, and as potential resources for challenging the orthodox approaches in the social sciences and humanities. Those discussions helped shape my thinking about politics; power; the relationship between race, gender, and class; and the increasingly hostile anti-Latino immigrant politics that had become evident. And I was more fortunate still to work with two colleagues, Richard Chabran from UCLA, and Luis Rubalcava from Cal State Northridge, in developing the initial research project in 1990 that eventually became the basis for *Transforming Citizenship*. Enabled by a nearly $300,000 grant from Hewlett Packard, we formed a team of three faculty and six graduate students, and over a three-year period studied the processes that transformed the industrial cities of Southeast Los Angeles from white working-class communities into overwhelmingly Latino neighborhoods; we also carried out a good deal of the fieldwork that I draw from in this book. The community formation model that I based the empirical work for the book on was essentially developed in collaboration with Richard and Luis, and so I am thankful for all I learned from their insights and critiques. The core argument we developed early on was that these changes were primarily driven by the interrelated processes of globalization, restructuring, and transnationalization. These attracted millions of immigrants from Mexico, as well as from other parts of Central and South America, who settled in cities and towns across the United States where virtually no Latino communities existed before. Using a mixed methodology that combined economic institutional analysis with ethnographies and life histories, we initially focused on studying the political economy of these processes, how they had transformed these communities, the impact on Latino households, and the types of strategies these households had developed to negotiate those changes.

However, once I began reviewing the different types of data we collected through those family and life histories, ethnographic studies of sites throughout the areas we focused on, participant observations, and informal discussions with a wide array of individuals, it became apparent that more than a process of adaptation was going on. There was a consistent pattern of behaviors, practices, and beliefs advanced by many of those we interviewed, that suggested a way of thinking about the meaning of the forms of exclusion they lived, about what it meant to belong in the United States, and about what it meant to have rights—all of which differed dramatically from how these issues and themes were understood and framed at that time in the literatures on citizenship, multiculturalism, immigration, and democracy.

It was the effort to make sense of this constellation of views, practices, and beliefs, and to relate it to those literatures that led to the development of the notion of associative citizenship, which is the core concept in the book. That notion developed late in the analysis, and so we did not enter the field with a theory that we wanted to apply; rather, the theoretical reformulation that the book advances grew out of the attempt to name and understand what was being articulated and often enacted by many individuals in these communities. Associative citizenship is essentially an alternative way of conceptualizing citizenship that is capable of accounting for the hierarchy of political status that is the real function of citizenship regimes, while at the same time identifying practices that challenge that hierarchy.

The current struggles to address the forms of marginalization that still affect large sectors of Latino communities take place within a framework and history that defines the political and discursive parameters of the conflict. While the issue of Latino citizenship is often interpreted as relating primarily to immigrants, the debates about the status of immigrants build on a particular discourse about who is an American, who belongs. The status of different groups that have a unique history in the United States has always raised questions about the ability of Mexicans and Latinos more generally to become "true Americans."

The fundamental concern with the question of "who belongs" from the earliest stages of U.S. political history is reflected in the fact that one of the first acts of Congress, the Naturalization Act of 1790, laid out the requirements for who could be considered eligible to become a member of the political community—essentially defining the parameters of political membership. And this issue has continued to be a major defining element throughout U.S. history—sometimes prominent, sometimes dormant, but always there as one of the constitutive factors that have influenced every scale of life up to the present day.

Finally, I want to acknowledge and thank some of the many colleagues, students, and friends who influenced my thinking about these and other related issues over the years. I once again want to acknowledge the collaboration and friendship of Richard Chabran and Luis Rubalcava, without whom the project that led to the book would have never been conceived and launched. My colleague and good friend of many years, Carlos Vélez-Ibañez, was also extremely important in my own intellectual and scholarly development. It was Carlos who taught me all I know about fieldwork, how to connect ethnographic study with theoretical frameworks. He taught me to listen and not just hear what the people we study say, and that it is not just data that we are collecting; the individuals who share their stories with us are collaborators and not subjects, and the best ethnographies help us to feel and understand the struggles, fears, joys, and pain of the people who trust us enough to share part of who they are with us.

Thanks to the many undergraduate students who over a period of several years were exposed to the ideas here, and who provided feedback, suggestions, and critique that forced me to sharpen my explanations. I am particularly grateful to the graduate students who were part of the first cohort of the new field of Race, Ethnicity, and Politics (REP) that we created in the Department of Political Science at UCLA in 2006. Despite considerable resistance from various quarters, they helped create a different and unique intellectual space in our department that made possible a truly critical and pluralistic option for the study of race and politics. I have been very fortunate these last few years to serve as the dissertation adviser to several students who have proven themselves to be exemplary scholars; they daily reaffirm through the seriousness and quality of their study and work that it is still possible to combine a strong political commitment to transformative politics with rigorous critical scholarship, and that the former in fact requires the latter. In particular I want to thank Raul Moreno, Albert Ponce, Alfonso Gonzales, Arely Zimmerman, Natasha Behl, Rita Rico, and several others who have been among the very best students I have worked with. They have begun their own intellectual and political journey committed to developing alternative ways of thinking, theorizing, and researching as the basis of a different, critical study of racialized politics. I should also point out here that the notion of exclusionary inclusion that I advance in the book is also used by Natasha Behl to describe the pattern of differential incorporation of Sikh women in her recent article (Behl 2014). While we developed and deploy the concept in quite different contexts, the initial formulation emerged from several years of collaborative discussion, teaching, and writing. I am very proud of these students, who are now colleagues and friends, for their courage to go against the grain, for their hard work, discipline, and faithfulness to the project we all set out to pursue. Working with them has been one of the highlights of my academic career and made the costs of the struggles to move in different scholarly and political directions more than worthwhile. The project of developing the new subfield would not have been possible without the collaboration and friendship of my colleague Mark Sawyer. Mark has not only provided both material and intellectual support for creating REP, but has also taught me a great deal about race, racial politics, and the challenges involved in developing theories and approaches that allow us to understand the complexity of the processes involved. Through our many conversations over the last fifteen years,

I learned about so many aspects of racialization that I had simply not been aware of, and so the central role of the notion of racialization in the analysis and argument of the book is a reflection of Mark's influence on my thinking.

I owe a debt of gratitude to the members of the IUP Working Group on culture, especially Renato Rosaldo, Rina Benmayor, Bill Flores, and Pedro Pedraza. The many conversations we had over a number of years resulted in a framework for connecting our individual ethnographically grounded research projects through the notion of cultural citizenship that laid the foundation for my own revised and extended version of the latter. So my thanks for their collaboration and willingness to share their work, ideas, and critiques. A different sort of debt is owed to Suzanne Oboler, who years ago invited me to be one of the associate editors of the then new journal *Latino Studies*, and especially for her counsel, support, and friendship since then. Thanks as well to the two other associate editors of the journal, Silvio Torres-Saillant and Mari Alicea, for the opportunity to work with them for the last several years. The intellectual vibrancy, joy, and good will that characterized our discussions of the broad range of themes and topics we encountered in the articles submitted to the journal greatly expanded my vision and knowledge of Latino studies as an emerging discipline; this gave me the opportunity to read and learn about aspects of the experiences and struggles of a much more diverse range of Latino communities than I had been familiar with. And thanks to Lourdes Torres for having the strength and courage to take on the task of being the new editor, and for her commitment to continue the journal's goal of promoting excellent scholarship as well as mentoring the many young Latino and Latina scholars who submitted their work.

I hope that the rigor, critical sensibility, and analytic clarity that characterized these colleagues' views will be reflected to at least some degree in this book. I also want to thank Rubén Martinez, my colleague and editor of Michigan State University Press's Latinos in the United States series, for his guidance and unwavering support for the project. And many thanks to the two anonymous reviewers who provided a series of recommendations that I have tried to incorporate; I believe that the manuscript is much the better for my having done so. I also want to thank Barbara Fitch Cobb and Elise Jajuga of the Michigan State University Press for their ex-traordinarily fine, detailed work of copy editing and final editing of the manuscript, which has undoubtedly made it a much more readable book. And thanks as well to Kristine M. Blakeslee, the managing editor of the Press, for her professionalism and support for the project.

But my greatest debt of gratitude is owed to my wife, Jackie, the most important influence on the development of this manuscript. Over the last twenty years, her love and friendship have provided unwavering, constant support for all that I have undertaken. Together we have faced and overcome professional and personal challenges, and have created a safe and loving space that has allowed us to grow and to pursue our individual goals and visions. There is no doubt that I would have never completed writing this book without Jackie in my life—without her encouragement, and the joyous home she has created for us. So I thank you for all the joy, laughter, travels, music, and dancing that has made our life together so special and made it possible for me to follow my own path.

Introduction

LATINO COMMUNITIES HAVE FACED A BROAD RANGE OF CHALLENGES AND obstacles in their long struggle to achieve equality, social justice, and equal membership in the major institutions of U.S. society. These have in fact been the primary normative goals that have animated and provided direction for the many different facets and forms of Latino politics. These efforts have been part of a broader pattern of transformative, oppositional politics seeking to democratize U.S. "democracy"— contesting a system of white supremacy based on wide-scale exclusion, repression, and subordination of communities of people of color that did not fit the ideological, normative vision of the national imaginary adopted by the elites who sought to extend their power and dominance throughout the hemisphere. The contradiction between the principles of equality and justice for all, and the reality of systematic forms of excluding large sectors of U.S. racialized populations, was embraced and justified without any sustained sense of shame or lament for what was at its core a politics of hypocrisy. This systematic racialization also led to the establishment of a form of incorporation based on practices of "exclusionary inclusion" of racialized populations. This book is a study of the processes of exclusionary inclusion of Latinos based on racialization, and of how these have determined their marginalized citizenship status; it also offers a framework for studying this dynamic. Contesting this fundamental condition has been at the core of Latino politics for more than 150 years. Pursuing the goal of achieving full, equal, and just inclusion or societal membership has been a constant in Latino politics, and it has thus been a major force in the struggle to realize democratic normative principles. I engage this problematic by examining the inherent limitations of the citizenship regime in the United States for incorporating Latinos as full societal members, and then offer an alternative conception that I refer to as "associative citizenship," which I argue already exists in embryonic form in Latino communities and which provides a way to account for and challenge the pattern of exclusionary belonging that has defined their position in U.S. society.

While there has always been a body of critical literature produced by Latinos advancing and justifying the principle of full and equal membership, these have until recently received scant attention within the orthodox, dominant academy. This is not surprising given that the academy not only shared but also was a principal source of developing ideological justifications for the forms of Latino exclusion and subordination.[1] But the civil rights struggles of racialized minorities in the United States made it impossible to ignore these contradictions, and provoked an engagement with the normative foundations of the system of "democracy" that exposed its often cruel and violent legacy. This was especially true in the field of political theory, which focuses precisely on normative discourse about the nature of political community. Theorists were slow to grasp the significance of these challenges to racialized forms of exclusion and its effect on the issue of political membership; initially they completely misunderstood what was in fact occurring. Thus one of the preeminent postwar political theorists, Robert Dahl, could state at the end of his influential book *Preface to Democratic Theory*, published in 1956, that the issue of racial conflict and division had been all but resolved. The events of the next fifteen years were to prove how deeply wrong he was. This inability to grasp the nature of the contestation, to engage the problematic, was perhaps why political theory became politically irrelevant until the publication of John Rawls's *Theory of Justice* in 1971, which has been credited widely with reviving the field of political theory in the contemporary period.[2] The constellation of concepts marshaled by Rawls to advance his argument—social contract, utilitarianism, intuitionism, good vs. right, principles of justice, efficiency, priority rules, the difference principle, the veil of ignorance, and civil disobedience—and the relationship between them—provided generations of political theorists with grist for their scholarly mill. Along with his substantially revised *Political Liberalism* (1993), Rawls provided one of the first efforts in political theory to deal with the contemporary condition of a deep cultural diversity that reflected strongly held, competing worldviews and values.

Yet strangely, but perhaps not unexpectedly given the isolated nature of the academy, Rawls never engaged or incorporated the processes of racialization as a fundamental constitutive factor or issue in his analysis—a serious flaw given the foundational role they played in the development of the West and modernity. At the time Rawls published his book, there was little literature within the academy that dealt with the issue of racialization, particularly in the areas of theory and philosophy. But since that time, the foundational role of racialization and colonization in the development of the West has received extensive attention and documentation in several other scholarly fields. The work of Edward Said (1978) was a watershed in this regard and has inspired a generation of literature in fields such as cultural studies and postcolonial theory that attempt to reconstruct the racialized historical trajectory of Western societies. Yet the field of political theory continues to be unable to incorporate this dimension in its work on political community. There are a few examples of efforts to do so, such as Charles Mills's *The Racial Contract* (1997) on the influence of racialization on the basic foundational theorists and philosophers of modernity. Thomas McCarthy, a leading figure and heir of the tradition of critical theory, recently published *Race, Empire, and the Idea of Human Development* (2009), tracing how the ideologies of race and empire were constitutive elements in the development of European and U.S. colonial expansion. But works like these continue to exist on the margins of the primary core of the field, and more than a few theorists refuse to recognize these efforts as legitimate works within the canonical tradition of political theory.

In her review of several volumes that attempt to create a space for racialization, Fogg-Davis comments on this marginalization in the existing state of political theory. The clarity of her summary merits quoting her at length.

Few contemporary political scientists would disagree that race has been a pivotal force in American politics since this country's founding. The magnitude and scope of its impact on current political life is, however, a matter of intense debate. Political theorists have conspicuously not been at the forefront of these race-specific discussions. This is not because political theory has ignored race per se. On the contrary, contemporary political theorists increasingly include race in their descriptive and normative analyses of democratic politics. Debates about identity politics, multiculturalism, the redress of invidious discrimination, and feminist discourse on intersecting social identifications have moved from the margin to the center of political theory and typically involve at least some attention to racial difference. But these discussions have for the most part not examined racial meaning in a sustained, focused manner. While there are exceptions, political theory, as a discipline, has not given theoretical priority to American race. (Fogg-Davis 2003, 555)

This is certainly the case in the mainstream literature on citizenship, one of the key elements of the modern nation-state, the primary form of political community that arose as part of the pattern of development of Europe since the sixteenth century, and which was imposed throughout most of the globe through the expansion of the European imperial project through colonization. Thus the efforts in political theory to examine the question of who is a member of the modern state, who can participate, and what form that can take, has for the most part ignored the role that racialization has played in determining the boundaries of inclusion and exclusion.[3] This occurred despite the fact that the establishment of racial subordination and hierarchy was an integral and vital aspect of the formation of the Western state. Goldberg has provided one of the few detailed analyses of this process in his *The Racial State* (2002). Yet the mainstream liberal, communitarian, and even radical analyses of citizenship have failed to engage this process in any sustained and comprehensive way. Instead, the mainstream works in political theory that have taken up the challenge they label "multiculturalism" have framed the issue primarily as one of "diversity," focusing on the differences of worldviews and values without, however, taking seriously the role that the structural conditions and politics of racialization have played in producing those differences.

Why should this matter to Latinos and the study of Latino politics? It matters because racialization was one of the main processes that determined the specific nature and level of exclusionary Latino membership in the institutions of society, such as not having access to jobs with higher wages; having their children attend inferior schools; not being able to live and purchase homes in some neighborhoods; having little or no access to adequate health care; often being unable to join labor unions. These and other practices clearly constituted a pattern of exclusionary inclusion, or an exclusionary form of belonging. It matters because these practices marginalized their participation in the political system, and because the institutional sites of quotidian experience in civil society were skewed against them in terms of full membership in the broader society. And racialization matters because Latino politics has been primarily about trying to change the obstacles and challenges that it produced. Studies of Latino politics, then, inevitably and necessarily require us to engage the normative dimensions that are the result of the range of exclusionary practices and ideologies that define the primary sites of Latino everyday life. The study of Latino politics has examined and documented the consequences of forms of marginalization in the areas of voting, organizational exclusions, educational policy, and access to the gate-keeping institutions that provide the path to better jobs and greater participation in the broader society. But in the area of political theory, there are very few efforts to engage directly the normative dimensions of these forms of Latino marginalization, or how they have affected the normative foundation of politics in the United States.

There is ample research documenting the rapid and extensive growth of the Latino population in the United States, and how this has transformed the racial and ethnic composition of towns and cities throughout the country.[4] The scope of the various ways that Latinos have changed the nation has raised a series of questions that the larger society will have to respond to in some way. It will have to decide what it means to be "a real American." What form of relationship should there be between the other sectors of the population and Latinos? What level of rights and access should Latinos, especially immigrants, have? Should the society adopt policies that embrace the diversity that Latinos and other nonwhites have brought about, or should the emphasis be on policies that promote assimilation to the dominant culture? The nature and meaning of the increasingly significant Latino presence in the United States is effectively captured in a recent essay by James Cohen:

> The changes now taking place in U.S. society under the impact of Latin@s are orienting U.S. society toward important choices with implications for the entire society. . . . [The] coming years will be a time in which U.S. society will be called upon to choose: 1) what sort of relationship it wants to entertain with its own immigrants, foreigners, ethnoracial minorities, etc., given that the latter are less and less in the minority; 2) what sort of relationship this society wants to entertain more generally with its own ethnoracial, cultural and linguistic differences; 3) how socioeconomic inequalities and inequalities of opportunity should be treated, given that they have steadily widened over the past few decades and maintain, as much as in the past, though in new contexts, strong ethnoracial connotations; 4) last but not least, important choices will have to be made regarding the types of relations the United States seeks to maintain with the countries of its southern periphery, and which are increasingly "inter-penetrated" with U.S. society itself. In short, Latinization is posing—and to some extent precipitating or radicalizing—choices that affect the heart of the established social and political system, the essence of U.S. citizenship, and imply at least a partial questioning of their bases. (James Cohen 2005, 169)

These questions and issues are dimensions that frame the broad parameters of the meaning of citizenship and the criteria for determining societal membership, and should be core concerns in the field of political theory. This book both advances a critique of the empty space in that literature and proposes a framework that provides a direction for rethinking the relationship between societal and political membership, and the form of citizenship that can organically embody that relationship. These are among the most essential of the elements that frame the boundaries of the notion of political community, the most basic concept in politics and political theory within which politics—"[our] deliberate efforts to order, direct, and control [our] collective affairs and activities; to set up ends for society; and to implement and evaluate those ends"—takes place.[5]

Thus my critique and intervention seeks to situate the study of Latino citizenship, and Latino politics more generally, within the context of a particular formulation of the political community. In my view, all other themes and discussions related to politics are implicitly or explicitly based on some notion of political community and on criteria for membership in that community. The book is thus part of the effort to open up that space—to encourage political theory to begin to incorporate the issues of Latino citizenship as a fundamental problematic.

Since my analyses throughout the book rest on this framework, it would be useful to provide a brief summary review of the specific fundamental argument, and the particular set of conceptual elements I draw on to advance it. The basic argument is that specific processes of racialization that have played a determinative role in creating and maintaining the pattern of social exclusions of Latinos have not been incorporated within, or accounted for by the dominant theories of diversity and citizenship as developed in the prevalent literature in political theory. This is in large part due to either incomplete or inadequate theoretical development and grounding of the relationship between societal and political membership—that is, between the levels and types of inclusion in social institutions, and levels of access and participation in the political institutions. I provide an overview of the patterns and forms of political, cultural, and economic exclusions of Latinos and argue that these constitute a pattern of *exclusionary inclusion*, a type of belonging that regulates and restricts the degree and nature of participation in the primary institutions of society. Latinos have been included in various aspects of U.S. societal institutions, but always on a limited and/or restricted basis. So they have been included, but on a differentially exclusionary basis. I also show that these patterns of exclusionary inclusion are based on a racialized ideological trope that has constructed Latinos *as perpetual foreigners* since the earliest period of contact between white settlers in the Southwest and Mexicans, and that this has been a constant factor affecting and framing the relationships between new groups of Latinos and whites up to the current period.[6] These forms and practices of exclusionary inclusion based on the image of Latinos as perpetual foreigners have resulted in a marginalized mode of Latino political membership that, despite significant progress since the 1970s, still characterizes the condition of a majority of Latinos to this day. So the concepts of *exclusionary inclusion* and *perpetual foreignness* are themes that lay the foundation for the rest of my analysis and provide conceptual pivots that anchor the other elements of the framework I develop. In order to account for this historical pattern, I advance an alternative formulation of the relationship between social and political membership that forms the basis of what I refer to as associative citizenship. These are practices that are based on associational networks characterized by relations of reciprocity, mutuality, and trust. The sites of performativity of the latter are located within the institutional spheres of civil society that serve as a mechanism of articulation between these sites on the one hand, and the economic and state structures on the other.

These arguments, analyses, and interpretations are developed in detail in a number of chapters organized as follows. Chapter 1 introduces the dilemma that the issues involved in Latino citizenship present for both the political system and for political theories that have attempted to address the condition of deep diversity that exists in the United States. It introduces the notion of citizenship as having both a regulatory and emancipatory dimension, and I argue that strategies to promote the latter can be pursued most effectively by adopting the normative ideal of full membership advanced by T. H. Marshall. I suggest the concept of *citizenship regime* to highlight the complex ways through which societal location and membership can and do affect the level of access to political membership. This formulation is then set within the specific institutional context of neoliberalism that defines the space within which a politics that contests forms of exclusion have to be organized.

Chapter 2 focuses on engaging some of the political theories that have sought to grapple with the challenge for liberal democracies of the conditions of deep and extensive cultural diversity that have resulted from the many changes induced by the related processes of globalization, restructuring, and transnationalization. Migrations of people of color from non-European countries have transformed the demographic and racial composition of the United States and resulted in a political backlash that relies heavily on a racialized, truncated, and flawed concept of citizenship to argue for containing or reversing that transformation. The theories and conceptual frameworks advanced by Rawls, Habermas, Taylor, Walzer, and Young are representative of the various approaches and parameters that have set the terms of discourse within political theory regarding the "new" reality. My analysis highlights the limitations of these discursive boundaries by focusing on their failure to offer a theoretical grounding for their assumptions regarding the nature of the relationship between societal and political membership, and/or the failure to incorporate the fundamental, constitutive role of the pattern and history of racialization.

In chapter 3, I first review the orthodox conceptions and/or approaches to citizenship and critique them for limitations similar to the diversity theories discussed in the previous chapter. I then develop a conception of what I call *associative citizenship* that offers a way to overcome the limitations I mentioned by incorporating four dimensions that are necessary to understand the configuration of elements that determine the degree to which "full" membership is achieved.[7] I argue that a conception of citizenship that is capable of explaining the experiences of marginalized populations like Latinos in the United States must include and be able to account for the following dimensions: the nature of societal and political membership, the pattern of inclusion/exclusion, modes of belonging, and the processes of racialization. The final section applies this approach to some of the main parameters characterizing the experience of Latino marginalization, arguing that each Latino group has a different history of articulation with the existing regime of citizenship.

Chapter 4 offers a way to empirically ground the elements of associative citizenship by developing a specific model of civil society that mediates between the macro-institutions of the economy and state, and the household. It is within the institutional, structured sites of civil society that these elements are present, and where their meaning, scope, and nature are both embraced and contested. Although the unequal relations of power are reproduced within these sites, they are also locations where a politics that contests forms of marginalization and exclusion can and has emerged. The focus here is on the emancipatory potential found in the practices and beliefs developed within Latino networks of reciprocity and trust; this can provide a way of perceiving and understanding the nature of prefigurative rights claims that can be, and have historically been, the precursor to expanding the democratic boundaries of citizenship proper.[8] These claims are enabled by participation in social networks based on trust and reciprocity—networks that both define and reflect societal location or membership. A final section discusses the connection between rights, civil society, and the development of a more inclusive form of democracy.

Chapter 5 focuses on using the model of associative citizenship to study the processes that give rise to a certain form of rights claims in a number of Latino communities, sometimes referred to as the "hub" cities in the southeastern sector of Los Angeles, and to the type of rights claims that have been advanced within the immigrant-rights movement. The discussion of the empirical material in this chapter is not intended to present a case study in the traditional sense. The in-depth, detailed, and sustained analysis that would be called for would require a different book organized around a different set of research questions. Instead, the purpose of the chapter is to *illustrate* the processes that affected the relationship between restructuring, immigration, and the formation of rights claims, and to relate sufficient detail from our interviews and research regarding the specific aspects of participants' experiences that led to their responses—including rights claims—to the effects of restructuring and immigration on their lives. Thus the focus is on the sets of interacting influences and processes.

The term "hub cities" refers to the fact that this region was the core of the Fordist industrial sector of the city from the late 1920s to the early 1970s. The communities at that time were heavily segregated and basically housed the white working-class labor force employed by the large number of industries in the area. The chapter describes in detail the forces that transformed this area into a region where by 2000, about 97 percent of the residents were Latino, a large percentage of whom were working poor. I describe the pattern of restructuring that brought about those changes, and then focus on the negotiation of conditions of poverty and other forms of marginalization brought about by the structural changes, which in turn led to assertion of rights claims and in some cases engagement in grassroots forms of politics. I do so by interpreting the results of a series of interviews, ethnographies, and life histories that focus on demonstrating that these rights claims were a response to specific material conditions and challenges experienced by the household members. I also discuss how the political context created by the anti-immigration politics of the last three decades led to the organization and mobilization of thousands of Latinos, and I focus on the role of networks as sites within which rights claims emerged. I argue here that these rights claims in fact constitute the core element of an alternative form of associative citizenship that is being enacted, and is rooted, in the everyday lives of Latino communities.

In the sixth and final chapter, I examine the challenges of converting rights claims into practices and action that lead to concrete changes in public policy. The assertion of rights claims will change nothing unless they are eventually embodied in laws, legislation, judicial decisions, and administrative law and practices that address the conditions that the rights claims were a response to. One of the obstacles that I focus on here is the challenge of creating a form of political solidarity in highly diverse Latino communities, and I contextualize the analysis of this challenge by situating it within the broader discourse on solidarity. I begin this section with a discussion of some key theories of solidarity at the general level, then focus more on the obstacles encountered in attempting to build forms of political solidarity within marginalized communities. I then discuss the particular issues that Latino communities face in their efforts to develop effective political action. I conclude with a review of some of the ways that rights claims have led to the creation of organized, formal groups and associations that became full participants in the public sphere, if not yet having full "membership" in it.

CHAPTER 1

Framing the Question of Citizenship

Membership, Exclusionary Inclusion, and Latinos
in the National Political Imaginary

It's great now that they're calling Jose Antonio a hero. But when he was up crossing the
border they called him a wetback. . . . In my mind, he was a hero when he chose to leave
the streets. The rest is just politics and window dressing.

—Bruce Harris, Director of Casa Alianza, in "From Illegal Immigrant
to Marines, Soldier's Death Spotlights Immigrants"

Whatever their legal citizenship status, and however many generations of American
citizens they can trace in their ancestry, Hispanics/Latinos in the United States are liable
to be treated as foreigners.

—Iris Young, *Justice and the Politics of Difference*

On Wednesday, April 2, 2003, the U.S. Bureau of Citizenship and Immigration Services awarded citizenship status posthumously to two young Latino
immigrants, Jose Garibay and Jose Gutierrez, who were serving in the Marines and
were killed during the first few days of the U.S. invasion of Iraq. The official reason
given for bestowing citizenship was that it was meant to reward them for losing

their lives in the service of "their" country. However, given the rise in anti-immigrant sentiment during the last few years, and the charges that Latino immigrants in particular have undermined the "American way of life" and drained our resources, and that the 37,000 noncitizens in the military pose a problem of "dual loyalty," these events presented an awkward situation for the government. Is it possible that the granting of citizenship was intended to reconcile the tension inherent in the fact that non-citizens died while performing duties normally associated with the highest loyalties of citizenship? Clearly citizenship has no meaning for these two Latinos now, so granting it to them posthumously was a symbolic act addressed to appeal to a national audience. Immigrants do not enjoy, to use T. H. Marshall's notion of citizenship, "full membership in the community" (Marshall 1950), so making Garibay and Gutierrez citizens posthumously appears to be a way to rectify what may seem to some as an unfair, perhaps even unjust situation, i.e., that these two were willing to risk their lives for a country that limited their ability to participate fully in its major institutions. At the very least, the action highlights the complex question of how the relationship between citizenship, identity, and the meaning of "belonging" to a political community applies to Latinos in the United States. But it is important to point out that the complex of issues concerning Latino membership and citizenship highlighted by this situation is not limited or relevant to only Latino immigrants. While foreign-born Latinos represent roughly 40 percent of that population, a majority of Latinos were born and raised in the United States. However, although there is great emphasis in the current period on the large number of recent immigrants, what cannot be ignored is that the history of Latino communities in the United States has been a long, complex, and diverse one in which the level and type of social and political membership of Latinos has been contested in various spheres of political and civil society—e.g., in the legal, economic, social, and cultural institutional sites of the society.[1] The "place," role, and institutional access of Latinos have been regulated and controlled through various institutional means and sites, such as treaties, court cases, legislation, labor-market policies and practices, and informal practices in civil society, and it is through the combined effects of these mechanisms that the level of Latino inclusion in U.S. institutions has been determined, and the effective citizenship status of Latinos defined. It is precisely this framing of the dimension of inclusion and exclusion that is the basis of Marshall's concept of citizenship, and it suggests that the study of Latino citizenship can provide a particularly useful lens for understanding the complex, multidimensional history of Latinos in the United States.

While I return to the issue of how to address this condition in the final chapter, let me clarify at the outset the basic purpose and framing of my study. This history of Latino marginalization and the relationship to citizenship can and has been interpreted in widely varying ways. What is distinct about my approach is that I view citizenship here as primarily a strategy for Latino empowerment. Adopting a Grams-cian perspective, I consider citizenship as a key element of the changing regulatory parameters of hegemony, i.e., the combination of force and consent through which the structure of privilege and unequal relations of power are enforced.[2] But my emphasis here is on examining how the struggle for citizenship can become the site of a counterhegemonic politics, i.e., a form of politics that challenges and seeks to transform that system of domination. While I engage the legal and social dimensions that are normally the focus of citizenship studies, my claim throughout the book is that a reconceptualized notion of citizenship can provide the basis for a set of political strategies that converge around the issue of exclusion and marginalization. Since the latter have been defining characteristics of the Latino experience in the United States, using citizenship as a generalized notion focused on the full range of practices and mechanisms of inclusion, and the relationships between them, could form the foundation of a counterhegemonic ideology and practice.

This issue takes on added significance in the contemporary period because of the rapid and extensive growth of Latino communities during the last three decades. Projections based on the 2010 Census suggest that the size and dispersion of Latino populations, and the key role they play in several sectors of the economy, mean that they have become a major, integral part of U.S. society. In the last decade alone, the numbers of Latinos grew 42 percent; there are expected to be well over 50 million when the current census count is determined, and they are projected to constitute over a quarter of the national population by 2050 (Passel and Cohn 2008; Passel, Cohn, and Lopez 2011; Motel and Patten 2013). Not only has there been a dramatic increase in the size of the Latino population, but significant Latino communities have developed in states that had virtually no Latino presence a short time ago. Latino restaurants, stores, churches, soccer leagues, home associations, as well as celebrations of holidays such as Cinco de Mayo are now a basic part of small towns in Georgia, North Carolina, Iowa, Kentucky, and throughout the South.[3] In places like Ames, Iowa, the Mexican Independence Day parades of the 16th of September are as visible and significant as those on the 4th of July. So it is clear that this population will have an ever-increasing effect on determining what kind of society the United States will become. This is particularly clear when one looks at the fact that 20 percent of schoolchildren and 25 percent of newborns are Latino.[4] When combined with statistics that show that Latinos between sixteen and twenty-five have a dropout rate of 17 percent, almost twice as much as African Americans and nearly three times that of whites, this portends an alarming future of even greater fragmentation, lack of opportunity, division, and inequalities, with all the ills and costs that these conditions entail.

It is important to note, however, that while these dramatic increases in the size, rate of growth, and spatial dispersion of Latina/o populations have played a fundamental role in transforming the configuration of political, cultural, spatial, and economic characteristics and relations of many of the important urban regions in the country, they are part of a much wider, complex set of processes of global transformations and restructuring embodied in a broad variety of institutional strategies, policies, and practices at both the regional and international levels (Smith and Feagin 1987; Sassen 1988, 1992, 1994, 1996a,1996b, 1998, 2000, 2001). While the causes of these large-scale reconfigurations are multifaceted, one of the key factors that has been both cause and effect of these changes is the massive and rapid increases in the level of nonwhite migrations from Latin America, Africa, Asia, and the Caribbean to the major cities of the United States and Europe. These more recent immigrant arrivals come from non-European cultural, social, and racial contexts dramatically different from those of the places they have settled. But this is not entirely new. Differences between Latinos and the rest of the population in the United States have existed throughout the history of Latinos in the country.[5] However, because of the conditions that I have reviewed here and the much greater prominence and presence of Latinos throughout the United States, this new reality, and the economic and political conditions of Latino communities and their capacity to become full and equal members of society, has to be a national concern and not treated as a "minority" issue.[6]

This disjunction or "difference" has generated a qualitatively different set of political issues and alignments, including the contestation of established notions of rights, responsibilities, obligations, entitlements, the relationship between the cultural and political realms, and identity. All of these are exactly the concerns that characterize the broader debate about the meaning of, and criteria for, societal membership and national belonging, and an ongoing, contested reexamination of the parameters of citizenship (Isin and Wood 1999; Isin 2000). However, while the specific parameters and context within which this has taken place may be recent, the marginalized position of Latinos—the difference they represent for the dominant institutions and majority white populations—has been part of the relationship between the latter and Latinos from even before the annexation of a significant part of Mexico. This difference has been a fundamental reason for legitimating and justifying the forms of discrimination and exclusion that have been a constitutive characteristic of the Latino experience in this country. Thus the struggle for inclusion, to become full members in Marshall's sense, has been a continuous, formative aspect of Latino history, and in this sense, the struggle for inclusion has been a struggle for full citizenship, with full and equal membership in all areas of societal institutions. My study is in effect an attempt to extend the discussion about the best ways of accomplishing that goal. However, I argue that achieving this is difficult within the parameters and functioning of the current citizenship regime because it is based on assumptions and normative beliefs that cannot easily or readily accommodate Latinos. Consequently, my study proposes that the explicit struggle for full incorporation needs to be organized around a concept of citizenship much more inclusive than that of the current regime. But this does not and cannot take place in a vacuum, and has to be situated within the larger context of the strengths and weaknesses of different political strategies that might be adopted in pursuit of attaining full membership.

There are different ways of framing this issue of inclusion that focus on distinct aspects. Because I will be looking at the ways in which quotidian practices within civil society and other informal spheres can be the basis of demands for inclusion, the relationship between those spheres and the notion of a public sphere is particularly salient. As is well known, Habermas introduced this idea as a way of examining how public opinion and forms of practices outside the sphere of the state are important for the development of a democratic populace and society (Habermas 1989a).[7] But the basic idea has been modified by a wide number of scholars who have adapted it to their particular concerns and foci. There is an overlap with many of the studies of civil society as a site of transformational politics, but as Craig Calhoun (1993) has pointed out in great detail, they are not exactly the same. Part of my analysis will follow Calhoun's caution and focus on the relationship between certain types of practices in civil society and how they become activated as part of the public sphere as citizenship-rights claims. However, much of this literature focuses primarily on behavior or practices that occur within organizations or formal associations. Much less emphasis has been placed on studying other forms of informal practices that develop particularly in marginalized communities, and that play a very important role in how groups develop political ideas and perspectives. The latter eventually are what enter into the public sphere and represent a different mode of participation in that arena.[8] The complex relationship between civil society, the public sphere, and rights claims to citizenship as full membership is one of the major aspects of this study. However, while I will engage the theoretical discussion of the intersection of these dimensions, I will also attempt to connect it to and ground it within the empirical conditions and real-life political experience of Latino communities.

Neoliberalism and the Structuring of Latino Politics: Membership, Incorporation, and Citizenship

One way to accomplish this connection is to preliminarily ground the discussion of this relationship by recognizing that at the most general level, there are two modal types of political strategies that are available for advancement toward the goal of full membership and citizenship. One is the traditional path of electoral politics, and the other I would identify as a community-based, often oppositional approach. These are not mutually exclusive and should be seen as two poles on a continuum, and groups often adopt a coordinated strategy that draws on both approaches. The electoral approach is based on the traditional ideology that the defining characteristic of democracy is based on the right to vote for elected representatives. Groups can promote their interests and affect public policy by mobilizing effectively to cast their votes for candidates who in theory can be replaced if they are not responsive to those concerns. This process becomes visible every two years at the federal level in the United States, and throughout the year at the local and state levels. The limitations and weaknesses of this approach as a strategy for groups with a history of being politically marginalized is that almost by definition they are not likely to be able to gain greater inclusion systemically using the very process from which they are marginalized. One of the characteristics of the electoral system as it actually functions is to maintain the structure of privilege of the status quo, as the history of elections and the legislative process demonstrates. The tactics and strategies for resisting demands for change are nearly endless, but the reliance on gerrymandering, voter fraud and suppression, intimidation, and misrepresentation are well known.

For the last few decades, as elections approach, attention to the role of Latinos in the electoral process increases accordingly. This is a familiar pattern, not only in the popular media, both English and Spanish versions, but also among mainstream academics and political organizations. The format and framing of these works represent a continuation of the approach adopted by the numerous studies that have documented the growth and behavior in the Latino electorate, particularly since the early 1990s.[9] These concerns focus on turnout, partisan loyalties and attitudes, pending or ongoing policy issues, elections or electability of Latino candidates, identifying local, statewide, and national elections in which Latino voters have the potential to be the "swing" vote, etc. While there are differences among researchers in their assessment of the degree of success or failure of these efforts, the underlying assumption of the vast majority of these studies is that the electoral process in the United States has the potential to promote the "interests" of Latino communities. Yet there are few efforts to link the functioning of these electoral processes to the broader characteristics and tendencies of the structural context within which these take place, and that may in fact circumscribe and limit the possibilities for addressing the broad and differing range of concerns that the many sectors of a very heterogeneous Latino population confront on a daily basis. Thus while we have a considerable amount of research on Latino electoral patterns, there is much less that attempts to situate these within an analysis of the potential effectiveness of the electoral process. The result is a truncated and limited view of Latino politics. While Latino electoral behaviors and trends are an important set of phenomena, they do not occur in an institutional vacuum, and they represent only one dimension of Latino politics, which encompasses a much broader terrain defined by the multiple levels and forms through which Latinos seek to promote their collective interests and affect the policies and practices that have a direct impact on their lives. A wide range of actions are undertaken by Latino community and neighborhood groups, CBOs, nonprofit organizations, home associations, immigrant-rights groups, student organizations, labor groups often linked to domestic and other nonunionized service sectors, and professional organizations to advance their concerns and to affect policies and practices of both state structures and institutions of civil society within which their daily lives are carried out. The kinds of actions undertaken, and policies promoted, by these types of groups and organizations imply a normative concept of Latino politics that is based on achieving full incorporation in all spheres of U.S. society and that views electoral behavior as an indispensable but also limited mechanism for pursuing this goal. It is this dimension of full incorporation, then—rather than any particular pattern of electoral behavior—that should be the measure of success and effectiveness of Latino politics. What is most often missing from works that focus on and emphasize the primacy of electoral activity is a sustained and detailed discussion of how electoral behavior is linked to this more fundamental question of incorporation, which is not the same as "political engagement." The implicit operative assumption seems to be that the increasing number of Latino voters will somehow translate into policies that will meet the variety of needs in these communities. But this overlooks the fact that despite the very significant increase in Latino elected officials, the record of responsiveness to Latino concerns is mixed at best. This is because this approach ignores how the structural features of the economy limit the reach of the electoral system and restrict the parameters of a policy agenda that can be pursued.

Instead, the discourse that focuses most directly on the level and nature of incorporation is that of political membership and citizenship. So it is really the issue of full and effective citizenship that provides the underlying normativity of Latino politics that is typically not addressed in studies or discussions of Latino electoral activity or patterns. The challenge, then, is to try to develop modes of analysis that seek to incorporate this broader conception of Latino politics, and to understand how the primary institutions of state, economic, and cultural power both impact the degree of Latino incorporation and often limit and contain the possibilities and strategies for social and political change. I want to provide a perspective that seeks to locate current Latino politics, including but not limited to electoral patterns, within the broader processes of U.S. neoliberalism that have defined economic and political agendas and policies since the late 1970s.

Clearly, the significant differences in class, race, immigrant status, gender, and national origin all make the development of a single "Latino" agenda that could address the manifold issues that affect Latino communities extremely unlikely. That is to say, the particular interests and needs of Latinos, as with other groups, differ according to their location along these dimensions. Yet, despite these differences, there are structural processes, policies, and practices that do affect the nature and types of opportunities, economic and social mobility trajectories, and life conditions of large percentages of Latinos. The literature on neoliberalism provides a way to identify and understand some of the key domestic structural phenomena and conditions within which Latino politics now take place.

Neoliberalism has been used to describe the linkage between the ensemble of changes in the structure of economic processes and relations that were promoted beginning in the late 1970s in response to the ineffectiveness of Keynesian policies that emerged from World War II. This includes the institutional and ideological practices and political policies of governance that were adopted as a result of the inability of state structures to address these problems.[10] These new policies not only guided the extensive and long-term restructuring processes adopted within both the economic and state spheres, but also coincided with the period of dramatic and rapid growth in the Latino population driven in particular by immigration. The key characteristics of neoliberalism are well known and have been documented in numerous studies (Harvey 2005; Leitner, Peck, and Sheppard 2007; Collins, Di Leonardo, and Williams 2008; Brenner and Theodore 2002). This does not imply, however, that there is a consensus on the meaning of neoliberalism, the interpretation of these characteristics, or the particular significance of the various components. This extensive literature on neoliberalism reflects a broad range of frameworks and an emphasis on different dimensions involved in these processes. Some studies focus on a set of economic policies while others use it as defining a particular historical period, and there are those who study it as an ideological phenomenon. I focus here on tracing how neoliberal economic policies and their consequences have severely limited the possibility that action that would seriously address the marginalized conditions of a majority of Latinos can be attained through the electoral process alone.

The primary assumptions on which neoliberalism is based are that an unregulated, free-enterprise economic marketplace is not only the most effective mechanism for economic and societal development, but is also the best way of promoting democracy and freedom here and abroad. All of the other defining characteristics of neoliberalism flow from these basic assumptions. Deregulation of industry and commerce in general, limiting the role of government in economic affairs, privatization, reduction in governmental responsibility for social services and community welfare, all are mechanisms and policies intended to achieve the ideal of a free market as the foundation for economic prosperity and democratization.[11] However, despite the fact that this view has been the guiding framework for the structure of governance under Presidents Reagan, Bush One, Clinton, Bush Two, and Obama, it has functioned, as David Harvey suggests, more as utopian ideology than grounded public policy (Harvey 2005). The spectacular failure of this ideology that led to the economic crisis of 2008 and the following years demonstrated that it is not government intervention in economic affairs that is rejected, but rather government intervention on behalf of the working class and minorities. The role of government under this neoliberal regime has been to promote, enhance, and facilitate the growth of corporate and financial sectors, while limiting support for social services, education, health, and welfare. The societal effects have led some to label this "predatory capitalism." The redistribution of wealth upward and the growing level of inequality have been so dramatic that even conservative thinkers such as Kevin Phillips, in his *Wealth and Democracy* (2002), have warned of the dire consequences for democratic governance.

One of the major effects of these processes and policies has been the redefinition of the purpose of governance that emerged from the period of the Depression through the early 1970s. The shift is clear when one compares the type of policies that reflected the notion of governance during the Depression and after with those adopted since the 1980s. During the former period, policies were adopted aimed at putting people back to work, addressing the issue of poverty, increasing the standard of living, and establishing strict regulatory regimes (reflected in legislation like the Glass-Steagall Act) to prevent the recurrence of the economic collapse of the 1930s. These policies prioritized strengthening the rights of labor, establishing a system of social security to ensure a minimum of economic well-being, dismantling legal structures of racial discrimination and supporting the expansion of civil rights, and establishing a health-care system intended to make sure that the elderly and poor would receive care. This contrasts markedly with policies advanced not only by Republicans, but by Democrats like Clinton, who pushed through NAFTA, primarily intended to open capital markets across borders; relied heavily on tax credits for the wealthy as a basis for influencing economic development; advanced legislation to dismantle the welfare system and replace it with the Temporary Aid to Needy Families programs; and embraced deregulation as a policy, most notably by the repeal of the Glass-Steagall Act. Many commentators blame this last action for the unleashing of the kind of financial-market behavior that could have led to the collapse of the entire financial system had there been no huge government bailout of those corporations that had in fact precipitated the crisis. And the policies of the Obama administration have been designed and promoted by advisers who come from the very same companies and sectors that orchestrated the near collapse. So the conception of governance as the guarantor of the corporate class that underlies and supports neoliberal economic and social policies remains largely unchanged.

These reflect two starkly different conceptions of the purpose of governance, and at least at present, there is little evidence to indicate that either dominant party is likely to offer or embrace anything other than the same type of neoliberal agenda and repertoire of policies. Given the likelihood that the Republican Party, with its reliance on failed policies of the past decade, will increase its number of elected representatives, there is little to suggest that even substantial increases in Latino voter turnout will result in any significant change in the ideological parameters within which the dominant public discourse and public-policy options will be advanced. I am not suggesting that voting and electoral behavior are unimportant—quite the contrary. This has been an important vehicle for promoting progressive legislation in the past that has resulted in greater levels of Latino incorporation. But in the context of the last thirty years, there have been few instances when either dominant party offered a serious challenge to the fundamental premises of neoliberalism. So one of the more important goals of Latino political actions needs to be supporting the kinds of changes that would make an alternative possible. But the fact that millions of people mobilized in support of immigrant rights, and responded to the vision and hope for change that they believed Obama represented, makes it clear that a politics based on providing an alternative to neoliberalism is indeed possible.

Latinos and the Impact of Neoliberalism

There is no lack of respected economists who consider the current situation in the United States to be not only an economic crisis but a crisis of governance as well (Krugman 2009; Stiglitz 2010).

As I indicated above, the policies and ideology of neoliberalism have clearly undermined the quality of life for millions of people. Unemployment has reached record levels, millions have lost their homes, and social services have been either eliminated or severely limited; most cities and many states are either on the verge of bankruptcy or unable to deal with crumbling infrastructure, faltering educational systems, inadequate medical and health facilities. This is the legacy of the neoliberalist policies of deregulation, privatization, and the promotion of greater levels of economic inequalities. And yet there is no prospect of addressing or reversing these as a fundamental part of the national policy agenda.

The particular pattern of growth and development of Latino communities since the 1970s has made large sectors particularly susceptible to these effects. There have, of course, been very significant advances made by sectors of Latino communities as a result of the changes brought about by the civil rights movements and legislation of the 1960s. A small but significant professional class has emerged that often plays a broker role, articulating their version of Latino "issues" and "needs" for mainstream institutions. And while the proportion of Latinos that have achieved middle-class status has increased significantly, it is important to keep in mind that a majority are still relatively marginalized. As I have already mentioned, the period of significant growth in the Latino population overlapped considerably with the period during which neoliberalism developed in the United States. This is no coincidence, since the demand for cheap labor was one of the central features of neoliberal restructuring policies that promoted large-scale immigration, serving as a magnet for workers from Mexico in particular. Given the size and dispersion of Latino populations and the key role they played in several sectors of the economy, they became an integral part of the neoliberal transformation. This population will continue to have a growing effect on determining what kind of society the United States will become. Because of this, the economic and political conditions of Latino communities and their capacity to become full and equal members of society has to be a national concern and not treated as a "minority" issue (Pew Hispanic Center 2009).

Economically, Latinos have been affected directly by neoliberal policies. A recent report published by the National Council of La Raza indicates that in 2007, about 41.8 percent of Latino workers earned poverty-level wages (set at approximately $10.20 per hour to support a family of four), compared to 34 percent for African American workers and 21.9 percent for white workers (Singley 2009). And Latinos tend to be concentrated in occupations that are not only on the lower end of the wage scale, with Latino men earning 68 percent of white-male wages and Latinas 77 percent of the wages of white women. But they are also overrepresented in jobs that have been particularly hard hit by the ongoing current recession, with a little over 20 percent of production and food service jobs, close to one third in construction and maintenance, and almost 40 percent in agriculture. And the AFL-CIO reports significant job loss in many of these occupations with a higher percentage of Latinos during the period between 2001 and 2005. So, for example, there have been 289,000 (19.9 percent) jobs lost in machinery, 220,000 (46.6 percent) in apparel, 58,500 (13.4 percent) in furniture products, 260,100 (36.7 percent) in semiconductor and electronic components, 235,200 (13.3 percent) in fabricated metal products, 144,800 (23.5 percent) in primary metals, 159,300 (19.9 percent) in printing, and the list goes on ("China Trade" 2009). In addition, 47.7 percent of Latino workers had no health insurance through their employment compared to 27.4 percent of white workers and 32.9 percent of African American workers. And two-thirds (65.4 percent) of Latino workers did not have access to retirement plans in their jobs. At a more general level, a recent measure called the Hispanic Inequality Index has documented the level of inequality of Latinos in the United States. Using a number of statistical indices comparing Latinos to whites in five different areas— economic standing, social justice, civic engagement, education, and health—the analysis concluded that the overall inequality index for Latinos is 71.8 percent, and is most pronounced in the areas of economics and social justice (National Urban League 2010).

Latino Politics, Citizenship, and Neoliberalism

If the measure of success of Latino politics is the degree to which it promotes full incorporation of all sectors of Latino communities into the major institutions that structure the quality of their lives, then even the brief review of the economic and material conditions of large percentages of Latinos presented here reflects a pattern of uneven, differential incorporation. And while a substantial percentage of Latinos have realized mobility and gained greater access to labor markets, schools, and political processes, a majority of Latinos continue to realize only partial incorporation. Neoliberal economic policies in the United States have caused the deepening of inequality among the lower two-thirds of Latino populations, resulting in formidable obstacles to full citizenship, membership, and incorporation, and continuing to make any significant reform toward greater incorporation highly unlikely.

The long-term, negative societal implications of these types of conditions were delineated over half a century ago by the British sociologist T. H. Marshall, who argued that the viability of democratic societies depends on developing a form of citizenship that goes beyond simply legal standing. Instead it is based on the principle of the full incorporation of the various different groups in all of the major institutional sites through which the distribution of power, resources, and benefits are determined. Marshall argued that legal or political formal citizenship is necessary but insufficient to achieve the type of *societal membership* that can sustain democratic governance while the kinds of material inequalities that affect Latino communities persist. This conception has been the point of departure since then for most analyses and studies of citizenship throughout much of the globe (Marshall 1950). And for at least the last two decades, the issue of incorporation has been a predominant concern among not only academics but also policymakers and politicians; furthermore this is, to a great extent, a function of the dramatic growth in the level of cultural, racial, and ethnic diversity that has been one of the unintended consequences of neoliberal economic-expansionist policies of the last thirty years.

While social-scientific studies and analyses of Latino electoral politics have provided useful knowledge about voting patterns, factors affecting choice of candidates, participation in campaigns, etc., they tell us little about whether these activities have any impact on the level of Latino societal incorporation. It might be contended that this latter dimension is a separate concern and is substantially a different research question. However this would be true only if the conception of the political embraced is by definition limited to phenomena related to the electoral approach. One way of understanding what is at stake here is to look at the process of framing involved in different conceptions of the political. In a recent set of essays, Fraser (2009a) uses the analytic of framing to unpack different dimensions of justice.[12] However, her approach suggests a way of understanding the different levels or registers involved in political analysis more broadly. Framing the political involves locating the relational intersection of the assumptions regarding three interdependent dimensions: defining what is its purpose, who is to be included, and how it is to be accomplished. Ineffective framing of the political results when any of these dimensions is either not addressed, or included in ways that either contradict or are inconsistent with the meaning of the other factors, resulting in a limited, distorted, or faulty analysis. Thus "misframing" the analysis of specific issues limits our ability to grasp the complexity and depth of how the political functions within the broader society. From this perspective, analyses or studies of Latino politics that focus on one of these dimensions without situating it within, and linking to, the other components of the relational conception of the political would be misframed.

A more ample, relational conception of Latino politics than what is typically advanced would allow us to see that the effects of neoliberal economic policies on Latinos make the realization of significant increases in the level of societal incorporation, and full citizenship for a majority of Latinos through electoral means alone, highly unlikely. As such, there needs to be greater attention, particularly on the part of academics and policymakers, both to the limitations of electoral approaches on achieving these goals, and to the many new forms of political advocacies that promote them.[13]

Neoliberalism, Political Theory, and Latino Citizenship

Citizenship, as I develop it here, addresses the most fundamental aspect of the experience of Latinos in the United States, because it focuses on the type of membership status, the level of access and participation in the major institutions, and the right to belong and be accepted as an integral and vital part of every facet of life at the structural, institutional, and quotidian levels. Achieving this goal is of importance or significance not only for Latinos but also for the well-being and deepening of democracy in the United States. Overcoming the barriers to forms of inclusion is key to the expansion of democratic governance and the achievement of a higher level of social justice. And this goal of gaining greater inclusion has been a defining characteristic of Latino politics since the initial stages of relations with the dominant institutions. The animating logic of Latino politics has always been based on achieving inclusion. And while it may not always have been seen as a force for greater democratization, indeed it has been a major corrective to the many failures of the United States to live up to its promise of a just, democratic society.

These relationships between democracy, citizenship, and social justice in a situation of deep diversity are some of the primary concerns of the field of contemporary political theory. But despite the pivotal role that Latinos have played in the development of the United States, they have been largely absent from the dominant discourses in the field. Thus one of my main goals in writing this book is to provide scholars, researchers, and students who study and write about Latinos, and who are concerned with the normative dimensions that characterize these kinds of questions, a way of engaging them without accepting the particular commitments and assumptions that underlie the dominant literatures in this area.[14] Without such an alternative, then, we allow a whole field of study to define issues of democracy, justice, and equality for us without its having engaged or accounted for Latino experiences. The framing of the questions and parameters that characterize these approaches reinforces the very marginalization that I discussed previously.

Despite the development of an extensive literature on the nature of citizenship since the early 1990s, there have been only a few works that focus on how theories and practices of citizenship have affected, and been affected by, Latino communities.[15] This lack of scholarly studies of those aspects of citizenship that have determined the varying levels of access that Latinos have had historically to the major institutions of society is particularly curious given that the specific nature of Latino societal membership has always been contested, unstable political terrain. While my primary concern is to develop a concept of citizenship that is able to account for the forms of exclusionary belonging that have characterized the way that Latinos have been situated in the United States, *Transforming Citizenship* argues that the study of Latino citizenship provides an opportunity to delineate the theoretical and practical reasons why the citizenship regime in the United States has been unable to develop a model capable of effectively incorporating the nature of alterity represented by racially marginalized populations throughout its history. I argue that this limitation problematizes the nature and scope of who constitutes the "we" that is discursively, theoretically, and politically presumed to be the foundation of the nation in the United States.[16] I contend that this results from the fact that the specific configuration of legal, social, cultural, and political elements and relations that define and form the context of both the juridical and societal dimensions of citizenship regime in the

United States, has received less than satisfactory theoretical accounts in some of the most influential analysis of the logic of citizenship in culturally diverse democracies. To be clear, I am not claiming that these dimensions go unmentioned, but rather that they are rarely integrated at the theoretical level of the analytics that are used in these studies. This limits the thoroughness and applicability of these works because it is the interacting influences of all these factors that I will refer to summarily as the "social and civil spheres," rather than simply legal or juridical status, that establish the criteria for determining the normative parameters of who legitimately belongs within the national political imaginary, and therefore demarcate the boundaries of citizenship.

In the chapters that follow, I will lay the groundwork and advance a concept of citizenship that situates it theoretically within the broader sphere of social and cultural relations, and will refer to this set of relationships as a *citizenship regime*, which I define as the *ensemble of societal practices and norms that regulate the nature and level of societal and political membership of differentially situated societal groups*. This notion of citizenship regime will serve as the basis for arguing that many of the works that have had the most influence on determining the types and boundaries of discourses are aimed at advancing conceptions of citizenship robust enough to promote effective levels of democracy in conditions of deep diversity. However, they have neither provided nor incorporated an adequate analysis of the tension between the criteria and practices that have defined the forms and levels of societal membership on the one hand, and political membership on the other. This disjunction between societal and political membership is the theoretical pivot for the analysis of Latino citizenship. While Marshall did not formulate his conception of citizenship as full membership in this way, he did argue that citizenship and citizenship rights could only be understood if they were situated within the institutional context in which they function. However, although he provided examples, he did not develop a detailed discussion of how to do this. Following this premise, I develop a model for the institutional grounding of the politics of citizenship or citizenship regime in chapter 4 and show why this is a more adequate way of approaching and understanding patterns and meaning of the form of exclusionary belonging—i.e., the marginalized, differential, and restricted forms of incorporation of Latinos. This pattern has, of course, been contested throughout the historical presence of Latinos in the United States, but it was the oppositional politics of the Latino civil rights movement that was in clear view by the 1940s, and was continued and extended by the social movements of the 1960s, that altered the pattern of incorporation of sectors of Latinos and opened up access to labor markets, housing, institutions of higher education, and so forth. While considerable class mobility occurred for those who were in a position to take advantage of those newly available opportunities, this has not been the case for the majority of Latinos, as I believe the figures I discussed earlier make clear.

The Resurgence of the Citizenship Problematic

In the broader field of studies of citizenship, it is now commonplace to observe that there has been a virtual explosion of studies of, and publications on, citizenship in the last two decades.[17] A number of reasons have been advanced for why this is the case, but they normally include globalization and transnationalism and their consequences, which are interpreted as either undermining or at least challenging the basis of modern citizenship. In his introduction to one of the earlier series of essays addressing the question of the resurgence of interest in citizenship, Beiner lists some additional factors: "Ethnic and sectarian conflict in northeastern and southeastern Europe; a redefining of national states at the heart of Europe, in a post–Cold War epoch that might have been expected to diminish political turbulence but seems instead to have generated *more* of it; dislocating shifts of identity provoked by mass migration and economic integration, accompanied by defensive reactions to bolster these jeopardized identities: all these political dilemmas have raised anew deep questions about what binds citizens together into a shared political community" (Beiner 1995, 3). But these factors are not in play universally or uniformly and affect different regions and states in quite distinct ways. Thus, for example, the dynamics of nationalist ethnic conflict and violence that plagued Eastern European countries for several decades had a much more significant effect on how the "crisis" of citizenship unfolded there than in the United States or Australia. And the ethnic nationalist divide in Canada has led to a quite different framing of the issues than in the United States. The variations and permutations in the dynamics that determine how questions of belonging, membership, and identity are worked out in different countries have led theorists such as Carens (2000) to conclude that there is no one formulation of citizenship that is applicable to each nation-state, and the analysis must incorporate and engage the specific and unique combination of historical, cultural, and economic factors of each state or region. While there are different perspectives in the literature regarding why the issue of citizenship has become a major concern in liberal democracies, for the United States, the most important factors have been the demographic and racial changes caused in large part by the consequences of the related processes of globalization, restructuring, and transnationalization. These in turn have given rise to conflict over the issue of national identity and deepened tensions between different racial and ethnic groups, and the question of "what it means to be an American" underlies much of both popular and scholarly discourse.[18]

The increase in the speed and range of the movement of capital, and changes in modes of industrialization and trade have both promoted migration and increased the levels of inequality. This has fostered tensions between, on the one hand, these types of movements across national, regional, and community borders and boundaries, and institutions and policies that continue to be based on the assertion of national sovereignty. The changes in the nature of international economic interdependence, and in the establishment of transnational communities and networks have altered the character of social relations, cultural frameworks, and political identities.

And the particular pattern that processes of restructuring have taken in the United States has also directly affected the development of Latino communities in both the United States and Latin America. There have been significant changes in the patterns of incorporation of Latinos into the workforce, the demographic composition and distribution of major cities, the nature of social relations in Latino communities and enclaves, and the emergence of Latino household and community survival and mobility strategies. As my brief discussion of neoliberalism indicates, restructuring has resulted in changes in Latino communities such as growth in size of Latino populations, the number of Latino groups (national origin), location, spatial pervasiveness, development of a middle and professional class, class differentiation, and a change in gender relations. These in turn have transformed the parameters of both local and national politics, particularly issues that deal with the relationship between community, identity, and civil rights. These changes in cities and neighborhoods set the context for the formation of social identity, and affect the bases and modes of establishing community linkages and ties, many of which reflect significant elements of Latin American culture and social relations. For some sectors of Latino immigrant communities, there is a tension between these community processes and the more traditional structures through which people can participate in politics and influence policy. The changing social bases of community formation have resulted in a much greater focus on the issues of citizenship, political participation, and human rights.

Following Carens's observation, the analysis developed in the subsequent chapters focuses on those aspects of the pattern of societal formation of the United States that have had the most significant formative impact on determining the level, type, and pattern of exclusionary forms of membership, belonging, and citizenship of Latinos since the early nineteenth century. In particular, I will concentrate on the following: how the U.S. conquest of Mexico and subsequent annexation of nearly 55 percent of previously Mexican territory influenced the historical framing of the racial, political, cultural, and economic locations of Latinos well into the contemporary period; the constitutive role of racialization in determining the structure of social and political hierarchies; and how the more recent related processes of globalization and restructuring have promoted a pattern of immigration of racially nonwhite peoples from around the globe, including Mexico, Central America, the Antilles, and parts of South America, as well as Asia and Africa. This last dynamic has been the most important proximate cause that has prompted and shaped the most recent discourse in the United States at both the theoretical and policymaking levels about issues of diversity, pluralism, difference, and otherness, and the convergence of these themes around the question of citizenship and the nature of societal membership more generally. These are the factors that have shaped the context in the United States within which what Beiner identifies as the core political and theoretical issue in the contemporary study of citizenship—i.e., "what binds citizens together into a shared political community"—has been engaged and contested not only in the rarified world of scholarship but also in state and federal legislatures, city councils, judicial and electoral arenas, and the media, as well as the manifold sites of quotidian politics in the streets, in the workplace, in universities, community organizations, and so on.

Citizenship as Contested Terrain

The notion of citizenship regime that I will advance here needs to be both situated within and distinguished from the various and different conceptions and approaches that characterize the broader field of citizenship studies.[19] I do so through a sustained engagement with, and rethinking of, a set of issues in political theory—such as multiculturalism, difference, identity, rights, and democracy—that are most often part of theoretical configurations within which conceptions of citizenship are developed. The changes brought about by the forces of globalization, restructuring, and transnationalization have generated conflict not only between different political groupings but also among scholars who have tried to make sense of these changes in terms of their effects on theories of democracy, on the appropriate role of cultural identities in politics, and on the political cohesion that is necessary for an effectively functioning democracy. For the purposes of this study, these different analyses can by grouped into works with an emphasis on the broader issue of diversity, and those that focus more specifically on citizenship. But both address the consequences and effects of similar processes. As a result, there is an inherent overlap between the two bodies of literatures.

Notions of citizenship either implicitly or explicitly rest on more general normative conceptions regarding the nature of belonging and societal membership, about inclusion and exclusion and the content of the political imaginary that defines the boundaries of these parameters, and about rights and ultimately notions of justice. These are some of the themes that pervade the works on diversity. My goal is to offer a framework for a concept of citizenship that provides an alternative to the dominant framings found in political theory, and that resonates with the Latino experiences of exclusionary belonging. Latinos have posed a dilemma for the notion of national identity based on white supremacy. This is because Latinos, like other groups who did not fit neatly within the normative national political imaginary on which the political system was based, have a history of being excluded and marginalized that is an indication of the flawed and limited conception of the relationships between national identity and membership and citizenship that exists in the United States. Thus Latino politics, with its emphasis on seeking full membership—and fulfilling the promise of democracy—has tended to be oppositional in nature, i.e., it has sought to challenge and change the norms of the political process that were designed to exclude Latinos.

This is why much of what follows in chapters 2 and 3 is a critical discussion and imminent critique of works in the field of political theory more generally, and lays the foundation for the model of citizenship regime that I advance in chapter 4. While the goal is to develop a theoretical foundation for conceptualizing citizenship in a way that is able to capture, account for, and engage the historical nuances of Latino experience in the United States, it is also meant to be an intervention in the field of political theory aimed at providing an alternative to many of the more orthodox conceptions of, and assumptions about, rights, identities, cultural and racial diversity, civil society, the public sphere, representation, participation, and democratic governance that characterize the field.

Diversity, Political Theory, and the Invisibility of the Social

Examining this broad range of issues that are contested, challenged, and debated within these different approaches to the study of diversity and citizenship, this book focuses on those aspects that are most pertinent and relevant to my argument regarding the central role of racialized alterity in mediating the tension between social and political membership in the case of Latinos and other racialized groups. Much of the work on citizenship is a response to the challenges presented to liberal democracies by deep forms of racial and cultural diversity and difference. The widespread qualitative changes in the racial and ethnic composition of liberal democracies of the U.S.-Euro center have clearly destabilized the normative conception of belonging embodied in the national imaginary that existed until it was challenged by the reality of deep diversity in both the realms of political and legal institutions, as well as in sites of everyday life that constitute the civil sphere.[20]

These conceptions of difference and alterity are key elements in the approaches to citizenship that I will engage, as well as in works that deal with the more general problem of social cohesion or solidarity in liberal democracies characterized by deep diversity. However, it is precisely these notions of alterity and solidarity that are undertheorized and inadequately developed. This limits the ability of these frameworks to fully account for or incorporate the qualitative nature of the Latino historical experience in the United States, let alone provide a conception of citizenship that can reconcile the systemic tensions between the political and societal membership status of Latinos that is the source of the forms of their societal exclusions. While these works reflect an acknowledgment that the homologous relationship between political and societal membership adopted by most modern political theory is no longer tenable, the various efforts to reestablish a stabilized relationship between political and cultural identities continue to be among the most contested conceptual and theoretical areas of concern in the field.

This limitation characterizes the work of some of the theorists who have had a major impact on defining the boundaries within which mainstream scholarly discourses and debates on deep diversity take place. Works by Rawls, Habermas, Walzer, and Taylor have played an important role in shaping the discursive parameters within which much of the contemporary analysis of the relationship between membership, difference, citizenship, and belonging has developed. While each advances a different particular theoretical argument and framework designed to reconcile the tensions of political and societal membership, they all share a common weakness. Despite the fact that these analyses of how to reconcile democratic inclusion in highly pluralistic societies all rely on some conception of reciprocity, solidarity, and/or mutual recognition as the basis for social solidarity and cohesion, the nature of this dimension is either unexamined or insufficiently developed. What ultimately undermines the effectiveness of these analyses is the failure to provide a satisfactory theoretical accounting of the nature, role, and significance of the specific construct of qualitative social relations—i.e., societal membership—on which their arguments are based. As a result, these theories and the analyses that are based on them are incapable of engaging or incorporating the radical nature of alterity of racialized others, including the figure of the racialized perpetual foreigner that has structured the political and cultural positionality of Latinos throughout U.S. history.

Pluralistic Alterity, Agonistic Solidarity, and Associative Citizenship

The challenge that these limitations pose is to develop a configuration of membership, belonging, and alterity that provides the basis for a theory and practice of citizenship capable of mediating the tensions that have arisen in liberal democracies around the issue of deep diversity. More specifically, this should provide a more complete understanding of the multidimensional processes by which Latino marginalization has occurred, focusing in particular on how the systemic and institutional disjunction between political and societal membership has produced the imaginary figuration of Latinos as racialized perpetual foreigners. One of the aims, then, of *Transforming Citizenship* is to provide a framework that develops and incorporates a notion of how alterity, membership, and belonging intersect that can more fully account for the dynamic of exclusionary forms of belonging that have marginalized Latinos historically and continue to affect a significant percentage of these communities. This effort requires a critical engagement with the question of what patterns of social cohesion and forms of solidarity are required to both create and sustain inclusive forms of democratic governance—an engagement that can provide the basis for the reformulation of the notion of citizenship as consistent with Marshall's normative notion of full membership. Such a conception can only be developed if the intersection between social and political membership is clearly delineated theoretically, demonstrating how the quotidian activities and relations of the civil sphere interface with the processes by which the boundaries of the political community are determined and discursively justified, enforced, and contested. What I advance in the following, then, is the idea of associative citizenship as a theoretical configuration that integrates particular conceptions of belonging, alterity, and membership to demonstrate the type of qualitative relations required for an inclusive form of democratic politics, and that is capable of accounting for the particular pattern of Latino marginalization that manifests itself in a specific racialized version of the "perpetual foreigner." By situating the traditional juridical notion of citizenship within the broader societal context from which both its meaning and practice derive, this framework and notion of associative citizenship provides a way of connecting the abstract, universalistic level of citizenship with its particularistic manifestations at the societal institutional level.

CHAPTER 2

Political Theory and Constructs of Membership

Difference and Belonging in Liberal Democracies

> The diversity of reasonable comprehensive religious, philosophical, and moral doctrines found in modern democratic societies is not a mere historical condition that may soon pass away; it is a permanent feature of the public culture of democracy.
>
> —John Rawls in *Political Liberalism*

> If America cannot confront the problem of pluralism, it is finished as a nation.
>
> —Bruce Ackerman in "Political Liberalisms"

ALTHOUGH THE UNITED STATES HAS ALWAYS BEEN A CULTURALLY DIVERSE country, that diversity has constantly presented a challenge to the normative political imaginary based on white supremacy that was such a fundamental aspect of the ideology that underlay the political and cultural system. One of the very first laws considered and passed by the initial Congress reflected the overriding concern about who qualified as a "real American," to use immigration scholar Bill Ong Hing's words (Hing 2004, 2). And Haney-López has written extensively on the fact that "In its first words on the subject of citizenship, Congress in 1790 restricted naturalization to 'white persons.' . . . From the earliest years of this country until just a generation ago, being a 'white person' was a condition for acquiring citizenship" (Haney-López 1996, 1). And far from having been resolved, this concern with "who belongs" continues to play a role in the contemporary period, as is reflected in Michael Walzer's essay "What It Means to Be an American," published in 1996. So the fact of diversity is not new. But culturally and racially distinct groups who were not considered to fit the normative political imaginary were regulated and marginalized from the mainstream of "American" life based on measures including force, legislation, and informal societal codes. That pattern of exclusion has always been challenged, of course, and since the social movements of the 1950s and 1960s, the demands for greater inclusion have been a constant source of division and conflict reflected in American politics.

Since the annexation of half of Mexico's territory in 1848, the cultural and racial features of peoples from Latin America were considered undesirable and did not fit into the normative idealized conception of who was a "real American." The subsequent pattern of exclusion has long been contested, but the rapid growth of Latino populations since 1970 has become one of the primary challenges and sources of political conflict and division in the United States. The challenge of accommodating and incorporating newly arrived immigrants, however, has been a consistent theme throughout U.S. history. And the mode and pattern of policies and ideologies to address the extensive growth of the Latino population that emerged in the contemporary period built on ideas, perceptions, and beliefs that viewed Latinos as a suspect group, whose identities and culture were considered foreign from the very first engagement with U.S. society. This is a crucial dimension that needs to be incorporated in any analysis of Latino political formation over the last 150 years. Given that historical pattern, the question arises of how best to account for and explain the nature of these relationships and positions. The conception of citizenship as full membership of Latinos in the entire range of societal institutions, implied in Marshall's framework, can only be realized if strategies and policies are pursued that promote the development of a set of processes and conditions designed to facilitate the creation of new forms of mutually acceptable, negotiated cultural and political space—that is, the kind of public sphere that not only can sustain real forms of interactive democratic inclusion, but in fact is constitutive of a form of citizenship that coincides with that kind of politics. While legal and juridical dimensions must be incorporated in such an effort, a broader range of social practices and structures that have an effect on the actual levels of access to the major institutions must also be developed in order to sustain the type of inclusive democratic citizenship advanced in my analysis. Because of the expansive nature of the problematic, much of the work on citizenship in societies characterized by deep diversity has drawn on a broader body of literatures that have sought to find ways to reconcile tensions arising from the new configuration of cultural, racial, and ethnic differences that increasingly characterize liberal democracies. The challenges these works address revolve around the question of what forms of belonging and membership can serve as the basis for the level and nature of societal cohesion or solidarity necessary for democratic governance to be viable and effective in states defined by deep racial and cultural diversities. While the emphases, approaches, and positions vary greatly in this literature, at the core of this problematic is the set of racial and ethnic tensions that have intensified in part as a result of the rapid and extensive migration of populations from racially distinct countries to the metropolitan centers of Europe, the United States, Canada, and Australia. The often extreme cultural and racialized disjunctions between the immigrant populations and the host society have resulted in the creation of spaces of liminality characterized by a topography of surface-level engagements floating above zones of, at best, anxiety, and at worst, suspicion and distrust.

The significance of the emergence of this polarization and these zones of liminality for democracy and societal membership has been addressed across many disciplines and fields, but has been a particular and major concern in political and social theory. Because of the centrality of the problematic of deep diversity in these literatures, I want to critically engage the fundamental positions that have been advanced by some of the major political and social theorists who have shaped the discursive parameters of much of the contemporary analysis of the intersection between membership, difference, citizenship, and belonging. My intention is not to undertake a review and analysis of the entire range of works in this literature, but instead to focus on those works that have been the major reference points for scholars who have studied the issue of deep diversity and division in liberal democracies. My goal here is to demonstrate the limitations of the way the issue of deep diversity has been framed in these works for addressing the nature and scope of Latino experiences in the United States.

While there are many classifications of the different approaches to the issue in the relevant extant literatures, my view is that the major works that have advanced broad frameworks for addressing the dilemmas posed by deep diversity in liberal democratic political societies have been configured in a number of often competing theoretical approaches based on liberal, communitarian, and radical perspectives. While not all of these engage the issue of citizenship directly, they lay out more general frameworks within which conceptions of citizenship have been developed. Although there is an extensive literature on various aspects of this kind of deep diversity, I focus here on the key foundational theoretical formulations developed by Rawls (1971, 1996); Habermas (1995a, 1995b, 1996); Walzer (1983, 1994, 1996,

1997); Kymlicka (1995a, 1995b); Taylor (1994); and Young (1990, 2000a, 2000b). These frameworks have had a major impact on defining the boundaries within which mainstream scholarly discourses and debates on deep diversity and citizenship have taken place. While the range of issues that have been addressed by these theorists, and the extensive literatures that engage their work, is quite broad, my intention is not to review the entire spectrum of the debates, but rather to focus on those aspects of the theories that are most salient to my analysis, namely, the theorization of the intersection between membership, democracy, and deep diversity and how these either advance or inflect conceptions of citizenship. Despite the different emphases, foci, and perspectives in these frameworks, they all center on the problematic of social and political cohesion as a fundamental challenge, and all rest on assumptions about the nature of qualitative relations that are necessary for a pluriversal democracy to function effectively. Each of these theorists organizes their analysis around different particular versions of concepts that are the basis of social cohesion, such as reciprocity, solidarity, and mutual recognition; but the theoretical work that these notions perform are quite similar. These in effect define the parameters of the idea of societal membership on which their arguments rest, but these notions reflect a number of the following limitations. Some are either not fully developed or not clearly delineated; most do not clearly link their positions theoretically to the implicit or explicit conception of political membership; and none address or account for racialization as one of the dimensions that have been fundamental, constitutive elements in defining the specific parameters of deep diversity in the United States. Each of these oversights severely limits the ability of these frameworks to provide an adequate understanding of the variable, complex, but essential ways through which societal relations structure and delimit the dynamic of citizenship more generally; each also fails to explain the patterns of exclusionary belonging that have defined the status of Latino communities. Neither are they capable of incorporating the radical nature of alterity of racialized others, including the figure of the racialized perpetual foreigner that has structured the political and cultural positionality and membership of Latinos throughout U.S. history. Thus the need to develop a new formulation of the relationship between forms of solidarity and belonging, alterity, and membership that delineates a configuration of these elements necessary for a conception of citizenship capable of incorporating and mediating the nature of the racialized form of alterity that Latino modes of membership have been based on, how that alterity is structured through institutions, and how Latinos experience and live it. As a first step in advancing such a formulation, I will examine the limitations of the way that the intersection between membership, democracy, and deep diversity are conceptualized in the following prevalent theoretical approaches.

Justice, Critical Theory, and the Fashioning of Political Solidarity: Rawls and Habermas

As indicated before, the works of both Rawls and Habermas have had a very significant impact on framing the discursive parameters of the debate on deep diversity. Rawls and Habermas have advanced complex theoretical frameworks that are designed to demonstrate that their different normative standards of justice and communicative rationality, respectively, can serve as the basis for meditating relations of deep diversity. Their formulations rest on a particular implicit conception of societal membership, and despite the difference in their theoretical projects, the validity of both these models depends on the existence of very specific types of qualitative social relations based on principles of reciprocity and/or mutuality. These are the axial pivots that define the cohesive parameters of their notions of societal membership. Yet Rawls simply brackets out this dimension and assumes its existence, while Habermas declares the need for a form of solidarity, but he provides only the briefest sketch of what this notion would need to look like, and does not demonstrate how it would be realized. The failure to provide a theoretical accounting of this dimension arguably results in both approaches having the same theoretical shortcoming. An analysis of how it affects and undermines the viability of specific aspects of the respective normative models of a culturally pluralistic society proposed by Rawls and Habermas is worth discussion.

Both Rawls and Habermas focus on the intersection between membership, democracy, and "multicultural" diversity in terms of a notion of public reason by which the validity or justification of the political claims or arguments of individuals is to be determined by standards of judgment that differ for Rawls and Habermas. In *Political Liberalism* (1996), Rawls presents a reformulation of the theory of justice he had offered nearly two decades before. In the more recent work, the goal is to defend a version of liberalism that addresses directly the new condition of deep substantive diversity—or pluralism, as he refers to it. Rawls states that the major question that his work addresses is: "How is it possible that there may exist over time a stable and just society of free and equal citizens profoundly divided by reasonable religious, philosophical, and moral doctrines?" (Rawls 1996, xxvii). This, he argues, is a problem of political justice, and Rawls advances a response by reconfiguring his notion of justice as fairness that rests on moral premises into what he calls a "freestanding" political concept of justice that "applies to the basic structure of society" (Rawls 1996, xliii). It is freestanding in the sense that it does not derive from a comprehensive substantive doctrine, but rather rests on its own "intrinsic normative and moral ideal" (Rawls 1996, xliv). Rawls then offers the following as the basis of his approach:

> Citizens are reasonable when, viewing one another as free and equal in a system of social cooperation over generations, they are prepared to offer one another fair terms of social cooperation (defined by principles and ideals) and they agree to act on those terms, even at the cost of their own interests in particular situations, provided that others also accept those terms. For these terms to be fair terms, citizens offering them must reasonably think that those citizens to whom such terms are offered might also reasonably accept them. (Rawls 1996, xliv)

This criterion of cooperation that Rawls refers to as "reciprocity" must ultimately find expression and be incorporated as rights and duties within the major institutions of society if pluralistic (multicultural) democracy is to function effectively (Rawls 1996, 16). Much of *Political Liberalism* is devoted to specifying and qualifying the conditions, characteristics, and concomitant factors that are implied by this premise and that are necessary to establish and sustain its connection to the political realm proper. This last point is important to Rawls since he wants to emphasize that the solution to the problem of fundamental differences in democracies must be located as a "political" solution that is forged within public institutions (the public sphere?) and not within the realm of civil society, or "background culture," as he calls it (14). Yet there seems to be a tension in Rawls's position here since he also holds that "the role of the criterion of reciprocity as expressed in public reason . . . is to specify the nature of the political relation in a constitutional democratic regime as one of civic friendship. This criterion, when citizens follow it in their public reasoning, shapes the form of their fundamental institutions" (Rawls 1996, li). However, the language of friendship is a curious choice for conveying the insistence that the political realm (as Rawls construes it) must be the forum for addressing differences. This reflects ambivalence at the core of Rawls's argument about the relationship between social and political membership. He does not want to be interpreted as accepting any particular substantive value or commitment, yet neither does he want to ignore the fundamental role of "background culture." And so he attempts to provide for a linkage by arguing as follows: "In a democratic society there is a tradition of democratic thought, the content of which is at least familiar and intelligible to the educated common sense of citizens generally. Society's main institutions, and their accepted forms of interpretation, are seen as a fund of implicitly shared ideas and principles" (14). Thus civil society can be the source of "shared principles," which I take it would provide a basis for an "overlapping consensus" but cannot itself be the site of the "public sphere." While Rawls seeks to construe reciprocity as a variant of a procedural contractualism, his conception of it nevertheless constitutes a qualitative concept rooted in a particular set of assumptions about what the substantive nature of social relations must be like for democracy to function effectively.

Like Rawls, Habermas has more recently attempted to rework some of his earlier formulations, and as part of that project has offered a wide-ranging articulation and defense of what he refers to as a "deliberative model of politics" (Habermas 1996).[1] Habermas considers both liberal and communitarian views of politics as incapable of providing the normative standards for the justification of democracy and to account for the reality of pluralism. While the former conceives of democratic politics in terms of the procedural dimensions for reaching compromises, the latter advances a concept that rests on principles of substantive ethical content. In contrast, Habermas provides an alternative formulation that he argues "takes elements from both sides and integrates these in the concept of an ideal procedure for deliberation and decision-making" (Habermas 1996, 26). He develops his position by elaborating the notion of "communicative rationality" that has been one of the cornerstones of Habermas's work for the last three decades. He argues that the core of this notion is "the linguistic medium through which interactions are woven together and forms of life are structured. This rationality is inscribed in the linguistic telos of mutual understanding and forms an ensemble of conditions that both enable and limit" (Habermas 1998, 3–4). From this notion, he has formulated a discourse ethics that establishes a procedure for justifying the norms of justice that must define the institutional basis of democratic legitimacy, and through which rational agreements between differing parties can be reached. Habermas elaborates the nature of this procedure through his construct of the "ideal speech" situation, which spells out the general conditions that must exist for this process to function effectively. Thus the model of deliberative politics proposed by Habermas rests on a discourse theory of ethics and society that derives the validity of political norms from the "very structure of communicative actions" (Habermas 1996, 26).

In contrast to Rawls, Habermas has argued for an institutionally expansive notion of the "political," and he has used the notion of the public sphere to develop an argument for the particular role that participation must play in democratic systems. For Habermas, the public sphere consists of those institutional spaces in society where individuals who are affected by collective decisions and societal norms have an opportunity to engage in public dialogue as a means to affect these. This is a form of democratic participation that must go beyond the formal institutions of government and that includes the realm of civil society. It is a recognition that democratic legitimacy must have a foundation in the realm of public life more generally defined, one that is rooted in the dialogical, intersubjective engagement of individuals seeking to find agreement through discourse. As a means for elaborating this process, Habermas relies on the notion of the ideal speech situation through which he establishes the specific conditions that must exist within the public sphere in order for this dialogical, intersubjective engagement to result in the validation of democratic norms. What are these conditions? In summarizing this aspect of Habermas's argument, Benhabib correctly observes that "the normative constraints of the ideal speech situation or of practical discourses have been specified as the conditions of universal moral respect and egalitarian reciprocity" (Benhabib 1992, 105). These two criteria and the relationship between them define, I argue, the way in which Habermas construes the intersection of membership, democracy, and plurality.

This aspect of Habermas's argument rests on the notion that for the ideal speech situation to realize its function of promoting the process of the resolution of conflicting values, there must first exist social bonds of mutual trust and reciprocity between those who engage in that public dialogue. And these in turn require an intersubjective network of mutual recognition, which Habermas has sought to elaborate through his discussion of the relationship between justice and solidarity. Adapting and modifying the work of Kohlberg on moral development, Habermas argues that individuals can only take form "by growing into a speech community and thus into an intersubjectively shared lifeworld" (Habermas 1989b, 46). Therefore any norm that governs behavior cannot secure the integrity of the individual "without at the same time safeguarding the vitally necessary web of relationships of mutual recognition in which individuals can stabilize their fragile identities only mutually and simultaneously with the identity of their group" (47). Thus justice, which is the realm of promoting equal treatment and dignity for individuals, cannot be realized without solidarity—that is, without at the same time pursuing the welfare and well-being of the members of a community without which the individual could not exist as himself or herself. For Habermas, then, the grounding of the legitimacy claims of democracy rests and depends on the existence of these qualitative characteristics of the social relations between its members that define the nature of societal membership. Without a form of societal membership based on bonds of respect, mutual recognition, and solidarity, the conditions for the realization of a just and democratic society would be absent.

The Politics of Recognition and Cultural Membership

Despite the considerable difference in the mode of argument and analysis, both Rawls and Habermas subscribe to similar premises that are fundamental to liberalism. Most scholars and critics agree that principles of universality, primacy of individual autonomy and liberty, and state neutrality are basic to the perspectives and framing of the issues of deep diversity that both theorists advance.[2] I would add that the specific form of the theoretical commitments make it difficult for Rawls and Habermas to fully account for the dimension of sociality and societal membership that I argue is crucial in developing an adequate analysis of the historical pattern of marginalization and exclusion of Latinos. However, Charles Taylor and Michael Walzer have both offered liberal approaches to framing the issue of deep diversity in liberal democracies that foregrounds community and group membership, and so merit a review of their positions to examine the extent to which they provide a more adequate theoretical framework for explaining the processes of marginalization of Latinos. While both analyses are rooted in strong commitments to individual liberty and autonomy, they nevertheless attempt to demonstrate that these can be reconciled with the broader contextual elements of culture within which those principles must manifest themselves. Taylor and Walzer advance, unlike the solely universalist premises found in Rawls and Habermas, arguments and frameworks intended to offer a way of mediating between the universal (embodied in rights of individual liberty and autonomy) and the particular characteristics of groups who make claims on the dominant political and cultural system. Both offer a conception of the basis of a liberal national community and propose a notion of the liberal state as a form of political community that is based on a set of common meanings embodied in a shared language, history, and culture—all of which means that the question and nature of societal membership is one of the major issues they address.

Let me take up Taylor's position in this section, keeping in mind that my focus is on those aspects of his theory that are most relevant for the issue of the relationship between societal and political membership. Taylor (1994) builds his response and prescription for dealing with deep diversity (what he designates the "politics of difference") on what he calls the "politics of recognition." In developing this position, Taylor adopts the idea of equal human dignity as advanced in modernity as a point of departure, arguing that this normative ideal focuses on establishing that all human beings share certain characteristics in common that establish their potentially equal moral value and worth. This belief in universal human potential emerged from the idea of an autonomous individual capable of self-reflection and self-interpretation, the foundation of modern individualist identity based on self-realization and development. This in turn led to the need and/or demand for recognition of the self by others, of the inherent value of the self. However, drawing on the influence of Hegel, Taylor argues that the development of the self as the basis of individual identity cannot take place outside of a dialogically constituted broader societal community of other selves. And so it is here that Taylor attends to the nature of community and memberships. It is the meanings of the community within which individuals exist that provide the basis of identity, but not in a static way. Instead, it is through dialogue with other selves that our sense of self is refined and emerges. And so language has a privileged role in Taylor's framework as not only the medium for the development of individual identity but also the way through which culture is transformed. Taylor holds, then, to a notion of an inherently intersubjective, dialogical notion of the self, not surprising given his Hegelian perspective. And following this line of thinking, this means that recognition by other selves is a need that individuals have, since it is only through this interaction with others that the self can emerge. Without the recognition of one's identity and self, then, the process of authentic identity development and self-realization cannot occur. As a result, withholding recognition can inflict a distinctive and fundamental harm on the individual. This dialectically changing relationship is the key basis for Taylor's notion of membership, for it is only through membership in the linguistically shared common culture that the autonomous self can emerge. And it is the ground for engaging the arguments advanced by the proponents of the "politics of difference."

Taylor takes the primary challenge that the politics of difference presents for liberal democracies, and the major axis on which it depends, to be the premise that difference-blind conceptions of rights and political principles cannot facilitate policies that address the specific needs of culturally "different" groups. Taylor basically agrees that universal standards applied to groups with different cultural values and beliefs can result in a form of collective denial of recognition of the identities of the members of those groups, so long as "fundamental" rights such as liberty, life, free speech, due process are not abridged. However, unlike the universalist positions found in traditional liberalism, the political system or state can and should enact policies that take into account cultural difference and are meant to protect cultural survival—what he calls the "right of cultural survival"—of minority groups, because, as he has already laid out, those cultural frameworks are the medium through which the minority self develops, and thus to deny it recognition would be to undermine the freedom to develop fully. Taylor refers to these types of policies as "immunities" and "privileges," a distinction crucial to his argument but never clearly delineated in a theoretically grounded manner. But in an important qualification, Taylor does not agree that his position leads to a form of cultural relativism that would immobilize the power of the state to protect more fundamental rights. So he rejects the idea that the right to cultural survival leads to the premise that all cultures are equally worthy or valuable. Instead, he argues that those in the dominant culture should immerse themselves in the culture of the other to discern what is worthy and what is not.

These are the basic elements of Taylor's conception of societal membership. While it represents a step in the direction of recognizing the importance of the organic relationship between societal and political membership, his formulation has fundamental flaws, different in nature than those that characterize the positions of

Rawls and Habermas, but that nevertheless limit its usefulness and effectiveness in addressing the specific type of historical marginalization experienced by Latinos. Let me outline the nature of the most basic limitations.

The first point is that while Taylor is attempting to incorporate the contextual dimensions that account for differential specificity of groups in society, he limits that context primarily to cultural factors. While he mentions that other factors can affect the cultural matrix of a society, there is no analysis of the economic and political dimensions that affect identity formation. Without articulating the interacting influences of these different realms of inherently related human activity, there can be no meaningful discussion or formulation of how exclusions or marginalizations in the societal realm, broadly defined, affect the level and nature of access to and participation in the political community. As an extension of this point, and as many critics of Taylor's work point out, there is no accounting for the issue of power and power differentials, and how these affect the cultural context that is the main focus of his position. This curious omission is one of the major criticisms leveled at Taylor's position by those who are advocates of a politics of difference.[3] What results, in the view of these critics, is a focus on "recognition" at the expense of an examination of what is involved in the process of "misrecognition." A more accurate rendering of the world of "realpolitik" clearly indicates that cultural formations are not neutral processes, and that the struggle to define the forms of representation of both normatively privileged and denigrated aspects of the society is a key factor in determining the definition of who the national imaginary is—the "we" that is acceptable and is in a position to do the recognizing. Because Taylor omits the issue of differential relations of power in the way he frames his approach, he completely overlooks the privileged position he accords to the culture of those who he assumes must do the "recognizing." This very framing of the issue obviously implies their superior position, and affirms and validates that superior position. Nor does he inquire into or examine the reasons why the politics of difference has emerged at this time, what were the political forces or dynamics that account for the assertions by marginalized groups at this particular historical juncture. The failure to make power issues and differentials central in his analysis renders Taylor incapable of engaging or even considering that the reason may have something to do with the hegemonic role of Western, Anglo-European culture, submerging and marginalizing cultures of non-European peoples and societies. In a scathing critique of this process as a reaffirmation of white hegemony, Bannerji asserts: "The central questions for Taylor are: do 'we' have any obligation to recognize 'them,' and do 'they' have any right to force this recognition from 'us'?" (Bannerji 2000, 134).

Contrary to Taylor's interpretation—or perhaps more accurately, misinterpretation—the point is that marginalized groups have not been refused recognition at all.

They have in fact been "recognized" quite explicitly, but in primarily negative terms that seek to rationalize and legitimize their marginalized status. This misrecognition is what is contested by these groups in the development of their oppositional political strategies. One does not have to subscribe to the entirety of Gramsci's (1971) analysis of hegemony to recognize that the struggle for the power to define normative representations and criteria is a key characteristic of modern politics, and certainly of liberal democracies. In his effort to reformulate a more realistic and feasible conception of multiculturalism, Parekh characterizes Taylor's argument as "sanitized" and observes that regarding the status of the "misrecognized," Taylor "seems to think that the dominant group can be rationally persuaded to change its views of them by intellectual argument and moral appeal. This is to misunderstand the dynamics of the process of recognition." And he adds that because misrecognition has "both a cultural and a material basis. . . . therefore, [it] can only be countered by both undertaking a rigorous critique of the dominant culture and radically restructuring the prevailing inequalities of economic and political power." He concludes that "No multicultural society can be stable and vibrant unless it ensures that its constituent communities receive both just recognition and a just share of economic and political power" (Parekh 2000, 342–43).

So both Taylor's analysis of the challenges presented by the politics of difference, and the formulation he advances to deal with them are seriously flawed because his framing reaffirms the marginalized economic and political institutional position of exclusion of "those" who are demanding recognition of their cultures. As a result, it completely negates the possibility of the type of mutuality that must characterize a democratic process capable of addressing the patterns of material inequality that characterize the position of these marginalized groups within the structure of liberal democratic polities.

Multiculturalism Lite: Kymlicka and the Discourse of Group Diversity

The work of Will Kymlicka provides an alternative to Taylor's erasure of the broader institutional factors that help create and maintain the kind of marginalization that defines the pattern of deep diversity. The goal of his analysis is to advance a reformulation of some of the positions proposed by the theorists I have discussed above, and he attempts to modify some of the basic tenets of liberal political theory to reconcile tensions arising from the new configuration of cultural, racial, and ethnic relations that increasingly characterize liberal democracies. As with my discussion of those theorists, I will focus only on those aspects that are relevant to the construct of societal membership that is adopted by Kymlicka. Unlike Taylor's restriction of his analysis of membership to the cultural realm, Kymlicka explicitly addresses the problem of deep diversity as a political phenomenon and develops the notion of multicultural citizenship to advance his argument. As the following discussion will demonstrate, Kymlicka's conception of multicultural citizenship incorporates a particular notion of reciprocity and/or mutuality as key elements. However, these figurations are limited in terms of providing a political solution to the "problem" of cultural diversity. Neither of them develops or incorporates a concept of alterity capable of accounting for the systematic, institutional, and individual effects of processes of racialization on the intersection between societal and political membership in the United States in particular. They also do not sufficiently recognize that as long as the conditions and terms of incorporation and inclusion are dictated by the dominant groups to marginalized populations and are not themselves subject to challenge, the mutual acceptance of a reconfigured national imaginary is not likely to emerge. Far from being exclusively the domain of the political or legal spheres, these terms of incorporation are rooted in, and enacted through, the practices and norms of the institutions in civil society.[4]

My critique might appear to be misplaced or a misinterpretation, since both Kymlicka and Taylor are concerned with the status of marginalized or subordinated groups. However, a closer look at Kymlicka's framing reveals that his conceptualization and formulation of diversity is of limited applicability to the case of groups other than African Americans that have been racialized, as well as how the structure of power based on the principle of white supremacy affects these groups. Let me first review Kymlicka's position; his work is important for my analysis because it is one of the leading referents for addressing the new terrain of citizenship in societies characterized by fundamental difference and deep diversity (Kymlicka 1995a, 1995b; Kymlicka and Norman 2000). It is through the institution of citizenship that Kymlicka connects the issue of deep diversity to the political realm. His work seeks to provide a way to bridge two major and seemingly irreconcilable perspectives on citizenship, and to advance a theory of citizenship that can account for the reality of deep diversity. The first of these positions, the liberal approach, is organized around the primacy of individual rights, and citizenship is construed in terms of the individual as the bearer of these rights. These rights ensure that private individuals can pursue their self-interests through the protection of the state, whose primary function is to mediate conflict and regulate activities. The opposing view is that proposed in the communitarian formulation, and although there are several versions of this approach, what is common to each of these is the conception of rights as a function of membership in a historically specific society, community, or state, as well as the emphasis on the formative role that cultural context plays in defining the nature and significance of claims to rights. It is only within the context of the specific configuration of social relations, institutions, and culture that the idea of rights can be understood and realized.

Kymlicka's goal is to advance a new "distinctively liberal approach to minority rights" that preserves the basic principles of individual freedom, but that is not limited by the traditional liberal conceptualizations of citizenship that insist that all rights must be "difference-blind," and that refuse to allow for any form of group rights (Kymlicka 1995a, 7). He notes that modern societies are increasingly "multicultural," but adds that the ways that this is formulated are exceedingly vague and ambiguous, primarily because the concept has not been grounded in an analysis of "how the historical incorporation of minority groups shapes their collective institutions, identities, and aspirations" (11). In order to overcome this lack of specificity, Kymlicka proposes four types of difference: separate nations within an existing state; immigrant ethnic groups; refugees and exiles; and the special circumstances of African Americans. The rights claims of distinct cultural groups need to be understood and evaluated in terms of the different institutional articulations that define each of these categories. But it is the first two that are primarily the focus of Kymlicka's concern. In developing and examining the situation of diversity that arises from the multinational position, the nation is understood as a "historical community, more or less institutionally complete, occupying a given territory or homeland, sharing a distinct language and culture" (11). The second source of cultural difference is immigration, a situation where groups seek affirmation of their ethnic identity but do not intend to establish a separate "nation" and instead aim to "modify the institutions and laws of the mainstream society to make them more accommodating of cultural differences" (11). Kymlicka identifies these as "two broad patterns of cultural diversity," and the specifics of the incorporation of these multinational and polyethnic groups require three forms of group-differentiated rights for these groups to acquire effective citizenship status: self-governmental rights, polyethnic rights, and special representation rights.

While this formulation represents a significant advance in the attempt to formulate conceptions of citizenship that can accommodate the challenges of diverse cultural identities, it is nevertheless limited by a set of specific problems. For while Kymlicka acknowledges the institutional dimensions of the problematic he confronts, his theorization of the structural changes that constitute the very context that he argues must be incorporated remains at a level of generality and abstraction that at best makes it difficult to determine the validity of this formulation, and at worst distorts or obscures the very reality it seeks to address. For example, Kymlicka acknowledges the vagueness of the ways multiculturalism has been used, and even alludes to the processes of "globalization" as having a determinative effect on the issue. "Globalization has made the myth of a culturally homogeneous state even more unrealistic, and has forced the majority within each state to be more open to pluralism and diversity. The nature of ethnic and national identities is changing in a world of free trade and global communications, but the challenge of multiculturalism is here to stay" (Kymlicka 1995a, 9). Yet nowhere in his work is there a systematic analysis of multiculturalism as a set of specific institutional social practices and power relations that are part of a broader process of social transformation. Even more problematic is the lack of specification of the processes of globalization that Kymlicka acknowledges are a crucial factor in producing the particular pattern of cultural differences that are now so much contested. And it is not simply that a more "complete" analysis of these phenomena would fill out the argument, for an accurate understanding of globalization at the level of institutional specificity of the practices that constitute it would in fact alter the very way in which the issue of citizenship in a multicultural context must be conceptualized. This is particularly crucial for understanding how patterns, practices, policies, and ideologies of racialization function in creating a particular type of alterity. What needs to be addressed, then, is how to ground the analysis of the practices of right claims within specific institutional sites that define the specific parameters of social membership within a particular multicultural society, and how to incorporate adequately this dimension of institutional specificity of social membership in the formulation of both the theory and practices of rights claims, which constitute the contested terrain of citizenship. This mode of theorization would thus account for these institutional sites, spaces, or places as constitutive of multicultural social relations rather than simply a contextual or additive dimension.

While Kymlicka acknowledges the significance of the issue of solidarity, the concept of citizenship he develops is not robust enough to deal with the nature of the disjunction between groups like Latinos and the larger society because he does not incorporate a notion of otherness or alterity that provides an adequate understanding of the racialized historical experience of Latinos. The notion of group-differentiated citizenship is too abstract to account for the nature of alterity that exists. "What is clear, I think, is that if there is a viable way to promote a sense of solidarity and common purpose in a multinational state, it will involve accommodating, rather than subordinating, national identities. People from different national groups will only share an allegiance to the large polity if they see it as the context within which their national identity is nurtured, rather than subordinated" (Kymlicka 1995b, 189). This makes clear the central role that the notion of solidarity plays in Kymlicka's notion of membership that underlies his construction of multicultural citizenship; but the fact is that despite its importance, it remains relatively unexamined, much in the same way that this dimension is assumed in Rawls and Habermas.

Arbitrating Membership, Nation, and Political Identities: Walzer

As I have shown in the previous sections, Rawls, Habermas, Taylor, and Kymlicka, all recognized as key figures in defining the parameters of the theoretical discourse on difference and deep diversity within the liberal tradition, develop their analyses and prescriptions based on certain assumptions about the nature of societal membership. While neither Rawls nor Habermas attends in any significant way to examining the latter, Taylor addresses it directly but frames and limits it in terms of primarily cultural identity, and Kymlicka advances a formulation that cannot account for the types of differences that Latino communities represent. And although he argues that a dialogical dimension must be part of developing a basis for "cultural survival" of marginalized groups, Taylor's framing of the issue in effect instantiates and affirms the subordinate position of members of those groups. We find a different strategy advanced in the work of Michael Walzer, another of the theorists who have helped define the discursive framing of the issue of deep diversity.

Walzer is one of the few political theorists who deals directly and explicitly with the issue of membership. Like the other theorists discussed so far, Walzer makes the social dimension of membership crucial to his approach by focusing on what he refers to as societal "shared understandings." But unlike them, he does have a sustained, detailed analysis and argues that this dimension is determined within the parameters of a particular model of civil society. This approach has the great merit of incorporating and rooting his analysis in the experiences and values of everyday life—a clear advantage over abstract models of subjectivity in the works of Habermas and Rawls, and the limited cultural framework adopted by Taylor. Walzer's notion of membership is framed within a broader theoretical framework that argues for a pluralistic concept of distributive justice quite different from that of Rawls, and that he develops on the basis of what he refers to as "shared understanding." While he presents this most fully in his influential book *Spheres of Justice*, he applies this to a broader range of issues, some of which are particularly relevant to my analysis (Walzer 1983).[5] Walzer views societies as distributive communities through which different social goods are allocated to various members. These goods are what are created through societal processes and are differentially valued according to the meanings ascribed to them by the members of the community. But these goods are so different in form and function that no one set of principles can adequately provide the basis of a just pattern of distribution. Instead, Walzer posits that there are three spheres of justice, and argues

> that the principles of justice are themselves pluralistic in form; that different social goods ought to be distributed for different reasons, in accordance with different procedures, by different agents; and that all these differences derive from different understandings of the social goods themselves—the inevitable product of historical and cultural particularism. (Walzer 1983, 6)

What emerges clearly from Walzer's argument and analysis is that there are no external standards for deriving these principles of justice. Instead, they must be rooted in the shared understandings that members of a community subscribe to. And so, societal membership is fundamentally defined by these shared understandings. But as a number of commentators have argued, this appears to be a completely relativistic position, incapable of providing standards external to a community. Indeed, the notion of "community" seems to hold a privileged position in Walzer's framework and serves as the referent for any normative considerations that arise. As such, the most important good to be distributed is societal membership itself, since that is what determines who can legitimately participate in the processes by which decisions about justice can be made.

Walzer is clearly aware of the issue of domination and subordination of groups within society and has written about the need for toleration and civility. Yet it is difficult to square his notion of justice with these analyses. The problem is that Walzer's scheme seems to assume that all members of a society can participate equally in the creation of "shared understandings" that are the basis of the principles of justice. But the historical record in societies like the United States is one where unequal levels of participation in this process are the norm rather than the exception. And the question of immigrants has been particularly salient in the last several decades because of the rapid growth in non-European-origin populations. These immigrants clearly arrive with a different set of substantive shared understandings. Through what process and at what point are they to be considered full members of the receiving "community?" These kinds of problems with Walzer's concept of membership are particularly evident in Walzer's short book *What It Means to Be an American* (1996). First, membership is tied specifically to only one form of political community, the nation-state, so there is no way, for example, to account for the growing numbers of individuals, particularly Latino and Asian immigrants, who have or want to have multiple memberships. An increasing number of Latin American countries encourage dual citizenship, for example. Mexico, Colombia, and the Dominican Republic are well-known cases, but the list is likely to grow because of the strong ties, particularly given the level of financial support Latino immigrants provide for families who are dependent on them. This, I believe, leads to a second weakness in Walzer's formulation, which is that while he claims that his approach adopts a pragmatic perspective, he seems to be unable to address the qualitative changes brought about by the very significant quantitative growth in the United States of populations with fundamentally different cultural frames, traditions, and beliefs. He simply assumes that despite this dramatic cultural shift, his original way of thinking about membership will be relatively unaffected. This is particularly problematic in dealing with those populations that have historically been considered borderline foreigners or not "real" Americans, but who have nevertheless become a very significant and functional part of the society. This leads to arguments that rest on virtually no understanding or historical knowledge of communities such as Latinos, reflecting the fact that Walzer's position is unable to mediate between the qualitative differences that exist within the cultural and social conditions on which the "sphere of justice" depends. For example, Walzer asserts the irrelevance of Mexicans (based on systems of exclusion) to the formation of American pluralism (Walzer 1996, 57). This is, then, an "American pluralism" that is not really pluralistic, that is in fact a form of "exclusionary pluralism" since, for example, Mexicans, as well as African Americans, have not been, according to Walzer, a part of developing that pluralism in the United States. This becomes a type of "selective pluralism" that by its very formation instantiates, reinforces, and justifies the exclusionary modes of belonging of Latinos that contradict the very notion of "pluralism" on which Walzer's argument is based.

On Young's Notion of Structural Differentiation

While all of the theorists I have discussed to this point advance different formulations for addressing conditions of deep diversity, these frameworks nevertheless rest on normative standards related in some way to notions of justice and its relationship to democracy. And as I have tried to demonstrate, they all have shortcomings that limit their ability to address the specific type of marginalization that has characterized the experience of Latinos in the United States. As I pointed out in the introduction, I believe that there is no avoiding the fact that the claims for inclusion that Latinos have made throughout their history are in fact normative claims based on standards of justice that not only give expression to a sense of exclusion, but that address the erasure from the national political imaginary that defines the societal "we" that is extended to the criteria of political membership. However the frameworks that these theorists offer do not provide a standard of justice that resonates with these kinds of claims rooted at the level of lived experience of marginalized communities, and certainly not that of Latinos. None of these theoretical analyses provide a detailed accounting of the relationship between societal and political membership, nor do they incorporate an analysis of the effect of processes of racialization in determining the variation in the level and type of incorporation of different groups. While I will take up the issue of racialization in the following chapter, I want to suggest here that the framework developed by Iris Young for examining the relationship between deep diversity, democratization, and standards of justice offers a more adequate foundation than the work of the theorists I have reviewed for understanding the nexus between societal and political membership that underlies Latino claims for inclusion—what Marshall's notion of full citizenship entailed.

Although I will not address all of the issues that Young engages in developing her framework, I do want to delineate in sufficient detail those aspects that are most relevant to my project. Young defines her primary task as examining the "implications for political philosophy of the claims of new group-based social movements associated with left politics" and adds that she seeks to uncover the nature of the implicit "conceptions of social justice" that these groups drew on (Young 1990, 3). She argues that this requires that the notion of justice be redefined, quite differently from the other theorists who conceive of it as a societal and political "good" and focus on the problem of how justice is to be "distributed." This, however, does not in Young's view seem to capture the nature of the claims to justice and inclusion that emerged as a fundamental, constitutive characteristic of the struggles of the social movements of the 1960s. Groups who had experienced forms of exclusion and marginalization, such as Latinos, African Americans, Native Americans, Asians, women, and gays, organized politically to press for greater access to, and inclusion in, the mainstream major societal institutions. Young refers explicitly to this pattern of historical marginalization and exclusion in the United States as oppression or domination.[6] This stance resonates much more directly with the kind of marginalization that has been central in the historical experience of Latinos. Young finds the root of that domination, as I do, to be in structural institutional relations. While this is a common position in political sociology, at the time Young was developing her analysis, few works in traditional political theory, including those discussed in this chapter, adopted an approach to the analysis of justice based on structural considerations. Young distinguishes her approach from what she considers the ahistorical orthodox perspectives, and identifies her approach as that of critical theory, by which she means "socially and historically situated normative analysis and argument" (Young 2000a, 10). She expands on this in the following:

A critical theory does not derive such principles and ideals from philosophical premises about morality, human nature, or the good life. Instead, the method of critical theory, as I understand it, reflects on existing social relations and processes to identify what we experience as valuable in them, but as present only intermittently, partially, or potentially. . . . Normative critical theory constructs accounts of these democratic ideals that render articulate and more systematic those feelings of dissatisfaction and lack which we normally experience in actual democratic politics." (Young 2000a, 10)

From this perspective, Young concludes that if a theory of justice is developed and presented as universal and not rooted in the specific elements of particular societal situations, institutions, or practices, "then it is simply too abstract to be useful in evaluating actual institutions and practices" (Young 1990, 4).

What, then, are the basic aspects of the alternative formulation that Young offers? She focuses on the way that groups are conceptualized in the various analyses of how to deal with deep diversity. While she agrees with those who point out the need to address the claims of culturally distinct groups in liberal democracies, Young finds that the emphasis on cultural identity limits the ability to understand the political and power dynamic within which marginalized groups function. Instead, Young makes a distinction between what she refers to as two different "politics of difference." The first is the politics of cultural difference that focuses on the challenge of promoting equality of freedoms of cultural forms and practices that are the foundation of cultural identities. The second approach is the politics of positional difference, and it is primarily concerned with the reality of structural inequality. While the politics of cultural difference foregrounds questions of identity, the politics of positional difference focuses on the location of a particular group in the hierarchy of power and inequality, which has an impact on life chances and opportunities, such as access to resources and labor markets, housing, health care, education, and so forth. This distinction is particularly significant for my emphasis on the relationship between societal membership (or social position, in Young's terms) and political membership. In this formulation, the claims to cultural recognition are not an end in themselves, but rather a means to challenge structural inequality and exclusion.

Instead of focusing on "identity" as a set of substantive attributes that are the basis of the oppositional politics of marginalized groups, Young asserts that groups need to be understood in relationship terms. Cultural groups are defined in terms of cultural differences, but structural groups emerge and coalesce as a function of social relations based on class, gender, race that are codified within the major societal institutions, and are thus groups identified on the basis of their common position in a structure of power. Even the salience of cultural difference only develops as a result of interaction with other groups. From a relational perspective, then, groups should not be understood in terms of a substantive logic, but rather in terms of what is needed to conceive of the formation of groups in terms of a relational logic where groups are differentiated from other groups on the basis of cultural forms and practices embedded within a specific structure of power.

> Considered relationally, a social group is a collective of persons differentiated from others by cultural forms, practices, special needs or capacities, structures of power or privilege. . . . In a relational conceptualization, what makes a group a group is less some set of attributes its members share than the relations in which they stand to others. . . .
>
> Cultural difference emerges from internal and external relations. People discover themselves with cultural affinities that solidify them into groups by virtue of their encounter with those who are culturally different in some or many respects. In discovering themselves as distinct, cultural groups usually solidify a mutual affinity and self-consciousness of themselves as groups. (Young 2000a, 90–91)

The political valence and implications of this formulation shift the theoretical and practical optic for interpreting the nature of Latino politics from one based on identity politics that has been commonplace not only among scholars, but within the realm of policymaking as well. So, for example, most of the opposition to, as well as support for, policies such as affirmative action are conceived as responding to Latino group claims based on a particular cultural identity. Indeed, Latino policymakers, politicians, and scholars buy into this framing of the issue. This is also apparent in claims that there is a pan-Latino base that can be mobilized solely on the basis of a common identity, when in fact, Latinos are a very heterogeneous, diverse population, marked by differences not only in country of origin, but also class and racial makeup.[7] But it is important to stress that adopting the conception of Latinos as a structurally defined group does not in any way mean that cultural identity is not a defining and fundamental characteristic of Latinos. The formation of Latino cultural identities is a crucial factor in understanding not only Latino politics but also the broader range of social and cultural practices that are core factors influencing behavior, beliefs, and perspectives. However, as I have already argued, the significance of Latino cultural identities and claims for societal recognition for the political sphere is their location within a hierarchy of power, and that they have become means to the end of challenging conditions of structural inequalities. The issue of the formation of Latino identities is a separate but obviously important issue for the question of how it influences the possibilities of both individual and collective political action. Understanding Latinos as a structural group facilitates the focus on, and analysis of, the processes of exclusion. It should be recalled that so-called identity politics emerged directly in response to the consequences of the images of perceived identity of groups, developed within the dominant culture, that were the basis of discrimination and marginalization. There would not have been any "identity" politics or need for it had it not been for the history of exclusionary practices based on "identities." Groups organized and mobilized around the factor that was the basis of marginalization. Thus it was the perception of Latinos and African Americans as inferior that, for example, led to their systematic exclusion. So it was logical for groups to organize around the characteristic that was the basis for that marginalization. Of course there were differences in identities among Latinos, but those differences were not salient to the dominant groups. For example, after the disappearance of Mexican elites in the Southwest, whites did not differentiate much between different Latinos in terms of class, gender, region, or national origin. It was the fact of being perceived as Latino that was the basis for discrimination. In the period since the 1970s, those differences in identities became more visible and salient within Latino populations and have been a source of division and conflict between different groups. And these became important for scholars studying the various Latino communities, and particularly important for the notion of Latino empowerment.

The notion of Latinos as a structurally defined group allows us to avoid a form of politics that is centered on the idea of a unified ideology based on consensus, and yet recognizes and acknowledges the perceived identity as the basis for institutional marginalization. Instead, we can account for the very significant differences in perspectives, class position, cultural identities and focus on addressing those aspects of social and political relations that produce and maintain the forms of structural inequalities that position Latinos within a hierarchy of power and privilege. It also means that we have to begin to acknowledge that some sectors of Latino communities will have much greater privileges and advantages than others, and that the political manifestation of these differences will influence the degree to which a politics of intragroup coalitions is feasible.

The importance of this distinction and the conception of social groups developed by Young for my study is that it provides a way to understand the relationship between social and political membership in structural terms, thus overcoming one of the primary limitations of the analyses of the major theorists of deep diversity I discussed. The idea that we are defined, and define ourselves, in and through our relations with others within institutional contexts allows us to connect the practices, behaviors, and beliefs that permeate social institutions and that define the social positioning of Latinos, to their status in the political community. My overview of the pattern of exclusionary inclusion of Latinos in chapter 1 was meant to demonstrate that not only has it been laws, official codes, and public policies that created this marginalization, but that quite often, these were created to enforce practices of exclusion that emerged in relations between Latinos and Anglos in civil society and served to justify forms of discrimination and segregation across the entire spectrum of societal institutions, housing, labor markets, education, and so forth.

CHAPTER 3

Reconceptualizing Citizenship

Membership, Belonging, and the Politics of Racialization

THE MAJOR CONCERN OF THE FRAMEWORKS DISCUSSED IN THE PREVIOUS CHAPTER
is the problematic of deep diversity of cultural groups that has characterized liberal
democracies for at least the last forty years. Each approach formulates the issue and
frames the challenge in different conceptual and analytic terms. But despite their
differences, they all fall short of providing a satisfactory theoretical account of the
relationship between social and political membership, and/or of incorporating the
effect of the processes of racialization in their analyses of the divisions, cleavages, and
conflicts that have been part of the formation of the United States and the politics
that provide direction for its positions and policies. However, many of the same issues
that these theorists engage have also been addressed by the recent literatures on
citizenship. Interest in the issues of citizenship arose for some of the same reasons
that gave rise to the theories of cultural difference that I have discussed. The latter
focused more directly on questions having to do with how to theorize the nature of
diversity than with its causes, and offered justifications for certain types of policies
and politics that they believed followed from their conceptualizations. But with
the exception of Kymlicka, these formulations do not address the linkage between
diversity and citizenship. The theorists of citizenship are concerned with the defining

parameters of political membership, but from a different frame of reference than the diversity theorists. The same kind of issues and challenges that diversity theorists engaged have led to a different set of questions about the nature of political standing within the political community, which have been explored so extensively in the last twenty years that there is now a field of citizenship studies.[1]

I have advanced the argument that the diversity approaches have limitations that make them inadequate theoretical guides for the study of the role of Latinos in the United States. In this chapter, I will offer a reformulation of the conception of citizenship as a way of overcoming those limitations. Before doing so, however, let me first review briefly the major theoretical approaches to the study of citizenship. While I will engage some of these throughout the book, a preliminary overview will help to locate my argument for the idea of associative citizenship within the broader literature. As a number of scholars have observed, there are many variations in these approaches, but for my purposes they can be thought of as falling into two major categories: modern/traditional and critical/radical.

Modern/Traditional

The works in the first category of approaches gravitate around debates regarding the significance and role of rights, obligations, responsibilities, and participation. This has been for some time the dominant framing of citizenship reflected in the works that have taken on "canonical" status in the field of political theory and are the predominant type of publications in the more established mainstream journals and scholarly presses. In Engin Isin's view, there are three perspectives that fall into this category: liberalism, communitarianism, and civic republicanism (Isin and Wood 1999, 7). What is generally at issue in the debates between adherents of these positions is the question of which of the dimensions of citizenship just mentioned are fundamental, and/or what the relationships between them are or should be. Despite the claims of "strong" differences between these positions, they all assume the individual and her relationship to the community as the primary axis for establishing the boundaries and defining parameters of citizenship.

LIBERALISM AND THE RIGHTS-BEARING INDIVIDUAL

Liberalism has been the dominant ideological framework in the West since the eighteenth century. There are, as with other schools of thought, different versions of liberalism, but there are nevertheless some common themes that are basic to this conception of society and politics. As is well known, liberalism arose as part of the transition to market-based societies and thus shared the emphasis on individualism, concern with state intrusion into the private lives of individuals, and an interest in establishing the state as guarantor of legal rights of persons. One version of the liberal conception of citizenship emphasized the rights to property and to enter into contracts. Delanty refers to this as the "bourgeois" conception (Delanty 2000, 13). Another version focused more on the republican aspects of citizenship connected with issues of democracy, and stressed civil and political rights. This perspective focuses on the legal representation of the citizen and on the need for formal equality in this realm, and this continues to be one of the traits of modern liberal notions of citizenship. Of course Marx presented one of the classic and enduring criticisms of the contradiction between insisting on formal equality while substantive inequality was a fundamental condition of capitalism (Marx 1848).

One finds mixtures of the two conceptions of liberalism in many liberal thinkers, but in the view of scholars of citizenship such as Delanty (2000) and Somers (2008), the market-based model has been the dominant tradition in citizenship and is deeply rooted and reflected in the political theories of Hobbes, Locke, and Adam Smith.

Despite these differences, all versions of liberalism make the rights-bearing individual the fundamental and unquestionable center of its conception of the political, holding that the individual has priority over the community or polity, and that the function of citizenship is to protect the primacy of the individual. In some ways, ironically, this frames citizenship as a prepolitical status. So whatever the configuration of rights, obligations, participation, and responsibilities developed and adopted by a political regime, these must be designed to maximize the protection of the individual from intrusions by both the state and by others. This is based on a notion of negative freedom—that is, freedom from governmental intrusion on the private rights of the individual. And since these must apply universally—i.e., they must regard all citizens equally—particularistic characteristics associated with variable identities are bracketed from having any serious political significance. Factors and differences based on race, gender, or any other culturally defined dimension must not have any role in the functioning of the political community. The institutional correlate of the liberal conception of citizenship is the liberal state, defined within this tradition as the primary guarantor and protector of the primacy of the individual. Scholars like C. P. Macpherson (1962) have demonstrated how this notion of market-based views of the relations between the individual and the state was enshrined as one of the primary principles in the development of the modern liberal state. And Somers (2008) has developed an extremely detailed analysis of the specific historical conditions that gave rise to the particular form of this market-based conception of citizenship. She argues that it continues to be the fundamental premise of Western conceptions of the political and as such, is one of the major obstacles to overcoming the forms of inequality and privilege that characterize modern capitalist societies.

COMMUNITY/MORAL COHESION/REPUBLICANISM

While Isin distinguishes between communitarian and civic republican versions of citizenship, the latter are really a subtype of communitarianism. The communitarian conception of citizenship emerged from a sustained critique of liberalism, focusing in particular on the ahistorical, acontextual, or "disembodied" conception of the individual embraced by liberalism. Although communitarians do not challenge the idea that it is the individual that is the "sole" bearer of the rights that define the basis of citizenship, they argue that the formation of the individual always takes place within societal structures and therefore can neither be prior to nor exist outside of a "community" of individuals. The liberal notion of the individual is rejected as being a mythical abstraction without qualities or characteristics that in fact are vital to defining the person. The challenge of citizenship from this perspective is to define a set of mechanisms that incorporate and integrate the individual within the broader society in a manner that does not undermine the individuality and rights of each person, but that nevertheless establishes a sense of obligation to the community at large—to a "common good"—and provides for the participation in the affairs of the community as a necessary component of democratic polities. The very nature of the critique of liberalism offered by the communitarians opens up a space for the issue of identity to take on a political valence. If the individual "self" can only exist within the web of societal interdependencies characterized by differences of race, gender, class, then these factors must somehow be incorporated in the strategies, practices, and policies that define the parameters of political membership. There is considerable emphasis in much of this literature on arguing for a "moral community" as the institutional mechanism by which the bonds between individuals and societal structures can be established.

One of the more influential versions of communitarian conceptions of citizenship is reflected in civic republicanism, a position that attempts to stake out an alternative to what is seen as an unnecessary binary framing of citizenship represented in the liberal and some of the communitarian perspectives. While in agreement with the general communitarian emphasis on the importance of participation and the sense of community on the one hand, and with the liberal focus on the state as necessary guarantor of individual rights on the other, civic republicans attempt to establish a form of mediation between these two positions. This is accomplished by arguing for the primacy of a form of "civic" identity—that is, a type of political identification with, and allegiance to, the fundamental principles and values of governance on which the polity is founded. While other "identities" based on such factors as cultural, racial, and gender characteristics are recognized as legitimate, they must be subordinated to one's civic identity as a citizen.[2]

Critical/Democratic

While the theoretical configuration of the issues engaged by both the liberal and communitarian approaches continues to be the point of departure for much of the mainstream work on citizenship, there is another body of studies that approaches the challenges of citizenship from a very different set of perspectives, and that my own conception of citizenship modifies and extends. Instead of framing the analysis in a way that privileges and prioritizes the notions of rights, obligations, moral community, and participatory loyalties, these works focus on the broader institutional dynamics by which the differential patterns of inclusion in and exclusion from societal institutions are determined.[3] These dynamics are framed and approached using a set of concepts that cohere around a different and distinct center of analytic gravity than those relied on by the modern liberals and communitarians. These concepts are mobilized to create an alternative discursive field organized around notions of democracy, diversity, difference, belonging, identity, solidarity, and recognition. The development of these configurations arose most directly from the challenges that the politics of the new social movements of the 1960s and 1970s posed to the multidimensional range of exclusionary patterns, and to both the intellectual and institutional infrastructures that maintained hierarchies based on gender, race, class, and other characteristics. Werbner and Yuval-Davis, for example, refer to these approaches as based on what they label forms of "democratic citizenship":

> As recent debates about the modern versus the late- or postmodern have highlighted, modernity was marked from its inception by contradictory tendencies: towards ordering, control and normalisation, on the one hand, and the toleration of uncertainty, scepticism, disagreement and difference, on the other. Democratic citizenship as a social and political construct encapsulates this modern aporia: it opens up spaces and arenas of freedom—of conflict, unpredictability, intimacy, the right to be different—while restricting and structuring these spaces by procedural hedges about limits. It orders conflict, channels and tames it; it labels and classifies collective differences; it determines how, where and when difference may legitimately be "represented," and who counts as "different" in the political arena, itself a social construct. Citizenship defines the limits of state power and where a civil society or the private sphere of free individuals begins. These opposed

> impulses are part of what makes citizenship, for subjects themselves, such a complex, ambiguous imaginary. (Werbner and Yuval-Davis 1999, 2)

The underlying political and intellectual thrust of these efforts, then, is the promotion of a form of citizenship based on a new politics of democratic inclusion.[4] As with the first approach to citizenship, there are considerable differences in the way these various ideas are theorized, and there has been an ongoing debate about how to conceptualize the appropriate analytic and political linkages between these dimensions. But despite these differences, the problematic of citizenship in these works is framed in a manner quite distinct from those analyses focused around rights and obligations. And this framing seeks to expand the parameters of citizenship beyond the juridical, formal conceptions in play within contemporary politics, for example, of immigration. These conceptions are primarily concerned with the relationship between citizenship and an inclusive form of democracy, and we can say that it is a form of democratic citizenship that they seek to advance. The perspective of democratic citizenship, then, tends to focus on the patterns of exclusion and marginalization, and on strategies for deepening the level of democracy. While the notion of citizenship I will develop in this chapter clearly falls within this category, I find that most of the democratic theories of citizenship, despite often focusing on the notion of difference, do not provide a conception of racialized alterity robust enough to adequately explain the particular historical relationship between citizenship and Latinos.

Latinos and Theories of Citizenship

Some of these limitations are addressed in a small but growing body of literature on Latino citizenship that focuses primarily either on the notion of cultural citizenship, or on Latino alienage, a condition closely linked with immigration and transnationalism. The conception of citizenship that I advance builds on and extends the work on Latino cultural citizenship while at the same time addressing issues raised by Latino immigration for citizenship theory and practice. This notion was advanced initially by cultural anthropologist Renato Rosaldo, and was developed by the members of a research working group that I participated in and that was funded by the Inter-University Program for Latino Research.[5] Adopting an orientation similar to that advanced by advocates of a more inclusive form of democratic citizenship, the group further developed the idea of Latino cultural citizenship to study the various efforts of Latinos to assert and affirm their cultural status, particularly as a means of confronting their marginalization within different public spheres of social interaction.[6] Latina and Latino scholars from Stanford University, UCLA, Hunter College, and the University of Texas, Austin, met regularly over a period of several years during the 1980s to discuss separate studies of Latino communities focusing on the emergence of different forms of cultural citizenship, and the results were eventually published in an edited volume, *Latino Cultural Citizenship: Claiming Identity, Space, and Rights.* In their synopsis of the processes involved in the working group's discussions and critiques of their research findings, Flores and Benmayor summarize the group's working conception of cultural citizenship as follows: "Cultural citizenship names a range of social practices which, taken together, claim and establish a distinct social space for Latinos in this country. Latino social space is evolving and developing new forms, many of them contributing to an emergent Latino consciousness and social and political development" (Flores and Benmayor 1997, 1). A few pages later they add: "Cultural citizenship can be thought of as a broad range of activities of everyday life through which Latinos and other groups claim space in society and eventually claim rights" (15). This group of scholars advanced this concept as a way to create an alternative discourse that made the pattern of exclusions from different realms and spheres of U.S. society the central, if not the organizing theme for explaining the Latino experience for the last 150 years. What emerged through the distinct but linked analyses of each group of researchers was the establishment of a way of conceptualizing Latino marginalization in a frame of reference and a distinct discourse that relied on related notions *of identity, difference, member- ship, belonging, rights, empowerment,* and *contestation* as these pertained to the specific characteristics of the Latino experience in the United States. At that time, this loosely defined discursive framework was in fact an intervention in the way that Latino history and politics had been framed by traditional disciplines in the humanities and social sciences, and different aspects of that discourse have been adopted and extended in a variety of works on Latino citizenship. For example, in *Latinos and Citizenship: The Dilemma of Belonging* (Oboler 2006), a collection of studies published nearly ten years after *Latino Cultural Citizenship* appeared, various elements of this discursive framing are adopted by all of the authors. The introduction to the volume by Oboler frames the studies around the common theme of "redefining citizenship as a lived experience" (Oboler 2006, 3). The analyses in these essays range across a broad set of issues and problematics, including the production of Mexican and immigrant "illegality," Puerto Rican struggles on the mainland to secure effective citizenship, transnational effects of welfare reform, dual citizenship, gender-based efforts and coalitions organized to promote greater practices of inclusion and belonging, struggles of undocumented youth to gain legitimacy, Mexican migration and transnational networks and their effects on the levels of political membership, and the mobilization of undocumented migrants in electoral politics. Despite the very different empirical foci of these works, they all studied how citizenship is engaged, contested, and lived at the level of everyday life, and how the regime of U.S. citizenship has directly and indirectly affected the entire range of experiences of Latinos in the twentieth century. And the analyses draw on various aspects of the discourse of cultural citizenship that I described—that is, membership, rights, marginalization and exclusion, identity, belonging, and contestation—to demonstrate how the practices and ideology of citizenship were encountered and engaged by different sectors of Latino communities.

Other recent works have drawn on the same discursive and theoretical framework. In *Remaking Citizenship*, Coll (2010) presents a detailed study of the efforts of a Bay Area grassroots organization, Mujeres Unidas y Activas, created by Mexican and Central American immigrant women to address the particular life challenges that their status entailed. Coll connects the life histories of these women to the anti-immigrant politics in California in the 1990s, and how the latter affected the way in which immigration and welfare-reform policies of that period impacted the everyday experiences of the women and their families. Focusing on issues such as child rearing, domestic violence, immigrant rights, these women drew on their sense of cultural identities as women, Latinas, and immigrants to contest the politics of exclusion and marginalization, asserting their right to full membership in the broader community, and transforming the way that citizenship has been traditionally defined. And in *Disenchanting Citizenship*, Luis Plascencia (2012) relies on similar conceptual and methodological tools to study the experiences of a group of Mexican immigrants who were either in the process of applying for citizenship or had recently been naturalized. He focuses on the relationship between citizenship status and the level of membership (what I refer to as "societal membership") in the broader institutions of society, arguing that the former does not necessarily lead to the latter. He argues that the central issues raised by his study revolve around the following questions: "How has the circle of membership been constructed in the United States? Does acquisition of citizenship create equality among citizens and erase other social hierarchies in the society? Does the obtainment of citizenship erase alienness?" (Plascencia 2012, 1–2).

Plascencia concluded that forms of discrimination, a sense of foreignness, and political and social inequalities continue to characterize the societal and political positionality of even those who acquire formal citizenship. This is due in part to what he calls the "Janus face of citizenship"—the fact that citizenship functions as both an exclusionary and inclusionary political practice and ideology, and that it is precisely the level of inclusion and exclusion that is contested by marginalized groups like the Mexican immigrants he studied. Like the works found in Oboler, Coll, and Flores and Benmayor, Plascencia's study focuses on ways that citizenship is played out and experienced at the level of everyday life, and how membership and inclusion are a function of the interaction between the dynamic relationships between identity, difference, rights, contestation, and empowerment.

While the conception of cultural citizenship reflected in these works provides an important alternative to traditional constructions of citizenship that did not resonate with the experience of marginalized groups, it does have important limitations. First, there is the failure to situate the enactments of cultural citizenship within a detailed analysis of the field of power relations, and particularly their relationship to state structures. This is, I believe, the point that Aihwa Ong makes in discussing the alternative conception of cultural citizenship that she develops. She observes that

> This notion of citizenship as dialectically determined by the state and its subjects is quite different from that employed by Renato Rosaldo. . . . who views cultural citizenship as the demand of disadvantaged subjects for full citizenship in spite of their cultural difference from mainstream society. While I share Rosaldo's sentiments, his concept attends to only one side of a set of unequal relationships. It gives the erroneous impression that cultural citizenship can be unilaterally constructed and that immigrant or minority groups can escape the cultural inscription of state power and other forms of regulation that define the different modalities of belonging. . . .
>
> In contrast, I use "cultural citizenship" to refer to the cultural practices and beliefs produced out of negotiating the often ambivalent and contested relations with the state and its hegemonic forms that establish the criteria of belonging within a national population and territory. Cultural citizenship is a dual process of self-making and being-made within webs of power linked to the nation-state and civil society. Becoming a citizen depends on how one is constituted as a subject who exercises or submits to power relations; one must develop what Foucault . . . calls "the modern attitude," an attitude of self-making in shifting fields of power that include the nation-state and the wider world. (Ong 1996, 738)

Second, there is a tendency to focus on the role of agency in these enactments without locating their strengths and limitations within a multiscalar framework that illustrates the relationship between different levels of analysis. While most of the studies of Latino cultural citizenship often provide detailed descriptions of the social and community context within which the enactments take place, these remain primarily context and are not linked theoretically to the rights claims to demonstrate how the processes involved at the two levels interact. This is a characteristic found in other studies where practices of contestation are central. Although Smith and Bakker focus on what they refer to as transnational citizenship, the practices they examine are similar to the kinds of claims and affirmations that cultural citizenship emphasizes (Smith and Bakker 2008). But like Ong, they attempt to situate these within the sphere of power configurations formed by processes of globalization and restructuring in which the state plays a fundamental role. Part of the problem, they suggest, is that many of the ethnographically based studies of immigrants have a "tendency to privilege a particular level of analysis and overemphasize the agency of the actors operating at that privileged level of analysis" (Smith and Bakker 2008, 19). They summarize the difference between the latter and their analysis by stating that their approach is a "clearly agency-oriented perspective that contextualizes the local and transnational practices of migrants within relevant historical, political-economic, and institutional contexts, without assuming that those contexts can be invoked to explain outcomes. Rather than presenting these contexts as determinative structures we conceive of them as factors that situate the acting subjects that form transnational networks and mediate their practices without determining them" (20).

Third, while the practices of cultural citizenship are construed as rights claims, there is virtually no analysis of how these particular rights claims are related to the broader field and literature on rights. There is an expansive literature on rights, and of particular relevance to the types of contestation that cultural citizenship are construed to embody, there is a serious debate among rights and social-movement scholars regarding the question of the emancipatory potential of rights claims. So, for example, some theorists that emphasize class-based social and political movements as the key to emancipatory politics view rights claims as a mechanism for stabilizing and reinscribing and reinforcing the status quo (Kennedy 2002). Others, like Patricia Williams, argue that without the rights claims, none of the advancements overcoming racial segregation and promoting civil and political rights would have been possible (P. Williams 1991).

And fourth, there is little in the way of connecting the claims of rights to the broader challenges of transforming those into effective policies. Unless those claims eventually find their way into the policymaking process, they are likely to be transient cultural affirmations without any lasting effect.

Both my critique of mainstream analyses of diversity and how they have complicated traditional theories of citizenship, and the reformulated conception of citizenship I offer later in this chapter are firmly rooted in the discursive framing and application of the notion of cultural citizenship that I have described above. However, I build on and extend the notion in a way that addresses some of these shortcomings. The concept of associative citizenship that I advance in this book emerged from my effort to address especially the first three limitations, and offers a reformulated, broader framework for the study of the kind of contestations that cultural citizenship was intended to highlight.

Latino Citizenship Theory Reformulated

I will argue here that theories of diversity reviewed in the previous chapter, and the approaches to citizenship that I reviewed above strongly suggest that the conditions of deep diversity in liberal democracies require a concept of citizenship that is characterized by a configuration of related dimensions, each of which cannot be addressed separately from the others, and that delineates the inherent relationship between the social and political dimensions of membership. In order to be capable of providing the basis for effective democratic governance in societies characterized by deep diversity, citizenship must be multidimensional and consist of those elements that define the contested aspects of that very diversity. In other words, citizenship must be able to address those issues and questions that conditions of deep diversity bring to the fore. So instead of thinking of citizenship in the United States as purely a legalistic phenomenon, or in other one-dimensional terms, the theorist needs to incorporate the dimensions that are constitutive of the range of issues that characterize the condition of deep diversity: the nature of membership and societal cohesion, patterns and strategies of inclusion and exclusion, forms of belonging, and the construction of alterity through racialization. These are the core elements of the form of associative citizenship that I will argue for here, and I will refer to them throughout the rest of the book as membership, exclusion, belonging, racialization.[7]

Both the diversity and citizenship perspectives deal with the question of how to incorporate and/or accommodate diverse populations within the confines of the national context, and by extension with the issue of membership and national cohesion, or what I will be calling forms of solidarity.[8] But the perspective of citizenship also focuses on the legal and societal parameters through which access and levels of exclusion, inclusion, and incorporation are formed, maintained, and modified. This means that in one way or another, the issue of social and/or political exclusion is at the heart of the studies of citizenship.[9] However, some scholars have argued in recent studies that effective citizenship requires the analyses of membership and exclusion, but that what they refer to as "belonging" must also be addressed.[10] These studies point to the history of forms of second-class or marginalized citizenship regimes, which demonstrates that groups can have ostensible and legal status without, however, being accepted within the broader societal institutions—not being seen as legitimately part of the "we" that constitutes the normative political imaginary. So it is possible to "be" a part of society without necessarily "belonging" to it. And finally, in the context of the United States, the processes of racialization have been a fundamental aspect affecting all spheres of society, but have been particularly reflected in the development of a hierarchy of citizenship from the beginning of the republic.[11] In the following discussion, I will review the key characteristics of each of these parameters and propose how they have affected Latinos in particular. It should be clear that these are not separate, discrete dimensions, but rather are intrinsically connected dimensions that define the regime of citizenship in the United States.

Latino Membership: The Nation-State and Citizenship

Citizenship is basically about membership in a political community. So the parameters of citizenship are completely dependent on the particular conception of political community that one is concerned with. Most of the discourses regarding modern citizenship have until recently been based on the assumption that the specific type of political community in question was the nation-state. Situating the discussion of Latino citizenship within this broader context is an important preliminary step in framing the relevant factors affecting the nature of Latino relations with the dominant institutions in the United States.

The parameters of the idea of the nation-state as the basic unit of political community were established by the Treaty of Westphalia in 1648. It should be recalled that the formulation and figuration of these elements were the product of a very specific set of political conflicts in seventeenth-century Europe that focused on rival claims precisely about the right to control and govern contested territorial areas. The Treaty of Westphalia was entered into as a means for ending the Thirty Years' War, and established territoriality, sovereignty, autonomy, and legality as the central principles of the nation-state that continue to be the basis of international political relations 350 years later (McGrew 1997, 3–60). This construction of the nation-state provided particular answers to fundamental political questions such as: How should we understand the meaning of political community? Where are power and authority to be located? and How is such power and authority to be legitimized? Despite the fact that these were answers that corresponded to a specific, bounded historical set of circumstances, this model of political community and organization became the modality that was imposed through conquest and colonization on societies and nations characterized by entirely different conditions, cultures, values, and societal practices.

One of the crucial elements of the modern notion of the nation-state was the right to determine and control the nature of both societal and political membership and thus establish criteria for who would be considered members of that society. However, this institutional structure in essence conflated two elements that characterized the condition of the societies that established it. "Nation" referred to the notion of "peoplehood," which Rogers Smith has examined in detail (Smith

1997), while "state" referred to an administrative and juridical apparatus. In fact, the construct of political community that the treaty established was based on the assumption that there is an isomorphic relationship between nation, territory, state, and political identity or culture. The cultural identity of the "nation" was assumed to be relatively homogeneous so that the "we" that constituted the "nation" was assumed to be relatively clear, but functioned more as normative criteria than as a reflection of matters on the ground. As a number of scholars have pointed out, political communities have rarely coincided with a sole cultural identity, particularly since the territorial boundaries have been arbitrary at best. Populations within those boundaries from different cultures and identities have been either the object of conquest or marginalized.[12] Instead, political communities emerge on the basis of a complex set of interactions between social practices, economic linkages, political power, cultural and ethnic loyalties, and military conquest. The modernist notion that territorial boundaries should coincide with the right of rule and governance developed as a specific element of the processes of nation-building in Europe during the period between the seventeenth and nineteenth centuries. Thus the particular way in which the relationship between power, governance, territory, identity, and membership evolved as part of a specific historical process of political and economic development in a limited region of the world, at a particular time, has been transformed into more universalistic claims that equate the dimension of explicit power and control with the dimension of territorial space.

But the rapid and extensive changes brought about in the contemporary period by processes of globalization, restructuring, and migration, as well as the extensive diversity that characterizes contemporary political environments, have led to intense questioning of the capacity and adequacy of the nation-state as a unit of political community to address and mediate the new configurations of political relations that often transcend its territorial boundaries. This is a view that has been advanced with increasing frequency in the literature on the political challenges arising from the rapid changes of globalization. As R. B. J. Walker states:

> It has been abundantly clear to many observers that the principle of state sovereignty is increasingly problematic. As a formalization of configurations of power and authority that emerged in a specific historical context, it has been criticized as an inappropriate guide to both theory and practice in an age of rapid transformation. It has come to seem particularly inappropriate in view of the current internationalization or globalization of economic, technological, cultural, and political processes. (Walker 1999, 161–62)

The debate centers on the extent to which this particular construction of the principles on which the nation-state continues to function can accommodate the new patterns of relationships and linkages that have resulted from the flows and diversity of peoples, technologies, capital, images, and ideas that increasingly define the global map. A variety of theoretical positions have emerged that challenge the forms of political discourse that have either ignored or been insensitive to these flows and the transformations they have initiated. Walker suggests that a central theme in these discussions is "how the questions to which the principle of state sovereignty has seemed to provide an uncontestable answer for so long—questions about who 'we' are, where 'we' have come from, and where 'we' might be going—might be answered differently" (Walker 1999, 160).

This presumptive "we" is thus a normative foundational element of the nation-state conception of political community that attempts to fuse the dimension of identity and jurisdictional elements. And it provides the basis of the specific nature of both membership and belonging in a given society. The form of state nationalism in the particular context of nation-state building in Europe adopted notions of membership and belonging that were essentially strategies that included promoting cultural homogenization as a means for regulating the level and type of societal membership in a given nation-state, and territoriality was key in articulating these two dimensions and incorporating them into the institutional basis of governance and control. The "we" that was privileged, and that defined membership in the initial formulations, has been consistently contested in most nation-states since then by the political coalescence of a series of different types of groups, such as labor, women, racial and ethnic groups, and more recently by immigrants. As a result, a vital element in the history of the development of the nation-state is the story of the various mechanisms, devices, laws, and regulations that have been created and relied on to contain the tension between the independent logics of nation and state. The goal in each instance was to make the forms of social and cultural bonding and solidarity that characterizes nations or peoples coincide with the jurisdictional prerogatives that established the right to govern through the control of the political institutions, including the control of the organized means of violence. This is why the issue of membership has been such a crucial element in defining the parameters of the nation-state. The substantive content of the "we" is created and maintained by the nation-state's claim to sovereignty and absolute autonomy in controlling membership, and although the means for doing so are varied, the regimes of citizenship adopted in each state have played a particularly important role in this area.

However, there have been few instances where this control has been completely effective. In fact, the popular notion of citizenship as a clear-cut status is mostly fictional. Citizenship is neither singular, discrete, nor unchanging. Instead, we need to understand the theories and practices of citizenship as developed by modern nation-states as primarily a set of political mechanisms intended to control and regulate the level, type, and range of not only political but societal membership as well. From this perspective, citizenship is not solely nor even primarily a legal status, but rather a political mechanism for the control and containment of the distribution of rights, benefits, privileges, entitlements, and resources to different sectors of the population who reside within the territorial, sovereign boundaries of the nation-state. This is the institutional logic that has affected the political and social cleavages, tensions, and conflicts that arose from specific parameters of inclusion and exclusion, as well as the corresponding differential levels of belonging. The specific dynamics and pattern of the process of national development vary, of course, based on different configurations of economic forces, political alignment of interests, cultural practices, and other historical factors. But the elements and functions that define the conception of the nation-state form of political community are similar: centralization of power, control of territorial boundaries, sole arbiter and enforcement of law, and the development of a "national imaginary"—or as Anderson (1991) calls it, "imagined community"—as an ideological representation of the normative conception of "peoplehood" that defines the criteria for determining who is to be included in the national "we."

How is the emergence of the nation-state as the sole unit of political community relevant for the study of Latino citizenship? The historical trajectory of Latinos in the United States has, of course, taken place within the broad context of the specific pattern of the development of the U.S. nation-state, but there are two aspects that are particularly important and relevant for understanding the marginalization of Latinos. First, the initial incorporation of Mexicans by the United States, as the result of annexation after the Mexican American War, occurred as part of the pattern of what was essentially a developing country concerned with all of the issues that nation-states attempting to establish their claim to sovereignty confront. In the United States, this included the vision of expansion of territorial control as well as a fundamental concern with the development of a national imaginary based on a white citizenry. The annexation of Mexican territory presented a challenge to the notion of establishing a homogeneous racial and cultural nation because Mexicans were considered foreigners by the majority of the white population, with a different racial makeup as well as a distinct and inferior culture. So from the outset, Mexicans, the first Latinos, presented a challenge to the type of nation-state envisioned by the majority of the political elites. The second manifestation of this challenge is really an extension of the same problematic but in a new and contemporary context. The issue of the political significance of cultural difference and alterity intensified as a result of the largest immigration of Latinos in U.S. history, beginning in the 1970s, which was to a significant extent the result of the particular pattern that globalization and restructuring took in the United States. The number of immigrants and their spread spatially across the country made it impossible to avoid confronting the issue of how these "foreigners" were to be incorporated.

Because this racialized conception of Latinos spanned the entire period of existence within the United States, the issue of what type of incorporation should be extended to them has been a constant in the relationship between them and the dominant white majority. And this tension has been one of the key elements that have both defined and reflected the citizenship status of Latinos. Thus questions regarding how Latinos fit, how they belong to the larger society, and what kind of membership should be "granted" to them have long defined the terrain of interaction and political relations between Latinos and whites. And this therefore has to be a key element in the study of Latino politics and Latino citizenship. Any study of Latino politics that ignores this crucial dimension would distort the oppositional nature of the context within which it emerged.

The kind of otherness that Latinos represent for the larger society, then, requires rethinking the challenge of reconciling diversity and difference with the boundaries of membership—of reassessing the parameters and criteria of membership, citizenship, and ultimately the kind of societal bases that foster the embrace of diversity. Each of these dimensions is in one way or another linked to the challenge of reconciling diversity and difference with the boundaries of membership. And these factors are what lead me to argue that the complex nature of the challenge that Latinos represent to the basic and traditional parameters of citizenship calls for unpacking and rethinking the elements that constitute the current citizenship regime.

Membership, Inclusion, and Belonging

The notion of citizenship that best explains the forms of exclusionary inclusion that has characterized Latino status needs to be based on understanding the dynamic interaction between social and political membership, forms of belonging, normative conceptions of cohesion or solidarity, and the form of otherness produced by racialization. The analysis of the issues related to Latino membership, citizenship, and political identity depends to a great degree on the particular interpretation of what the nature of Latino historical experience has been in the United States, and in particular, the nature and degree of incorporation of Latinos in both the civil and political spheres of society. One-dimensional conceptions of citizenship are unable to capture the breadth and range of the factors that determine and influence the level and nature of Latino inclusion and exclusion in U.S. society. So I propose to take up these issues by advancing an alternative conception of citizenship framed by the four elements that I discussed earlier (membership, exclusion, belonging, racialization) in a way that corresponds directly to key characteristics of the experience of Latinos. As an initial step, I return to T. H. Marshall's conceptualization of citizenship as "full membership" in societal institutions, because it is particularly relevant to the issues of incorporation that have been a point of contention between Latinos and the society as a whole (Marshall 1950, 28–29). While much of the literature that uses Marshall's analysis of citizenship as a point of departure focuses on the role of rights in securing full membership, there is less attention to that part of Marshall's work that attends to the meaning of "full" membership.

As is well known, Marshall does indeed trace how different rights evolved in liberal democracies to expand the modern concepts and practices of citizenship. While civil rights developed to secure certain protections for individuals from arbitrary intrusions or encroachments by the state or other citizens, and political rights were most relevant to gaining greater levels of access to and participation in the structures of governance, what is often overlooked is that one of Marshall's key points was that these could not be effectively performed without citizens having a minimum of material resources, and he argued that social rights developed as a mechanism to do just that. But the broader implication of Marshall's framing of his analysis of rights in terms of "full membership" is that the viability of democratic societies depends on developing a form of citizenship that goes beyond legal standing or status alone, and includes the principle of full incorporation of the various different societal groups in all of the major institutional sites through which the distribution of power, resources, and benefits are determined. Marshall argued that legal or political formal citizenship is not sufficient to achieve the type of societal membership that can sustain democratic governance if significant sectors of society remain excluded from the processes and institutions through which benefits are accessed. What is primary and foregrounded in this conception of citizenship then is the issue of societal incorporation or membership, and not only political or legal incorporation.

This reading of Marshall expands the scope and nature of citizenship and makes the nexus between membership in the political sphere and membership in the broader arena of societal institutions a crucial aspect of democratic citizenship. However, much of the literature on liberal citizenship reads Marshall in a more narrow way, focusing primarily on the civil and political dimension, and works that address social rights do so normally in terms of the relationship between individuals and welfare-oriented states (for example, Katz 2001). What is missed in this position, and limits its usefulness in addressing modes of exclusion as theoretically integrated components of citizenship, is the inherent relationship between political and social membership. Approaches that attempt to bracket the two, to study one in isolation from the other, result in distorting our understanding of how the parameters of citizenship are actually determined. I stress this point to address the criticism that expanding the theoretical dimensions of citizenship beyond the political and legal terrain in effect dilutes its meaning to such an extent that it become analytically useless. Quite the contrary; relying on conceptions of citizenship that ignore the interaction between the social and political spheres of membership provides an incomplete understanding of how social and cultural factors impinge on the way citizenship is performed and maintained.

While Marshall provides the initial insight that citizenship requires full societal and not just political membership, the notion is underdeveloped theoretically in his work. However, a number of social and political theorists influenced by Marshall's work have addressed the issue directly, and provide a way to advance a notion of membership that is both more comprehensive and resonant with the project of understanding and expanding democratic forms of citizenship. For example, in arguing that the levels and types of interdependencies promoted by globalization require us to rethink the defining parameters of what constitutes a "political community," David Held writes that political communities are not solely defined by juridically established boundaries, constitutional and legislative processes, and patterns of policymaking, but instead are constituted by "social practices, economic linkages, political power, cultural and ethnic loyalties" (Held 1999). From this perspective, then, full membership must be a function of the interaction between the levels of participation in and access to these spheres of societal organization. Other scholars have expanded on the idea of what is entailed in the notion of full membership, and how this is related to the issue of exclusion and inclusion; they have proposed that a more complete understanding of the disjunctions and conflicts that arise over the normative parameters that bound conceptions of citizenship requires introducing the additional dimension of "belonging."[13] In his discussion of the role of citizenship in the relationship between nationalism and political community, Craig Calhoun states that "Membership in a society is an issue of social solidarity and cultural identity as well as legally constructed state citizenship. This is all the more important to recognize in an era shaped both by new cultural diversities and new challenges to the abilities of states to maintain sharp and socially effective borders" (Craig Calhoun 1999, 219). And in a particularly useful perspective for pressing my argument, Nieguth advances an analysis that concentrates on the role of power in determining the dynamics of inclusion and exclusion in the relationship between nation and membership, and describes the nature of societal membership and citizenship as follows:

> Membership is a condition for individuals to gain access to societal goods and power. As such, it is a multidimensional phenomenon: the organizing principle guiding processes of boundary construction in a given society manifests itself not only in who is admitted physically from a spatial outside, but also in the relative societal status enjoyed by

members of different social groups within a state, in other words, admission. Hence, no measurement of the distribution of membership in a specific nation can rely on legal definitions of membership alone, such as political citizenship. Instead, it will have to take into account the distribution of political, economic, social, and cultural status among individuals. (Nieguth 1999, 157)

According to these more expansive perspectives, understanding and explaining the particular nature, scope, and type of citizenship in any given political community requires taking into account much more than legal factors and political policy. In particular, conceptions and practices of citizenship need to be articulated in relationship to the broader context of societal membership. To the degree that cultural differences become the basis of modes of exclusion and contestation, the notion of cultural identities must be included as one of the fundamental bases for the cleavages that are incorporated and reflected in the process of defining the boundaries of the forms of membership that constitute the notion of citizenship that I am advancing here. So the study of citizenship not only must include attention to legal status, but must recognize the fundamental and constitutive role of cultural differences and identities in affecting the nature and practices of membership and citizenship, as well as the challenge these differences represent for the task of establishing forms of solidarity that can sustain a pluralistic democratic society. These factors are constitutive of the determination of the normative boundaries of membership and citizenship, defining who will be considered part of the "we" that can inhabit the public sphere.[14]

It is precisely these dimensions of the relationship between citizenship and membership that are considered problematic by critics of what they consider a tendency among Latinos to nurture their cultural difference rather than to assimilate and accept the normative cultural framework in the United States.[15] However, the difficulty with these positions is that they assume a homological relationship between culture, identity, and citizenship on which their conceptions of national belonging are based, a position that is simply no longer tenable.[16] The fact is that this assumed relationship has functioned as an ideological trope and fiction throughout U.S. history, since diversity has always been a defining characteristic of the society. But that diversity was suppressed, silenced, ignored, or erased throughout most of the country's history until the cultural politics and social movements of the 1960s contested and rejected the established political conditions within which cultural engagement between groups was supposed to take place. It is this inability and/or unwillingness to acknowledge that the cultural diversity that now exists is neither a passing phase nor epiphenomenal, but in fact has redefined the basic structure of national identity that lies at the core of the anti-immigrant, anti-Latino ideologies that are reflected in works of neoconservative scholars. Instead of lamenting the fact that societies inevitably change, what is called for is a reconceptualizing of the meaning of political community, citizenship, membership, and belonging in a way that resonates with and corresponds to the deep, thick nature of cultural difference that now defines U.S. society, as well as developing alternative narratives of national belonging that incorporate and valorize these differences as constitutive of a truly multicultural democratic system.

Conceptualizations of membership such as those advanced by Calhoun and Nieguth support this kind of reconceptualization by expanding the boundaries of what are considered the defining parameters and practices of membership and citizenship beyond the limits of state-based identities and the focus on the level and nature of incorporation into the state structures. Instead, the terrain of citizenship practices is expanded to incorporate the qualitative nature of associational and cultural practices within the institutional sites of civil society that serve to reproduce the hierarchies of race, class and gender, as well as the political contestations that challenge those hierarchies. As such, they introduce notions of belonging and solidarity as constitutive of the nature of societal membership that is the foundation for the specific parameters of regimes of citizenship.

Expanding the scope of membership on which citizenship regimes are based requires a strategy that David Held has referred to as a process of "double democratization" (Held 1991). This conceptual expansion does not contend that the legal and juridical dimensions of citizenship are unimportant, or that they are mechanistically derivative from these associational practices. Rather, it rejects the one-dimensional conception of citizenship on the grounds that it obscures the real political nature of citizenship because it is incapable of capturing the contextual figurations that enable its essentially regulative function of controlling and containing societal membership. It also fails to capture the forms and characteristics of cultural identities considered acceptable and compatible with the "national" identity.[17] Positions such as Held's reinterpret citizenship as consisting of the two elements of legal status and forms of belonging and solidarity that function primarily as a political practice and strategy whose meaning changes over time as it is contested by a variety of claims and political actors, including by the presence of cultural "others."[18] The pattern of changes in the meaning of citizenship in the history of the United States certainly supports this interpretation. While I am not in complete agreement with the particular interpretations offered in Rogers Smith's *Civic Ideals*, his research clearly traces in meticulous detail the ways in which the meaning of citizenship has shifted in response to specific political interests and marginalized cultural groups (R. Smith 1997). And the comprehensive study by Evelyn Nakano Glenn documents how changing formulations and interpretations of citizenship have played a basic role in legitimating and sustaining unequal and oppressive race and gender relations in the United States (Glenn 2002). While traditional concepts of citizenship assume the coincidence of political identity derived from state membership with cultural identity derived from group membership, the construct advanced in these perspectives conceives of citizenship as consisting of the full range of practices and policies designed to mediate the tensions between political and cultural identity.

However, as scholars such as Nieguth and Craig Calhoun indicate, societal membership also entails a range of modes and types of belonging. If, as the perspective advanced by Held and others argues, there is a hierarchical structure of differential forms of societal membership reflected in the unequal levels of access to the major institutional sites of society, this suggests that we must expand our notion of membership to include the dimension of how groups belong in a different way. One of the factors that literatures on marginalized groups in the United States have made clear is that members of these groups have a sense of not being "accepted by" or "acceptable to" members of the dominant group, and that this unacceptability is incorporated as informal norms and codes of practice in the sites of civil society. So while the sense of belonging is a subjective dimension of societal membership, it is clearly rooted in objective institutional practices.[19]

Several recent works have attempted to provide the conceptual ground for reevaluating the link between citizenship and structures or forms of belonging and solidarity from perspectives similar to the one adopted here, and thus provide support for the normative project of democratic revitalization (Baumeister 2003; Orchard 2002; Thomas 2002; Shachar 2001). Thomas, for example, proposes five competing conceptions of political membership, or as she puts it, "five distinct ways of understanding what it means to belong to a given polity." She adds, "Clearly distinguishing between these separate notions is a necessary first step toward understanding the conceptual roots of contemporary membership conflicts" (Thomas 2002, 328). The first mode of national belonging is based on "descent"—i.e., a form of solidarity based on either ancestry and/or race—and so membership grows or diminishes as a function of birth or death. A second modality construes the bonds of citizenship as more flexible, and focuses on the attachment to a particular way of life, or culture. The third form is distinguished by adherence to a certain set of beliefs about the "founding" principles of a nation, which are typically thought of as the "political" culture underlying the form of solidarity. This is quite different from the fourth type of belonging, which is based on the idea of "contract" as the basis for conceiving of citizenship as establishing a set of equal rights and duties that serve as the foundation for "living together cooperatively." And finally, a fifth mode of national belonging is based on "monetized contract," where the connection to the polity is conceived of as a kind of investment in, or consumption of, the state's resources.

While this typology is suggestive, it is limited because it does not account for the kind of conflicts and disjunctions that revolve around racialized identities and cultures in pluriversal democracies, which require a different and more expansive formulation of belonging. The source of this inadequacy, I believe, is that there is no engagement with, or incorporation of, a notion of "otherness" or alterity that informs the notion of deep diversity and cultural differences at issue in liberal democratic societies, and in particular, racialization as otherness. So there is no way to incorporate the existence of these kinds of exclusionary forms of belonging, or exclusionary inclusion. This is a weakness that also characterizes and undermines the effectiveness of arguments of theorists such as Rawls, Kymlicka, Raz, Kukathas, who specifically address the issue of how to reconcile cultural forms of pluralism with democratic principles of governance; yet none of them give serious consideration to the specific historical experience or present circumstances of Latino populations.[20] At one level this is puzzling, given the presence of over 50 million Latinos throughout the United States. But at another level, it reflects a kind of theoretical blindness and lack of scholarly engagement with the rapidly changing cultural and demographic empirical realities on the ground. As I will argue, this is in part due to the fact that Latinos continue to be ideologically constructed by both popular culture and mainstream academia as perpetual racialized foreigners, and as a result, remain the "brown Other" in the social imaginary of national belonging.[21] Oboler's analysis of Latino otherness in U.S. society provides a clear delineation of the various dimensions or axes of otherness along which Latino identities and incorporation in institutions are construed, pointing out how class, gender, immigrant status, country of origin, and race are all at play in the dynamic processes of othering Latinos (Oboler 2002).

To summarize, then, I adopt Marshall's conception of citizenship as full membership and extend it to cover not only legal, juridical, and political institutions but also the civil sphere of quotidian action and practices.

Racialization, Belonging, and Citizenship

Adopting the notion of full membership as the primary conceptual lens for this study calls for a focus on the patterns of inclusion and exclusion (what I refer to as citizenship regime) that have been a central component in influencing the historical formation and development of Latino communities in the United States. These patterns have also determined the nature and level of incorporation of Latinos in the major institutional sites of both political and civil society, i.e., societal and political membership. And while many factors have affected the particular strategies of exclusion that were relied on to contain Latino institutional access, most have been linked to and depended on processes of racialization. While the history of the patterns of discrimination has been extensively documented and is a core part of the scholarly literature on Latinos, it is necessary to provide an overview since it has rarely been taken into account by theorists who have defined the canonical normative parameters of the discourse on multiculturalism, democracy, and citizenship that I engage in this study.

However, much of the literature that documents these patterns of exclusion has not, until recently, focused on the constitutive role of the processes of racialization. This is in part due to the fact that conceptions of Latinos as a racialized minority run counter to much of the more traditional social-science literature that categorized Latino populations as ethnic groups, and thus framed the study of Latinos as an extension of the conceptualization of European immigrants to the United States.[22] However, more recent studies have focused on racialization as a fundamental aspect of Latino experience in the United States. Some describe in particular the processes that established the specific form of racialization of Mexicans in the early nineteenth century as the formative period. I want to examine this set of dynamics in greater detail because this established the racialized framing for the pattern of exclusionary forms of inclusion and belonging reflected in ideological beliefs, economic restrictions, political marginalization, and social segregation, that future Latin American immigrants would confront. I refer to the particular configuration of these forms of exclusionary inclusion as the construct of "perpetual foreigner." This notion is a way of capturing and highlighting the image of Latinos and other racialized groups in the United States as not being able to assimilate.[23]

Recent studies have examined the processes by which this view of Latinos as racialized perpetual foreigners was constructed.[24] In one of the first systematic analyses of Latino racialization, Almaguer's detailed study of the various modes by which racialization processes established the system of white supremacy over Mexicans and other groups, shows that explanations that attempt to fit these patterns into the "ethnic" models that have dominated studies of Latinos present limited or distorted interpretations of the formation of what Alcoff calls the "real identities" in play (Almaguer 1994; Alcoff 2006, ch. 4). And in her recent study of the ideological construction of the Mexican "race," critical race theorist Laura Gómez develops a framework that focuses on the combined effects of colonialism, law, and racialization, and argues that "the construction of Mexicans as an American racial group proved central to the larger process of restructuring the American racial order in a key period stretching from the [Mexican-American] war to the turn of the century" (Gómez 2007, 5). While her study focuses on the region of New Mexico, Gómez provides a reconstructed explanation of racial dynamics more generally by demonstrating that it was the interaction between a variety of groups, including American Indians, African

Americans, Asians, Mexicans, and Euro-Americans, that established the specific parameters of the racialized system in the United States. She adds that "Excavating the nineteenth-century history of Mexican Americans as a racial group erases their racial invisibility and thereby reveals the complex, sometimes contradictory evolution of nineteenth-century racial dynamics as involving both multiple racial groups and competing racial ideologies" (6).

Other studies focus on the contemporary period, particularly on the rapid and large expansion of a more diverse Latino population since the 1970s. In their introductory essay in the collection of studies titled *Latinos: Remaking America*, Suárez-Orozco and Páez (2002, 9) argue that the experience of immigration, the changing nature of U.S. relations with Latin America, and the processes of racialization as Latinos are "at the heart of the Latino experience in the United States." Focusing on the interactive processes by which Mexicans and Puerto Ricans have been racialized in contemporary Chicago, De Genova and Ramos-Zaya (2003) provide a detailed analysis of how the unequal but different relationship each group has had to U.S. citizenship has been meditated through their positioning in the larger racial order. Their research reveals that despite the often negative images that the Mexicans and Puerto Ricans they studied have developed of each other, the racializing processes each undergoes have established a tenuous but nevertheless real sense of Latinidad, i.e., a sense of commonness or even solidarity, albeit one that is situational. So that racialization not only affects the relationships between Latino groups and white populations, but is clearly a factor affecting the intragroup relations between Latinos. A different framing of the issue of Latino racialization is advanced in the work of sociologist Ramon Grosfoguel, who traces the contemporary racial positioning of Latinos to the legacies of a colonialism in which racial differentiations and racist ideologies were constitutive, defining elements. This work focuses in particular on accounting for the ways that racialization has affected different Latino groups, each with a distinct history of articulation with, and incorporation into, the dominant institutions in the United States, and thus treats these racializations as important elements in the contemporary formation of Latino communities (Grosfoguel 2003, 2004).

While these various studies focus on processes of Latino racialization, it is not always clear exactly how they are using the term. So it would be helpful to specify how the concept is deployed in the following analysis. Recall that I have argued that citizenship must be understood in terms of both the legal, juridical component, and the quotidian practices that both define and regulate the level of membership and participation in the institutional sites of the civil sphere. So the concept of racialization I adopt has to resonate with, and be linked to, both of these dimensions. This type of formulation is advanced by Omi and Winant's conception of racial formation, which proposes that processes of racialization operate both at the level of the state and in the realm of civil society. They identify key mechanisms by which racialization is enacted and reproduced as racial projects, which "connect what race *means* in a particular discursive practice and the ways in which both social structures and everyday experiences are racially *organized*, based on that meaning" (Omi and Winant 1994). This approach combines representational forms with their manifestation in both the making and enforcement of state policies and their incorporation in the relations of everyday life that take place within the civil sphere, and rejects any notion of essentialized or biological conceptions of race.

Alcoff's (2006) recent important reconstruction of the way we think about identities extends and elaborates this position in a way that delineates the dimension of visibility in racialized processes. She demonstrates how racial categories and distinctions operate to mark different groups, and positions them within a hierarchy of power relations characterized by differential access to societal institutions—precisely the emphasis in my study of the continuum of inclusion and exclusion in this book. While recognizing the complexity and ambiguity of racialized identities, Alcoff nevertheless roots her analysis in the significance of physical differences that are connected to, and function as, coding mechanisms. Disputing the idea that perception is somehow politically, discursively, or ideologically neutral, she argues that visible perception and perceptual difference "represents sedimented contextual knowledges" (Alcoff 2006, 184), and further that "it is an indisputable fact about the social reality of mainstream North America that racial consciousness works through learned practices and habits of visual discrimination and visible marks on the body" (196). So it is not the physical difference itself that creates "naturalized" categories of "races," but instead the differential valorization and meanings that are attached to them.

Building on and adapting the perspectives advanced by Omi and Winant, and Alcoff, I will use *racialization* as constituting a configuration of social, cultural, and political processes by which specific perceived visible differences are imbued with racial significance and meaning that then are incorporated in a racial hierarchy both within the macro-level of economic, state, and cultural institutional structures, and within the interstitial nodes of quotidian experience and relations that take place in the sites of civil society. These macro- and micro-level racialized codes and practices function as sedimented forms of socially, politically, and culturally produced "knowledge," or more accurately, "common sense," that are then naturalized through a learned process and become the representational mechanism for coding the differential location in the racial order.[25]

Racialization of Latinos and the Regime of Citizenship in the United States

I now want to relate and draw on this particular conception of racialization to provide an overview of those aspects of the particular pattern of the racialization of Latinos that I believe to be the most salient for understanding the processes of exclusionary inclusion that have characterized the nature and level of Latino societal membership. The modes of Latino incorporation into U.S. society have always been marked by conflict, contentiousness, and contestation.[26] It is a history replete with systematic forms of discrimination, exclusionary practices, and ideological denigration of Latinos. And racialization as described above has been the primary form of establishing both the discursive and material modes of exclusionary belonging that have characterized Latino experience in the United States. These have manifested themselves in both the political and civil spheres in different configurations that have varied historically. Because the dramatic increase of Latinos in the United States during the last forty years has had an effect on so many aspects of the society, there is considerable attention to the current situation, conditions, and political potential of the various Latino communities.[27] Each Latino group has a different history of articulation with U.S. society, and this heterogeneous nature of Latinos is reflected in the very different patterns characterizing each group's incorporation into U.S. institutions. This is further reflected in the distinct ways in which the citizenship status and forms of belonging of each group have been defined. Different constitutional, legal, and political mechanisms and strategies have been used to determine the citizenship status of each Latino group, ranging from concerns with dual citizenship to racialized forms of constructing variable citizenship status for specific groups. However, despite these differential modes of articulation and incorporation, the staging of the cultural identity of each group has converged around a particular mode of racialization that is configured on the basis of the notion of Latinos as racialized perpetual foreigners—a framing that has its roots in the nineteenth century and still resonates with the tensions between Latinos and the broader society, particularly but certainly not limited to immigrants.

It is crucial to recognize that the current pattern of politics of contestation over the level and role of Latino membership has been framed and shaped by the modes of racialized exclusion that were established during the period when political, economic, and cultural dominance of the Southwest was established by the new Anglo political elites and settlers, structuring a particular mode of incorporation that set the framework for future relationships and societal location. In particular, the initial cultural and ideological construction of the Mexican population in the region as racialized "foreigners" has been a continuous thread in the historical relationship between Mexicans and the political and legal apparatus, as well as with the general Anglo population that became the majority and dominant sector in the Southwest shortly after the Mexican-American War.[28] This initial racialized construction established the discursive parameters within which later-arriving Latino groups have been conceptualized.[29] This is not to imply or ignore the heterogenous nature of Latino communities and the very different histories of articulation with, and modes of incorporation into, the United States of the different Latino communities, each of which requires its own more specific and detailed analysis. My claim here is that despite these differences, the majority of Latino groups have been categorized within a preexisting racialized cultural imaginary produced, limited, and modified by the dominant cultural institutional apparatus such as the media and legal and educational spheres.[30] This racialized conception of Latinos challenges the categorization of Latino populations as ethnic groups, which is an extension of the conceptualization of European immigrants to the United States. Instead, it is based on the fact that there was a clear pattern of relations that established the initial set of parameters that defined the "place" of Mexicans in the transformed landscape of the Southwest, and that was racially as well as class encoded. It was obviously a different mode of racialization than that of African Americans that structured the institutional basis of the social order in the southern and northern states, but functioned much the same way in defining the hierarchical structure of the racial order.

Differential Patterns of Racialized Incorporation

THE FOUNDATIONAL MEXICAN EXPERIENCE

One of the primary claims of Gómez's very detailed analysis of the formation of Mexican communities in New Mexico is the argument that the cultural and political racialization of Mexicans that was constructed during the nineteenth century established the discursive framing through which the cultural image of other Latino groups would be developed in the future. As she points out, "The mixed Spanish, indigenous, and African ancestry of the Mexican people opened the door to questions about where they would fit in the American racial order" (Gómez 2007, 83). Thus it was clear that visible differences, of the type that Alcoff makes central in her analysis of racial hierarchies, were the major reason for the racialization of Mexicans and became one of the basic sources of conflict with Anglos.

While there are several elements that influenced this process, three are particularly relevant for my argument. First was the reality of conquest and colonization that defined not only the political relations between Mexicans and the U.S. state apparatus, but also the pattern of social relations between Mexicans and the newly arrived but expanding population of Anglos, particularly after the Mexican-American War of 1848. Second, and related to the first point, was the ideological vision of the "founding fathers" of the United States as a white nation, which was the basis of the system of white supremacy that was imposed on the nonwhite populations. Third, many policymakers and a large sector of the public in the United States believed that Latin American cultures and societies were inherently inferior, particularly because of the racial mixtures and indigenous peoples.

On the first point, the engagement with and the effects of racialization were complicated by the reality of what Gómez calls "double colonization." Although it may seem to some as historically remote, Gómez convincingly demonstrates that the dynamic of racialization of Mexicans cannot be explained without taking into account the way that colonization influenced the processes involved. She introduces the notion of double colonization to describe the particular mode of racialization that took place. The region and peoples of what is now the U.S. Southwest experienced, and developed in the context of, two conquests and colonizations—first by the Spanish, and then by the United States after the Mexican-American War of 1848. Gómez notes that "Both the Spanish and American colonial regimes imposed a system of status inequality grounded in racial difference. While a central aspect of both the Spanish and American conquests was a racial ideology of white supremacy, the particular variants of the ideology differed under the two regimes. Double colonization meant that the various racial groups who inhabited the region in the mid-nineteenth century were forced to navigate two different racial regimes simultaneously" (Gómez 2007, 27). Mexicans and native peoples in the newly conquered Southwest were already part of a strict, caste-like racial order of subordination that the Spanish colonizers had established, and it was from within this preexisting frame of reference that they had to learn to negotiate a different mode of racialization. But in both cases, what provided the normative foundations of the racial order was white supremacy. While this took different forms, after the annexation the process of racialization quickly produced a racial order with white Europeans at the top and in control of the major positions of power and most material resources, followed by Mexican elites, Mexican mestizos, and indigenous groups. Visible differences became primary markers for locating and positioning individuals and groups within the racial hierarchy, and were embedded within the practices and rule of state institutions, as well as within the cultural framing of these different racialized populations that mediated the relations between them and Anglo society.

A second feature that influenced the political relations that Mexicans developed with the institutions of the state, and the social relations established with the Anglo populace, was the view of many of the founding fathers and of prominent political leaders and politicians that the United States had to remain a white nation. This influenced public opinion regarding non-European sectors of the society and was reflected directly in the jurisprudential principles embodied in the interpretation of constitutional and court rulings more generally. In a discussion of what he calls "los olvidados" (the forgotten ones), Perea provides a brief but revealing exposition of the widespread conception of the United States as a white nation—what became known as "manifest destiny" (Perea 1995). He argues that the history of this idea began with the "Framers' plan for America" (Perea 1995, 972). He cites John Jay from Federalist No. 2, who articulated a vision of the United States as consisting of a people with a common ancestry, language, religion, and similar "manners and customs"—all of which refer to whites. Perea argues that this was a view commonly held by others who created the constitutional foundation of the United States. Of course there was already a considerable degree of diversity, and so what Jay was giving expression to is a normative racialized national imaginary. Perea also discusses the racialized view of the United States advocated by Franklin, who played such a significant role in framing the debates in the Constitutional Convention. Jefferson shared essentially the same notion of a white United States, but worried about the "blot" and threat that African slaves were to this vision. This was a view that essentially justified the expansion of the U.S. borders through conquest and violence, culminating in the attack on Mexico and declaration of a war of annexation. It was reflected in the laws that the states and local jurisdictions created regarding issues such as land grants and property rights, and which enabled the stripping of Mexican control of virtually all of the natural resources. It was also embodied in the cultural figuration and representations of Mexicans at the popular level.[31]

The third element that affected the mode and pattern of racialization of Mexicans in the nineteenth-century Southwest was the widely shared view that Mexicans and other Latin American peoples were inherently inferior. Recent works on the transformation that the Mexican population underwent in the nineteenth-century Southwest provide strong evidence of this claim. Although Almaguer acknowledges that the particular mode of racialization of Mexicans varied by region, and that Mexicans were legally defined as "white" at the conclusion of the Mexican-American War, nevertheless his study of the origins of white supremacy in California, and the framing of Mexicans as foreigners, clearly shows the foregrounding of racial imaging in the process by which the modes of access and incorporation of the majority of Mexicans were established (Almaguer 1994). Anglo settlers did make a class distinction between the small Mexican elite who had controlled virtually all of the land-based form of capital and who were considered acceptable in terms of status and interaction, even intermarriage, and the rest of the working-class, mestizo population. But that sector quickly continued to shrink until the vast majority of Mexicans became racialized wage laborers. In another study, Vélez-Ibañez also documents some of the prevailing cultural constructions of Mexicans that developed, particularly in the latter half of the nineteenth century. He quotes Henry Lewis Morgan, who greatly influenced the early stages of the development of anthropology in the United States, to the effect that the racial mixing of European and Indian evident in the majority of Mexicans produces a racially inferior "breed." While there were variations of this racial stereotype in Texas, Arizona, California, and New Mexico, there was nevertheless convergence on the basic premise of Mexican racial inferiority. David Weber's study of the U.S. frontier also highlights the centrality of this theme, demonstrating that most Anglo-Americans considered the racial mixture that characterized most Mexicans as "violations of the laws of nature" (Weber 1973, 337). And in an earlier study, Barrera demonstrated the significance of the role of the ideology of white supremacy in establishing a racialized Mexican labor force during the latter half of the nineteenth century (Barrera 1979). Menchaca's analysis of racialization processes affecting Mexicans in the newly reconfigured political order demonstrates, through detailed historical analysis and documentation, the centrality of race, and its embodiment in the notion of foreignness, in establishing the forms of hierarchies that led to the political and economic marginalization of Mexicanos in the Southwest (Menchaca 2001). These studies delineate in considerable detail how the mode of subordination of the Mexican population was accomplished not only through legal and political strategies, but also because the sites of civil society were major spaces for regulating the nature and level of Mexican access to, and incorporation in, the emerging social order on a racialized basis. The combination of formal state policies, on the one hand, and restrictions and racial coding through which social relations in the civil sphere were regulated, on the other, in effect created the foundational framing for the specific strategies, practices, and ideological tropes by which the nature of societal membership was contained and defined.

While many of the practices and ideologies reviewed here took place within the civil sphere, the configuration of the three elements described above—i.e., the consequences of double colonization, the normative vision of the United States as a white nation, and the belief in the inferiority of Latin Americans, and in particular Mexicans—also found expression in the political realm, especially the decisions rendered by the legal system. From the very beginning of the appropriation and "official" occupation of previously Mexican territory, the legal citizenship status and forms of belonging to the new society of Mexicans was consistently problematic for the dominant political order. The origins of this ongoing site of contestation is described clearly and succinctly by Haney-López.

In the early 1800s, people in the United States ascribed to Latin Americans nationalities and, separate from these, races. Thus a Mexican might also be White, Indian, Black, or Asian. By the 1840s and 1850s, however, U.S. Anglos looked with distaste upon Mexicans in terms that conflated and stigmatized their race and nationality. This animus had its source in the Anglo-Mexican conflicts in the Southwest, particularly in Texas and California. In the newly independent Texas, war propaganda from the 1830s and 1840s purporting to chronicle Mexican "atrocities" relied on racial disparagements. Little time elapsed following the U.S. annexation of Mexican territory in 1848 before laws began to reflect and reify Anglo prejudices. Social prejudices quickly became legal ones, highlighting the close ties between race and law. (Haney-López 1996, 169)

As a result of this positioning in the social imaginary and hierarchy of the expansionist U.S. project, and despite the fact that the terms of the Treaty of Guadalupe Hidalgo that concluded the war guaranteed equal property and other rights to the Mexican inhabitants of the new U.S. territories, most never really enjoyed full membership in the society. Román concludes his study of Latinos and legal citizenship by citing Delgado: "The Mexicans' rights were denied, language and culture suppressed, opportunities for employment, education, and political representation were thwarted" (Román 2000, 98).

However, the enabling mechanism for this racializing of the legal citizenship status and belonging is found even earlier. Curiously, the original U.S. Constitution does not define the parameters of citizenship, but the racialized normative conception of white supremacy was embodied in one of the initial acts of legislation passed by Congress that established that naturalization leading to U.S. citizenship would be restricted to "white persons." While the specific applications of this legislation have varied significantly over the years, the racial restriction on citizenship was not completely eliminated until 1952, reflecting that racialization was one of the primary and constitutive dimensions for determining citizenship status in the United States for most of its history. This prerequisite that all naturalized citizens be white created a constitutional dilemma for the United States concerning the legal citizenship status of Mexicans. Determining the latter was complicated by the fact that the original version of the Treaty of Guadalupe Hidalgo included language in article 9 that guaranteed the full rights of citizenship to those Mexicans who stayed in the new U.S. territories. This was in response to the Mexican government's concern about the protection of the status of its conquered peoples. However, that article was changed to give Congress the discretionary power to decide when and how Mexicans would be granted full rights as U.S. citizens. The language states that Mexicans "shall be incorporated into the Union of the United States and be admitted at the proper time [to be judged of by the Congress of the United States] to the enjoyment of all the rights of citizens of the United States, according to the principles of the Constitution; and in the mean time, shall be maintained and protected in the free enjoyment of their liberty and property, and secured in the free exercise of their religion without restriction" (Treaty of Guadalupe Hidalgo, article 9). In his study of Latino rights, Morín argues that this was done "to appease the concerns raised in Congress over the racial threat that Mexicans represented to Anglo-American rule" (Morín 2005, 23). Even though the time frame for granting citizenship was left ambiguous, the fact that the treaty stated that Mexicans could become citizens meant that they would have to be considered "white" to be consistent with the 1789 naturalization legislation, which stated that only whites could become citizens of the United States. The dilemma came to a head in 1897 in the ruling *In re Rodriguez*, by a federal court in Texas, that granted citizenship to "the 'pure-blooded Mexican' applicant," but remarked that "'if the strict scientific classification of the anthropologist should be adopted, he would probably not be classed as white. The court allowed the applicant to naturalize on the basis of a series of treaties conferring citizenship on Spaniards and Mexicans in the wake of U.S. expansion into Florida and the Southwest. Rodriguez was thus admitted despite the court's belief that he was not White" (Haney-López 1996, 161). So the initial framing of legal citizenship as the mode of belonging suitable for Mexicans was founded on a fictional construction of a nonwhite, "white" Mexican subject who, while defined as white, did not receive the benefits or full membership associated with that racial status in the society. What this underscores is the clear and close connection between the way Mexicans were "situated" and restricted within the spheres of civil society, and the legal construction and framing of the level and type of state membership embodied in their citizenship status. The constitutional and legal construction thus both reflected and helped construct the mode of belonging thought to be "appropriate to Mexicans."

The interacting and combined dynamics of double colonization, the normative construction of the U.S. nation as white, and the view of Latin Americans as inferior all found material and ideological expression in the sphere of legal and political policy, as well as the social mechanisms of marginalization operative in the sphere of civil society. The substantive nature and consequences of these processes were all predicated on the belief that despite the provisions of the treaty and the legal positions advanced in several judicial decisions, Mexicans were not actually white. This therefore staged Mexican identity as basically and irremediably foreign—that is, they did not fit within the normative cultural matrix developed and embraced by both the state and civil institutions, converging around and creating the imaginary construction of Mexicans as "perpetual foreigners." Since this made it impossible to grant *effective* full membership and citizenship to Mexican-origin peoples, what resulted was a pattern of modes of exclusionary belonging as the boundary conditions for the level and type of incorporation of Mexicans into the United States.

PUERTO RICAN COLONIALITY AND MIGRATION

As I indicated earlier in this chapter, Latinos are a heterogenous population with very different specific histories of incorporation into U.S. society. After Mexicans, Puerto Ricans have the longest history of Latino settlement in the United States. Even though the historical situation and the specific modes of incorporation of Puerto Ricans has been quite different than those of Mexicans, some of the same factors that framed Mexicans as perpetual foreigners nevertheless also influenced the mode of belonging and citizenship status of Puerto Ricans. The foundation of the mode of citizenship and belonging created for Puerto Ricans has its roots in the colonial relationship between the United States and Puerto Rico, and its subsequent "peculiar status within the U.S. political system" (Meléndez and Meléndez 1993, 1). The status of the population of Puerto Rico became a political concern in the United States during the conflict with Spain at the end of the nineteenth century. The invasion of Puerto Rico by U.S. troops in 1898 was part of a more general plan of imperial conquest of the strategically important islands of Cuba and Puerto Rico. While the treaty of peace signed in Paris that brought an end to the hostilities left Cuba free, Puerto Rico, along with Guam and the Philippine Islands, was ceded to the United States as a dependent territory without any promise or provision allowing for future citizenship for its inhabitants. However, within two years of the treaty agreement, a proposal to grant citizenship to Puerto Ricans was brought before the U.S. Congress by Senator Foraker; this was considered in the broader context of the question of how to deal with the other acquired territories. The basic issue that arose was one that all empires have to confront, that is, determining the status of racially and culturally distinct populations brought under U.S. sovereign control through conquest (Cabranes 1978).

This became a contentious issue involving numerous interests and concerns over a period of sixteen years. Every congressional session between 1900 and 1917 took up and hotly debated the issue of the status of Puerto Rico and its inhabitants. Finally in 1917, Congress passed the Jones Act, granting greater governmental autonomy to the island and conferring "citizenship" status on Puerto Ricans—but a type of citizenship that was quite different than that which had previously been elaborated through legislation and judicial decisions. It was not based on the principle of incorporation as full membership and equal standing, but was driven by political considerations regarding the appropriate strategies for dealing with "foreign" territorial possessions of the United States. This difference was apparent from the very start of the debate in 1900 and was ratified in the final form of the legislation; it is described clearly by Cabranes in his discussion of the initial congressional debate on the issue.

> The author of the first legislative proposal to make Puerto Ricans citizens of the United States thus acknowledged, as others would in the years to come, that the principal objective of granting American citizenship to Puerto Ricans was neither to incorporate Puerto Rico into the United States (and thereby to have the Constitution apply in all respects to the island and to its people) nor to grant Puerto Ricans political and civil rights equal to those of citizens in the American Union proper. The objective, rather, was "to recognize that Puerto Rico belongs to the United States of America." (Cabranes 1978, 427–28)

Senator Foraker, who Cabranes quotes in the last line, made it clear that the particular concept of citizenship being considered for Puerto Ricans was a very restricted one. In his remarks to the Senate, Foraker stated that "In adopting the term 'citizen' we did not understand, however, that we were giving to those people any rights that the American people do not want them to have" (quoted in Cabranes 1978, 428). He also made clear that the intention was not to integrate or incorporate Puerto Ricans into U.S. society; instead he saw the granting of citizenship as a way of asserting and affirming complete control over the fate of Puerto Rico and its people. In addition, extending this particular form of citizenship precluded the option of national independence for Puerto Rico. So in effect, the Jones Act and the type of citizenship bestowed on Puerto Ricans simply reaffirmed the island's status as a U.S. colony. Thus this peculiar construct created what can only be thought of as a form of second-class citizenship, a status with legislative rather than constitutional grounding and therefore subject to legislative reversal. Clearly this form of citizenship was not intended to create a space of belonging for Puerto Ricans within U.S. society, but instead framed them both legally and in the social imaginary of U.S. culture as *citizen foreigners*, "'living in an unincorporated territory,' belonging to, but not being a part of the United States" (Meléndez and Meléndez 1993, 1). Although Congress passed legislation in 1950 changing the status of Puerto Rico to a commonwealth and granting a greater degree of control over the internal process of governance, the form of citizenship remained unchanged. A number of plebiscites have been held since then giving the people of the island the opportunity to voice their preferences about statehood, independence, or remaining a commonwealth, and although the status quo has been generally upheld, the population continues to be seriously divided over the issue, which dominates in many ways the domestic politics of the island. Needless to say, this construction of the status of Puerto Rican citizenship has affected the pattern of incorporation of Puerto Ricans into the domestic institutions of the United States. Although quite restrictive, Puerto Rican citizenship nevertheless facilitated

Table 1. Immigrants to the United States from El Salvador and Guatemala, 1970–2010

	1970	1980	1990	2000	2010
El Salvador	15,717	94,447	465,433	817,335	1,648,968
Guatemala	17,356	63,073	225,073	480,665	1,044,209

Source: Mahler and Ugrina (2006); Ennis, Ríos-Vargas, and Albert (2011).

the process of migration of large numbers from the island to the mainland during the 1940s and 1950s. Since then, the number of Puerto Ricans in the continental United States has grown to 4.7 million, representing nearly 56 percent of the entire population of Puerto Rican origin, so that over half of Puerto Ricans live in the United States (Motel and Patten 2012, 4). Like the cultural imaginary of the Mexican-origin population as the "perpetual foreigner" that has its roots in the pattern of initial contact, the "citizen foreigner" continues to be a vital element in the constructed identity of Puerto Ricans adopted by the dominant cultural frame.

THE CENTRAL AMERICAN EXODUS AND LIMINALITY

The pattern of incorporation of Central Americans presents a very distinct mode of articulation with the United States compared to that of either Mexicans or Puerto Ricans. Despite some popular misconceptions, significant numbers of Central Americans migrated to the United States as early as the 1950s, when some 45,000 entered the country legally. That number increased to 100,000 in the 1960s and to more than 130,000 in the 1970s (Hamilton and Chinchilla 2001, 29). Still, the most noteworthy growth occurred in the 1980s, during the most violent turmoil and civil wars in Guatemala, El Salvador, and Nicaragua.

Because these internal struggles took place in the context of the Cold War, the response from the United States to immigrants from Guatemala and El Salvador was quite different from the response to those coming from Nicaragua. Many of those fleeing Nicaragua after the fall of the right-wing dictator Somoza were considered by the Reagan administration as "freedom fighters" and were given preferential treatment in terms of their immigrant status. The proportion of these that received asylum was higher than the proportion of either the Salvadorans or Guatemalans, who arrived in the United States during the same period and were fleeing for basically the same reasons. Several scholars argue that the reason that migrants from these countries were labeled "economic migrants" and denied asylum status was because the United States had strong ties with the right-wing dictatorships in power in El

Salvador and Guatemala. The fact is that the majority of migrants fleeing the civil wars in these countries did not qualify for any type of legal protections in the form of asylum, and were for the most part labeled as undocumented. That denial of claims for asylum by migrants clearly fleeing the violence in their countries essentially reflected the policies that had been adopted by the U.S. State Department. This situation was amended in 1998 and 2001 for basically humanitarian reasons that arose from the effects of natural disasters in the region. The government created the category of Temporary Protected Status, and it is estimated that over 370,000 migrants from Central America currently live in the United States under this rubric. While those who come under the jurisdiction of this policy are protected from deportation for a specific period of time, and are entitled to receive work permits, there has been no mechanism that would provide for permanent residency, let alone naturalized citizenship.

The INS estimated that close to 60 percent of Salvadorans and Guatemalans were undocumented or protected only temporarily. Menjívar has documented in great detail the contradictory maze of complex legal obstacles that have created a condition she refers to as "liminal legality," and she describes the effects of this legal uncertainty on the everyday lives of Salvadorans residing in the United States (Menjívar 2006). Other scholars have framed this experience in similar terms, referring to "spaces of nonexistence" and "being neither here nor there" as ways of describing the uncertainty that pervades individuals and families who live in these immigrant communities (Coutin 2003). What this does, of course, is define societal membership of these groups in an ambivalent and unstable frame, marked by an ongoing tension that permeates the networks of families and neighborhoods where Salvadorans and Guatemalans reside.

Despite this very different modality of unstable membership, these groups also confront the processes and experiences of racialization similar to Mexicans and Puerto Ricans. While there is not yet an extensive literature on this aspect of their unstable societal membership status, a recent essay by Rodríguez and Menjívar (2009) provides a detailed discussion of how Salvadorans and Guatemalans have been affected by and positioned within the processes of Latino racialization. They point out that

> For many Central Americans, new racial experiences are transpiring in the United States. In the span of just a couple of decades, thousands of Central Americans have been introduced to the racial and ethnic matrices of U.S. society at various social, cultural, and economic levels. The integration of Central American newcomers into the U.S. racialized social structure also creates consequences for later immigrant generations. (Rodríguez and Menjívar 2009, 187)

They indicate, as other scholars studying Central American immigrants have, that these groups are often "invisible" as separate Latino groups and are most often assumed to be part of the Mexican immigrant community. And so they face the same racialized images that have animated the nativist anti-immigrant movement that coalesced in the early 1990s and has gained considerable strength since then.[32] Central American immigrants, including those who have secured legal status or citizenship, have been subsumed as part of the generalized "Latino immigrant" who has been subjected to increasing hostility, exclusionary laws, and ordinances that, despite the denials of anti-nativists, are based on the assumption that these immigrants are racially distinct and identifiable, and that they are essentially unassimilable foreigners. While the proponents of these exclusionary tactics and measures claim that they are concerned with "undocumented" Latinos, the rhetoric and actions of many of these groups, clearly reflected in the popular media and Internet, belie that assertion and create a climate of fear where even Latinos who are citizens are subject to suspicion and scrutiny (Chavez 2008).

Although the specifics of the particular histories of articulation with the majority-controlled institutions in the United States of each group of Latinos reviewed here are completely different, they nevertheless converge around the form of racialized othering, as racialized perpetual foreigners. Thus diversity at one level does not preclude commonality at another. What the different modes of incorporation have in common is that Mexicans, Puerto Ricans, Salvadorans, and Guatemalans in the United States have been construed culturally and ideologically through the prism of racialized foreignness; they are thus perceived as cultural groups that are suspect in terms of willingness or ability to accept and conform to the established rules of cultural engagement with the dominant society as "true Americans," the normative national imaginary defined in terms of whiteness. And while the particular factors that have had the greatest effect have varied over the last 150 years, the societal positionality of significant sectors of Latino populations continues to be primarily determined by material and cultural dimensions of these processes, albeit in a different form and register. Later-arriving Latino groups have been situated within, and framed as, an extension of the racialized notion of foreignness that developed at the representational level to situate and homogenize Mexicans, Puerto Ricans, Salvadorans, and Guatemalans—and by extension other Latino groups as well—within a specific position in the U.S. racial order. As long as this remains the case, a form of authentic and truly inclusionary democracy, capable of incorporating all groups on an equal basis, will remain an illusory and unattainable goal.

If we view this pattern of Latino experience in the United States using Marshall's basic premise of citizenship as full membership, it becomes clear that a comprehensive understanding of the political valence of this pattern requires a concept of citizenship that can capture the various dimensions involved. Thus the need for the reformulation of the concept of citizenship as including the nature of membership and societal cohesion, patterns and strategies of inclusion and exclusion, forms of belonging, and the construction of alterity through racialization. However, the question arises about how to examine the interaction of these dimensions, and I take up this issue in the following chapter.

CHAPTER 4

Associative Citizenship

Civil Society, Rights Claims, and Expanding the Public Sphere

THE FOUR DIMENSIONS OF THE REFORMULATED CONCEPTION OF CITIZENSHIP I developed in the previous chapter (membership, exclusion, belonging, racialization) should not be viewed as only theoretical elements, but should also be understood as taking on meaning through the institutional contexts within which they function. Citizenship is ultimately a set of practices, the specificity of which are determined by the particular norms and characteristics of the particular institutions where these practices are enacted. In other words, we need to find a way to focus on the institutional sites and practices through which societal location and membership, and political membership mutually influence one another; where the differential pattern of belonging takes form; and where patterns and strategies of inclusion and exclusion become incorporated as ongoing practices, ideologies, and policies. We need to explore how the form of racialization as foreignness functions. These investigations address specifically the elements of membership, exclusion, belonging, and racialization as the constitutive elements of associative citizenship. Such a theory also has to be capable of accounting for the dual historical roles of citizenship regimes, that while they have been a form of control and regulation, at the same time they have provided a means to make claims for greater societal and political inclusion.

I argue in this chapter that a specific conception and model of civil society can provide a way to ground these dimensions empirically within specific institutional contexts. This approach is suggested by some of the very works on diversity and citizenship that I critiqued earlier. However, while these perspectives are suggestive, they do not develop a specific way or approach for linking their positions to particular institutional frameworks and contexts. This is one of the reasons that the inherently reciprocal relationship between societal and political membership has not received the kind of theoretical elaboration that would illuminate how that relationship plays out empirically on the ground. The key point here is that in most of these works, the formulations, analyses, and prescriptions regarding political membership rely on the preexistence of certain kinds of qualitative relations—particularly forms of mutuality, trust, and reciprocity—in the realm of societal membership. The problem is that the latter are either not mentioned at all or are assumed to exist, without any detailed analysis. But what if these societal relations do not exist? Since they are vital to the notions of diversity and citizenship these theorists argue for, should attention not be paid as seriously to the nature of these relations, and how they can be nurtured and fostered? For example, the normative formulations that Habermas and Rawls propose as the foundation for just, democratic societies rely on the preexistence of some form of trust and/or reciprocity. If these are indeed preconditions, and if without them there can be no just, democratic society, should this dimension not be analyzed as rigorously as the other elements in the theories proposed? Much like Habermas and Rawls, most of these theorists locate the site of these societal relations within civil society. Yet they fail to develop a conception or model of civil society as part of their analyses. What I propose here, then, is to develop a model of civil society that not only incorporates the four dimensions of citizenship that I propose, but also allows us to delineate the dual function of citizenship regimes, and can provide an account of the institutional conditions necessary for the type of qualitative relations that are required for a just, democratic society. But I first want to elaborate on the need for this institutional grounding, and then address the question of how best to institutionally situate these four dimensions.

Institutional Context

The theorists who advance analyses of diversity and citizenship that I discussed in chapter 3 have different positions regarding the issue of institutional context. The liberal approach focuses on the primacy of individual rights and citizenship and is thus construed in terms of the individual as the bearer of these rights. These rights ensure that private individuals can pursue their self-interests through the protection of the state, whose primary function is to mediate conflict and regulate activities. But the emphasis is on the nature of these rights, and few of the theorists in this tradition elaborate in any depth as to how the actual institutional context works in terms of the practice of citizenship rights. The communitarian formulations, on the other hand, tend to interpret the conception of rights as a function of membership in a historically specific society, community, or state, and emphasize the formative role that cultural context plays in defining the nature and significance of claims to rights. It is only within the context of the specific configuration of social relations, institutions, and culture that the idea of rights can be understood and realized.

However, while the variations of the communitarian positions I reviewed in chapter 2 are all based on the assumption that some aspects of institutional context are vital, as I pointed out there, none of them provide a sufficiently developed analysis of this dimension to support their arguments. Kymlicka and Taylor make the cultural component of institutional context a central part of their argument, but ignore how state and economic factors shape and interact with cultural configurations. Although Walzer recognizes the importance of the economic sphere, his notion of "shared understandings," on which his analysis of the issue of deep diversity rests, is essentially another conceptualization of the cultural dimension of social relations that does not situate it with the broader institutional system within which it functions. The liberal positions that Rawls and Habermas develop depend on a preexisting societal context, but both either assume its dimensions or bracket it out of their analyses. The theories of citizenship do not provide much more attention to the economic aspects of institutional context and how these might affect their conceptual constructions of citizenship.

An effective approach to the challenge of developing a conception of citizenship that is responsive to the conditions of deep diversity needs to theorize these institutional sites, spaces or places, as constitutive of diverse social and political relations, rather than treat them as simply contextual or additive dimensions. The study of Latinos and Latino citizenship in the contemporary period must be situated within the specific institutional characteristics that have had a formative impact on them. In the next chapter, I will argue that these are related to, and the product of, the processes of globalization, restructuring, and transnationalization. But I first want to establish a theoretical defense of the approach that I will adopt regarding the relationship between institutional context and the emergence of rights claims that is the basis of associative citizenship.

There are several literatures that suggest ways to accomplish this task. One of the approaches focuses on the constitutive role of the spatial dimension in providing the "grounding" of these relations. Of particular relevance to efforts to understand the form of exclusionary belonging of Latinos are the various attempts to theorize spaces of difference and exclusion as third space, hybridity, borders, the "in-between," or margins (Soja 1996, Kraidy 2005, Brah and Coombes 2000, Saldívar 1997). These constructs have emerged from efforts, often but not always under the rubric of postcolonialism, to rethink, retheorize, and rearticulate the disjunctions between Eurocentric and Third World constructions of cultural formations and configurations so as to capture the complexity of the conditions of articulation. This is particularly salient for Latinos since there have always been a mix of native- and foreign-born, and the fact is that even native-born Latinos are often perceived as "perpetual foreigners," as existing outside the normative national imaginary based on Western conceptions of superiority.

These approaches attempt to theorize the complexity of these relations in terms that reject the privileging of Western culture, and that delineate the nature of institutional locations of Third World peoples. While not arguing for the reductionist conflation of these terms and the complex theoretical frameworks within which they have been elaborated, and without assuming a sameness of content, it is nevertheless clear that these operate within a field of constructs that overlap considerably. This overlap is noted in a recent essay on boundaries.

> A jumble of cultural-political practices and forms of resistance have emerged that have variously been named hybrid, border, or diasporic. The most creative and dynamic of these resistances are located on the borders of essentialism and conjuncturalism. They refuse the binarism of identity politics versus post-modernist fragmentation. . . . We name this terrain of practice and theory, this zone of shifting and mobile resistances that refuse fixity yet practice their own arbitrary provisional closures, the third timespace. (Lavie and Swedenburg 1996, 154)

And social theorist Ed Soja reviews a group of affiliated positions that he designates "thirdspace" and provides the following description, which although advanced in the discussion of bell hooks, nevertheless captures the central thrust of his own conceptualization. He states that hooks "attempts to move beyond the modernist binary oppositions of race, gender, and class into the multiplicity of other spaces that difference makes" (Soja 1996, 96). In their study of popular culture in Latin America, Rowe and Schelling propose a useful definition of cultural hybridity as "the ways in which forms become separated from existing practices and recombine with new forms in new practices" (Rowe and Schelling 1991, 231). But this deceptively simple definition does not convey the complexity of both the processes involved and the modes of theorizing them. Works by theorists such as Bhabha, Spivak, and Said have sought to delineate these in great detail. These conceptualizations all reject binary theoretical constructions and the privileging of monocausal factors, and insist instead on the notions of multiple subjectivities and voice, on complex modes of positioning.

However, these concepts, and the frameworks they are nested within, are clearly not without difficulties. They have been the subject of wide-ranging critiques from a variety of positions, and the shortcomings of these formulations have been amply delineated. One line of critique is particularly relevant to the focus of my study. A position advanced by Hall, and by Frankenberg and Mani, maintains that while the notions of the margins, borders, hybridity, and third space seek to address fundamentally important phenomena, these relations are even more complex than many formulations maintain (Hall 1996, Frankenberg and Mani 1993). What is called for is careful attention to, and delineation of, problems that arise in applying these concepts to issues of, for example, periodization, historical appropriateness and correlation, and both historical and institutional contextualization. For those of us exploring these themes within the context of the United States, one of the most helpful efforts to delineate the difficulties in applying these notions is found in the critique of postcolonial theorizations advanced by Frankenberg and Mani. They point out that terms like "postcolonialism" and affiliated notions need to be situated within the specific and particular historical circumstances and experiences that are being addressed. And they specifically focus on the issue of the appropriateness of the concept of postcolonialism in comprehending the U.S. situation. They provide a summary of the historical and political elements that such an endeavor would have to account for.

> White settler colony, multiracial society. Colonization of Native Americans, Africans imported as slaves, Mexicans incorporated by a border moving south, Asians imported and migrating to labor, white Europeans migrating to labor. U.S. imperialist foreign policy brings new immigrants who are "here because the U.S. was/is there," among them Central Americans, Koreans, Filipinos, Vietnamese and Cambodians. The particular relation of past territorial domination and current racial composition that is discernible in Britain, and which lends a particular meaning to the term "postcolonial," does not, we feel, obtain here. Other characterizations, other periodizations, seem necessary in naming for this place the shifts expressed by the term "postcolonial" in the British and Indian cases: the serious calling into question of white/Western dominance by the groundswell of movements of resistance, and the emergence of struggles for collective self-determination most frequently articulated in nationalist terms (Frankenberg and Mani 1993, 293).

They suggest the use of the term "post–civil rights" as a possible way to talk about the U.S. case, but immediately indicate their reservations regarding its adequacy.

> Let us emphasize at the outset that we use the term 'post-Civil Rights' broadly, to refer
> to the impact of struggles by African Americans, American Indians, La Raza and Asian
> American communities that stretched from the mid 1950s to the 1970s. . . . However, the
> name, 'post-Civil Rights,' would only grasp one strand of our description of the US. The
> term would have to be conjugated with another, one that would name the experience of
> recent immigrants/refugees borne here on the trails of US imperialist adventures, groups
> whose stories are unfolding in a tense, complicated relation—at times compatible, at
> times contradictory—with post-Civil Rights USA. (Frankenberg and Mani 1993, 293)

It is in these substantially different, particular (local) historical and institutional
circumstances that one of the major difficulties is encountered by efforts to characterize and theorize notions of borders, margins, third space, hybridity. There are two
dimensions of this problematic in particular that need to be addressed and disen-
tangled: the connection between the colonizing-decolonizing contexts and histories
that are the root of much of the theorizing about these concepts; and the connection
between the longstanding populations from formerly colonized countries, and the
most recent immigrants from both the same countries, and others from distinct
regions and with substantially different cultural contexts. Again, Frankenberg and
Mani put the issue succinctly and clearly. In referring to recent immigrants to the
United States, they state that

> Their travel to the U.S. has been occasioned by a history related to, but distinct from, that
> of people of color already here. Their historical experiences stretch existing categories—
> "Hispanic," "Asian"—inflecting them with new meanings. Relations between recent
> immigrants/refugees and those already here, whether whites or people of color, are
> constituted through discourses that draw heavily on colonial and racist rhetoric both in
> form and content. . . . *Nothing but the most complex and historically specific conceptions
> of identity and subjectivity can sufficiently grasp the present situation and articulate a
> politics adequate to it.* (Frankenberg and Mani 1993, 301 [italics mine]).

The question arises as to whether the notions of these spaces have been
theorized in ways that can adequately account for the realities of the substantive
experiences, particular networks, modes of engagement, and relations of political
configurations that revolve around historical and institutional axes and moments.
To repeat, "nothing but the most complex and historically specific conceptions of
identity and subjectivity can sufficiently grasp the present situation and articulate
a politics adequate to it." My premise here is that while some of the formulations
of citizenship in deeply diverse societies move in the right direction and articulate
positions that are adequate at one level of theory, they are still incomplete in terms

of elaborating and providing for the institutional grounding/dimensions of these concepts. An empirical example of this occurred when I confronted this dilemma in developing my analysis of the processes of transformation of Latino communities in Los Angeles, where one of the most difficult dimensions to explain is the dynamic between recent Latino immigrants and earlier generations of Latinos, who have a long history of engagement with U.S. culture and its system of subordination and power. These are two different yet complexly related trajectories or axes of engagement, and these in turn provide conditions and opportunities for cultural and political strategies that have qualitatively distinct centers of gravity.

In addition to this aspect, we need to suspect that some of the accents, emphasis, and limitations of theorizing third space, spaces of marginalization, have to do with another factor that is less often discussed. The critical examination of both colonialism and decolonization is hardly a new focus of attention, particularly in decolonized Third World countries. But it appears that the reason this concern has become a major preoccupation in the present historical moment of the Eurocentric academy has less to do with theory than with demographics. It is the enormous and rapid migration of Third Word peoples to the heart of Euro-U.S. cities that has burst the boundaries of canonical paradigms. The pervasiveness of radical cultural differences in the major Euro-U.S. metropolitan centers has sounded a dissonant chord for some, brought welcome decentering for others, but it can hardly be ignored by anyone. The world has changed, and sooner or later, theory has to confront it. The grounding of this particular theoretical enterprise in this reality requires not only that the parameters of these spaces be delineated but also, to paraphrase Michael Kearney's critique of ethnography, that the theorizing "must situate the production and consumption of representations of [subaltern spaces] within the relationships that join [the theoretical self to the subaltern] other it presumes to represent" (Kearney 1996, 3). There needs to be, in other words, an accounting as well of the ways in which the theorizing itself may function as what Jameson calls strategies of containment (Jameson 1981).

Both of these dimensions—expanding and deepening the boundaries of the conceptions of third space, and including the self-reflexive moment as part of that enterprise—can be advanced by delineating their specific institutional grounding. With regard to the former dimension, the necessity to move in this direction is reflected in the following:

> Third spaces, third texts, third scenarios are concepts articulated in the interdisciplinary field of Minority Discourse through usage of Cultural Studies methodologies. Thus the cultural materials currently analyzed by using the modalities of "the third" are highly stylized domains of knowledge, framed as dramatic, literary, cinematic, artistic and

musical texts. Bridging Ethnography, Cultural Studies, and Minority Discourse will be possible if we return to the primary daily realities from which such textual representations are derived. We call for reconceptualization, from lived identities and physical places, not just from texts, of the multiplicities of identity and place. As they are forced into constantly shifting configurations of partial overlap, their ragged edges cannot be smoothed out. Identity and place perpetually create both new outer borders, where the overlap has not occurred, and inner borders between the areas of overlap and vestigial spaces of non-overlap. (Lavie and Swedenburg 1996, 168–69)

The "lived identities" and realities of these hybrid and third spaces, of the margins, the borders, of the spaces "in-between," are not random, epiphenomenal, or transient. They are institutional spaces, structures of cultural, economic, and political practices that simultaneously limit and enable the parameters, conditions, strategies, and options for social and political action. And their quality as spaces of the hybrid, border or margin, are directly linked to the variety of changes in the nature of the relationship between territory, space, identity, and community that have resulted from the processes of globalization and transnationalization. I am not positing a simple, linear causal relationship here, but instead a complex set of interdependent and multidimensional constellations of institutional practices. The theorizations of third space, borders, marginalization, then, must be reconfigured to incorporate these institutional spaces as necessary, inherent, and internal dimensions of the organic discursive and material complexes that constitute societal relations. I want to make clear that I am not calling for a return to binary or totalistic constructs of society. Instead my view reflects the following premise articulated by Bhabha.

> It is only when we understand that all cultural statements and systems are constructed in this contradictory and ambivalent space of enunciation, that we begin to understand why hierarchical claims to the inherent originality or "purity" of cultures are untenable, even before we resort to empirical historical instances that demonstrate their hybridity. (Bhabha 1995, 208)

In other words, the articulation of theorization is neither reducible to nor dependent on a mechanistic or reductive conception of empirical "reality." Rather, it is a constitutive element of that reality (constitutive and not causal, which would return us to the tradition of idealism), and as such it is not sufficient to situate third space within the "transnational" or "global" context—the modes of discourse and frames of representations of third space themselves need to be part of that same process of contextualization. This is not a novel position, although the problematic within which I have developed it is (that is, explaining the processes of transformation of Latino communities in Los Angeles). Thus, for example, Dirlik argues that "with rare exceptions, postcolonial critics have been silent on the relationship of the idea of postcolonialism to its context in contemporary capitalism; indeed, they have suppressed the necessity of considering such a possible relationship by repudiating a foundational role to capitalism in history" (Dirlik 1994, 331). And in a much earlier critique, Benita Parry points out that postcolonial writers like Spivak and Bhabha share a "programme marked by the exorbitation of discourse and a related incuriosity about the enabling socioeconomic and political institutions and other forms of social praxis" (Parry 1995, 43).

Now the characteristics of fragmentation and cultural disjunction, and the emergence of these third spaces that contest U.S.-Eurocentric representations and dominance, are indeed constitutive of the social relations in large urban centers in the United States, Canada, and Europe. The theoretical formulations reviewed above are useful precisely because they establish a discourse that enables the analysis of the complexity of the consequences of the transformations in social patterns, now characterized by a series of elements that have either emerged or intensified within the last forty years, including globalization, restructuring, and transnationalization. And the literature on these processes has demonstrated the centrality and importance of the patterns that have characterized the globalization and transnationalization of both capital and labor since the late 1960s (Cox 1997, Featherstone et al. 1995, King 1996, Knox and Taylor 1995, Sassen 1988, 1992, 1994).

The specific institutional grounding, then, for the field of forces, practices, and theorizations that are the axes of these theoretical constructions of third space is the particular configuration of interrelated processes of the restructuring and transnationalization of global capitalism. To recognize the centrality and influence of these processes does not necessarily privilege them or reduce the theorization of third space to a mere ideological expression. It is precisely to avoid this facile dismissal of the complex reality that theorizations of third space attempt to account for, that I propose to delineate a more structurally rooted elaboration of these relations. To ignore them, or to construct them in institutionally ungrounded ways, leads to an incomplete analysis at best, or the obfuscation of the reality of domination at worst. Margins, borders, and third spaces need to be framed and contextualized as components and expressions of how these processes of social transformation, of globalization and transnationalization, are being lived. Nederveen Pieterse observes that "Hybrid formations constituted by the interpenetration of diverse logics manifest themselves in hybrid sites and spaces. . . . Global cities and ethnic mélange neighborhoods within them (such as Jackson Heights in Queens, New York) are other hybrid spaces in the global landscape" (Nederveen Pieterse 1995,

51). The emergence of these new types of institutional spaces or sites challenges traditional ways of understanding and explaining culture, identity, and community, primarily because they are expressions of a different relationship between space and place that characterizes the dynamics of transnationalism. The degree, extent, and pervasiveness of the changes in patterns of social relations, cultural configurations, and forms that are part of the processes of globalization and transnationalization, have disrupted long-established boundaries that assumed specific representations and constructions of those populations that were constructed when "they" were "there," and "we" were "here." But the viability and adequacy of these constructions have been undermined now that "they" are "here" and have challenged the notion of who the "we" are. Hence, although the focus of analysis of these concepts of third space has been on those who are marginalized in different ways, in fact the emergence of transnationalism has impacted long-established populations as well. Thus the meaning of, and hence the stability and orientation provided by, established notions of "here" and "there," of "we" and "them," have been fundamentally decentered and problematized.[1]

Gupta and Ferguson have advanced a convincing critique of contemporary forms of cultural analysis that continue to assume an isomorphic relationship between nations, territory, space, and identities.

> In a world of diaspora, transnational culture flows, and mass movements of populations, old-fashioned attempts to map the globe as a set of culture regions or homelands are bewildered by a dazzling array of postcolonial simulacra, doublings and redoublings, as India and Pakistan apparently reappear in postcolonial simulation in London, prerevolution Tehran rises from the ashes of Los Angeles, and a thousand similar cultural dreams are played out in urban and rural settings all across the globe. (Gupta and Ferguson 1992, 10)

And while they appreciate the effort to describe this dislodging of identities from a fixed and stable territorial "place" through the notion of deterritorialization, they opt instead to characterize this dimension as "reterritorialization" to avoid the connotation that space and place no longer are significant dimensions of social formations. Space and place still matter, but in a different way.

What all this means is that the changes brought about by the processes, various dimensions, and manifestations of globalization, restructuring, and transnationalization, need to be understood as they are lived and experienced by the communities affected by them. This requires that we rethink the concept of what constitutes a nation, of what role territory plays as well as the nature of the claims of sovereignty, and how these are related to the processes of community and identity formation. And as the particular configuration of these factors change, so too must our conceptions of the complex ways that these dimensions are incorporated in the institutional structures of the state and of civil society. Since these factors affect how characteristics of the concept of citizenship are defined, as they change, so must the way we think of what it means to "belong" to a given society. But in developing this reformulation, the central role of institutional specificity expressed in and through particular places must be incorporated. One way of addressing this project is found in the more recent work of the urban theorist Saskia Sassen, who after concentrating on explaining the specific dynamics of globalization for several years, has joined the effort of a growing number of scholars who have focused on analyzing the implications and consequences of these processes for both the discourse and institutional arrangements of citizenship (Sassen 1996a, 1996b; Garcia 1996; Holston and Appadurai 1996).

Let me briefly outline her argument. One of the major objectives of Sassen's work is to use the notion of situated space, or "place" as she calls it, to ground the specific processes that constitute globalization. Referring to the reason she adopts such a position, she indicates that it "allows us to recover the concrete, localized processes through which globalization exists and to argue that much of the multiculturalism in large cities is as much a part of globalization as is international finance" (Sassen 1996c, 206). By examining the actual practices that constitute globalization, she demonstrates that it is defined by a very specific configuration or pattern of trans-national relations and actors, and adds that in many analyses, it is normally only the relations and activities of transnational capital that are focused on as constitutive of globalization. This is understandable since the new forms of transnational legal regimes "privilege the reconstitution of capital as an internationalized actor and the denationalized spaces necessary for its operation" (Sassen 1996c, 217). What is obscured by these formulations is the fact that not only has the configuration of capital changed, but the spaces and places that serve as the basis of their practices and activities have also been altered fundamentally, because the nature of what binds people and places together in these spaces has changed—as have the corresponding forms of the claims made on economic, social, political, and cultural dimensions of these spaces. Thus these conceptualizations or theorizations of globalization have overvalorized the role of capital and undervalorized that of labor as a necessary and constitutive element. The phenomena of immigration and ethnicity that are in fact constitutive of globalization are construed and positioned theoretically by writers such as Kymlicka, who uses these factors as major elements in his attempt to reformulate citizenship. He describes ways that limit the ability to perceive the reconstituted spaces that emerge from these processes of globalization, wherein different types of claims to citizenship are pressed by the cultural others that typically inhabit these spaces. What we still narrate in the language of immigration and ethnicity, I would argue, is actually a series of processes having to do with the globalization of economic activity, of cultural activity, and of the changing parameters of identity formation. Too often immigration and ethnicity are conceived of as processes that produce a form of otherness, but without rooting them in some kind of institutional context. Understanding them as a set of processes whereby global elements are localized, international labor markets are constituted, and cultures from all over the world are de- and reterritorialized puts them at the center along with the internationalization of capital as a fundamental aspect of globalization (Sassen 1996c, 218). Thus while the new claims of transnational capital on the state are represented as a major component of globalization, both the spaces and the claims being made in them by immigrants and other disempowered sectors are either erased, ignored, or construed in terms of a discourse that is anchored in figurations of social and economic relations long ago eclipsed by the forces of globalization. Instead, we must recognize that the spaces created by the complex and multidimensional processes of globalization have become strategic sites for the formation of fluid and complex identities and communities, and for the corresponding emergence of new types of claims within these transformed spaces.

Although they do not emerge from the same type of detailed analysis of restructuring and globalization that ground Sassen's position, there are other works that argue for a similar notion that new and different types of citizenship claims are part of this process—claims that are difficult to conceptualize in terms of, or reconcile with, the assumptions of the liberalism that underlie efforts like Kymlicka's. In their introduction to an issue of the journal *Public Culture* devoted to citizenship, Holston and Appadurai argue that the transnational processes constitutive of globalization have generated claims to "new kinds of rights outside of the normative and institutional definitions of the state and its legal codes" (Holston and Appadurai 1996, 197). And in her essay on "Cities and Citizenship" that introduces a special issue of the *International Journal of Urban and Regional Research* on that theme, Garcia reviews the debates about the "rapid changes in the practice of citizenship" and argues that these require the development of new forms of conceptual and empirical analysis (Garcia 1996, 7). From this perspective, then, it is crucial that attempts to reformulate our conceptions of notions of citizenship incorporate the contending claims of all the actors that occupy different spaces in the new globalized city, a process of political contestation that is likely to change the boundaries and parameters of the discourse of sovereignty and citizenship.

The challenge that emerges from these analyses that either suggest or explicitly call for the reformulation of the parameters of citizenship, then, is to develop a theoretical framework that allows us to perceive and examine these types of new claims and their relationship to the processes of globalization and restructuring, one that enables us to ground the social practices of these sectors and the processes that produce them within specific institutional sites, "spaces" or "places." I believe that such a framework can be formulated by drawing on some of the insights and arguments found in the various ways that the discourses on civil society configure the relationship between citizenship, the state, and democracy.

Civil Society, Institutional Context, and Rights Claims

Let me take up the question of what kind of institutional model can accommodate the four dimensions of citizenship I proposed, and delineate the processes by which they are determined. One of the main points of my critiques of both the diversity and citizenship approaches to deep differences was the failure to provide a theoretically grounded account of the development of the relationship between social and political membership. This was crucial since nearly all the formulations of, and approaches to, the issue of political membership that I discussed rely on certain preexisting social conditions, especially forms of mutuality,[2] trust, reciprocity, and solidarity as characteristics of the qualitative social relations or linkages in a society that are the necessary preconditions for a just and democratic polity. By doing so, these theorists implicitly assume that these very same processes will also define the appropriate basic boundaries of *societal membership*. However, what is called for is to make this relationship explicit by incorporating the institutional dimension and demonstrating how the extent to which these conditions are realized is determined within the institutional, particularly informal, sites of civil society. While the regulative function of a citizenship regime is generally considered to develop within the state, it is also reinforced within the institutions of civil society. Like some of the diversity and citizenship theorists I discussed earlier, I also want to look at the nature of the processes within civil society where the qualitative nature of the social relations that must exist between members of a society who hold fundamentally different moral and cultural values can develop in order to achieve a legitimate, just, and inclusive form of democracy.

The claim I advance in the following is that existing conceptions of citizenship are limited in their ability to recognize rights claims that arise from within marginalized social, political, and cultural locations, as providing alternative forms of citizenship, and that by taking seriously the notion of "institutional place" and context, some of these limitations can be addressed.[3] Even work that is sympathetic to this effort remains at a level of abstraction that makes it difficult to clarify and assess the nature and significance of these claims. However, a question remains regarding how to incorporate institutional place as a theoretical opening that facilitates incorporation of these new types of claims as part of the field of discourse regarding citizenship and rights. One approach that addresses this issue is suggested in the critiques and formulations of Sassen reviewed earlier that argue that rights and citizenship claims arise from the associational practices and activities of communities.

Since the nature and role of associational practices and activities that take "place" outside the sphere of the mechanisms of the state and marketplace is the primary focus of recent analysis and debate regarding civil society, I believe that we might find there some of the elements needed to understand the process of expanding the conceptions of rights claims and citizenship in a way that allows us to account more adequately for changing institutional contexts brought about by the processes of globalization, restructuring, and transnationalism, all of which are related macro-phenomena that set the broader contours of the institutional spaces within which Latino politics have developed since the early 1970s.[4]

Civil Society and Trust

The associational basis of civil society is reflected in Walzer's description of it as "the space of uncoerced human association and also the set of relational networks— formed for the sake of family, faith, interest and ideology—that fill this space" (Walzer 1995, 153). Although most theorists of civil society would agree to this formulation at the most general level, beyond that there are a host of differences in the way that civil society has been conceptualized, and the uses to which it has been put. Since the late 1980s, civil society has become one of the key contested concepts in social and political theory, and was adopted in a wide variety of ways throughout the social sciences and humanities. I do not intend to offer a review of the full range of these different positions, but rather to draw on those aspects of the literature that resonate with my underlying emphasis on providing the institutional context within which rights claims and citizenship practices are advanced. In particular, I will focus on conceptions of civil society developed within critical theory that emphasize the emancipatory potential of practices within this associational sphere, and that provide a way to elaborate the relationship between rights claims, citizenship, and the institutional sites of civil society.[5]

This relation between associational behavior and democracy has been a major concern in the writings on democracy for the last two centuries. The most well-known and influential formulation was de Tocqueville's *Democracy in America*, where he attributed much of the vitality of democracy in the United States to participation in non-state associations. This theme has continued to be the focus of a large body of works, and the current emphasis on civil society is an extension of that discourse. Mark Warren (2001) has recently provided a detailed study of the different forms of association and how they function, distinguishing which types of associations and associational networks promote democracy and which undermine it. Rosenblum's *Membership and Morals* (1998) complements Warren's work in her comprehensive survey by extending the analysis to engage the relationships between different forms of associative behavior and theories of pluralism and voluntary associations. But perhaps the best-known contemporary attempt to link these kinds of associational behavior and sites to the processes of democratic practices is Robert Putnam's work, which emphasizes the role of reciprocity and trust in this relationship. Putnam contends that "networks of civic engagement and norms of reciprocity" are crucial to promoting the expansion of democratic participation and "good" government (Putnam et al. 1993, Putnam 1995). "Networks of civic engagement, like the neighborhood associations, choral societies, cooperatives, sports clubs, mass-based parties . . . are an essential form of social capital: the denser such networks in a community, the more likely that its citizens will be able to cooperate for mutual benefit" (Putnam et al. 1993, 173). Thus social capital, which Putnam defines as "features of social organization, such as trust, norms, and networks" (167) that establish relations of reciprocity, is activated by social trust, which according to Putnam arises from "two related sources—norms of reciprocity and networks of civic engagement" (171). He proposes that social relations that embody these characteristics offer the best path to democratic self-government.

But this emphasis on the associative dimension of social relations as the basis for expanding the scope and responsiveness of democracies also has a long history in theories of social organization extending back to the nineteenth century. Hirst (1997) argues that associationalism was then a major framework that competed with collectivism and individualism as normative forms of societal organization. It grew from a critique of a pure market-based society where the function of the state was to use its power to protect the economic interests of the elites. It differed from collectivist and individual critiques of the same phenomena by arguing that associations were the primary foundation of a true democracy, and that they should be the basis of all societal organization, including the state, economy, and private realms. At root, associationalism was an agenda to democratize the sites of everyday activity, and civil society was a key component. The argument had strong and well-known proponents such as Robert Owen, Harold Laski, and G. H. D. Cole, all of whom argued for the need to base democratic reforms on organizational structures that rely on and foster associative relations, that is, on organic networks of social relations based on the lived experiences of the members of it. This perspective has received renewed attention more recently in a number of works by Hirst (1994, 1997) and Cohen and Rogers (1995). The lead essay on secondary associations by Cohen and Rogers in the latter, and a set of critical responses to it by nearly a dozen well-known political scientists, provides a detailed discussion of the wide array of issues that are raised by the question of whether associational behavior is supportive of democratic forms of governance, and if so, what conditions and characteristics are required for associations to enhance the effectiveness and responsiveness of democratic organization.

These approaches all focus on formal, organized associations, and while they make valuable contributions to our knowledge of the relationship between that sphere and democracy, they overlook the role of associational behavior that takes place within informal networks. A number of critical theorists have provided alternative ways of framing the relationship between democracy and civil society. Their concerns with both the regulative and emancipatory functions of civil society have given rise in the last two decades to a very substantial literature. This is reflected in the significance that civil society has in the work of a number of theorists who address the issue of deep diversity in liberal democracies. Theorists such as Young (1990, 2000), Benhabib (1992, 1994), Cohen and Arato (1992), Barber (1983), and Walzer (1983) have all developed approaches that incorporate conceptions of civil society in different ways, while attempting to move beyond the limitations of works influenced by Rawls, Habermas, and Putnam. Although they differ on the specific elements involved, the critical theorists nevertheless all conceive of civil society as a set of sites where relations of power are reproduced, and within which a democratic politics of contestation can emerge. And relations of trust, reciprocity, and solidarity that are rooted in civil society play a central role in many of these analyses.

While these political theorists have elaborated a clearer notion of civil society at the theoretical level and have emphasized the role of trust and reciprocity, it is not always clear how it is that these practices and values promote the development of a more inclusive, just democratic system. This issue is taken up by Jean Cohen, who provides one of the most useful analyses of different aspects of the problematic. She advances her own conception of civil society through a critique of both the theoretical and political weaknesses of what she regards as two of the most important conceptions of civil society, the first being what Cohen calls the "neorepublican stance of Robert Putnam and his school," and the second the communitarian version advanced by a number of theorists who have published in the journal *The Responsive Community.* But it is clear that her critique is intended to apply to the tendencies in the broader discourse on civil society within the United States. Unlike the social theorists who advanced broad-based and multidimensional conceptions of civil society in the nineteenth century, the neorepublicans and communitarians offer a narrow and conservative vision of how to reverse the decline of traditional values as the basis of social integration.

"Civil society" in these approaches has become so reduced and so romanticized that the normative thrust of the concept, along with its relevance to contemporary problems, is being obscured. Nearly everyone in the current discussion has come to equate civil society with traditional forms of voluntary association (including "the" family). And nearly everyone assumes that the "intermediary bodies" created by voluntary association, the alleged sources of social trust, the guarantor of responsive government, and the key to civic virtue, are in decline in contemporary America. The debate is over the causes of the decline and what to do about it. (Jean Cohen 1999a, 212)

This emphasis on decline has skewed the interpretation of civil society in such a way that it focuses only on participation in formal voluntary associations, and as a result, Cohen argues that this approach actually undermines and obscures the democratic and emancipatory potential of the associational sphere.

Cohen contrasts this vision with the Gramscian conception of civil society that provides a way to understand the dual functions that it plays in liberal democracies: that of regulation and control to maintain the status quo, and also as a site for contesting the structure of privilege and domination that characterize it. Cohen summarizes this position as follows:

Civil society is construed both as a symbolic field and as a network of institutions and practices that is the locus for the formation of values, action-orienting norms, meanings, and collective identities. But the cultural dimension of civil society is not a given or natural. Rather, it is a site of social contestation: Its associations and networks are a terrain to be struggled over and an arena wherein collective identities, ethical values, and alliances are forged. (Jean Cohen 1999a, 214)

The emphasis on civil society as a contestatory site of transformative politics has been extended and developed in studies such as Melucci (1989) and Touraine (1981), and in Cohen and Arato's (1992) comprehensive analysis. What their research has made clear is that while formal voluntary organizations are important, they can often actually reinforce the unequal relations of power, and that a great deal of the creative, oppositional potential is found in informal networks and practices and in the social movements they sometimes lead to.

This dimension has been addressed in a number of applied analyses, such as some of the case studies in a volume on social movements in Latin America that focus on civil society as the basis for an expanded conceptualization of the public sphere (Alvarez et al., 1998). These essays all underscore the central role of associational behavior and practices based on relations of trust, reciprocity, and other forms of mutuality in the development of new forms of political expression. The introductory essay in that volume states that these chapters "call attention to the cultural practices and interpersonal networks of daily life that . . . infuse new cultural meanings into political practices and collective action. These frameworks of meaning may include different modes of consciousness and practices of nature, neighborhood life, and identity" (Alvarez et al. 1998, 14). These practices have become mechanisms to articulate claims that contest the societal boundaries established not solely by institutions of the state, but in the realm of everyday life as structured by civil society. Sites normally construed as apolitical were transformed in these cases as rearticulated public spaces, where "market stalls, local bars, and family courtyards" served as localities where processes of both political affirmation and contestation were enacted and resulted in politically salient claims (Rubin 1998, 155). Similar conclusions are advanced in a recent volume that focuses on civil society in non-Western societies, arguing that "there is . . . a need to shift the debates about civil society away from formal structures and organizations and towards an investigation of beliefs, values, and everyday practices" (Hann 1996, 14).

These studies converge around the premise that the fostering of democratic relations and forms of government requires a broad network of activities and practices that are rooted in "the submerged networks of daily life" (Alvarez et al. 1998, 14). This approach argues for a broader concept of the political than that found in much of traditional literature in political science and political sociology, which conceives of the political primarily in terms of the primacy of the formal, institutional apparatus of governing. The implications for understanding the dynamic nature of the processes that define the boundaries of the "political" are summarized by Roniger in his study of civil society and clientelism:

> The "construction of reality" hinges on social interaction and exchange as a contextual, pragmatic phenomenon. It is at this level of interplay between the logic of modern constitutional democracy and the praxis and pragmatics of everyday life and social action that moral obligations and commitments are enmeshed and can be reformulated in recurrent patterns of action and exchange through a complex web of movements, communities, associations, and interpersonal relations. (Roniger 1994, 8)

These approaches, then, suggest a way of expanding the theoretical and conceptual parameters of the notions of citizenship and rights claims. This enables a level of analytic and empirical specificity that can account for the new strategies of political inclusion and rights claims that are rooted in the associational strategies and practices characterized by relations of trust, reciprocity, and mutual exchange, and that are developed within the sites of civil society in response to the effects of globalization and restructuring. These associational networks function within very specific institutional sites or "places" that mediate the relationship between the household and the institutions that control the primary resources of economic, political, and cultural power. Referring to the political significance of the relationship between the state and civil society, Chandhoke writes that

> states invariably seek to control and limit the political practices of society by construct-
> ing the boundaries of the political. The state attempts in other words to constitute and
> contain the political discourse. However, politics as articulatory practices which mediate
> between the experiential and the expressive are not only about controls and the laying
> down of boundaries. They are about the transgressions of these boundaries and about
> the reconstitution of the political. The site at which these mediations and contestations
> take place; the site at which society enters into relationship with the state can be defined
> as civil society. (Chandhoke 1995, 9)

While I agree with this position, I would amend it to include the mediations not only with the state, but with the macro-institutions of economic and cultural power as well. These sites of mediation are the "places" of everyday life, where individuals and groups engage and encounter the norms, boundaries, customs, and networks that define institutional relationships, where they experience the consequences and effects of economic and political policies. Schools, churches, the workplace, parks, are all sites not only where the activity of everyday life is carried out, but where the effects of the practices of power are experienced, where the boundaries set by the configurations of privilege, status, and access are encountered as the limits of action. And these are sites where the impact of globalization and restructuring takes effect, and where strategic community responses to these consequences are developed. But they are also the sites of association, where individuals and groups establish a wide variety of relatively stable networks of activities that not only sustain their survival, identity, and sense of worth, but have also served as the basis for the development of practices and activities that are concerned with the direction of community and collective life, with the constitution of a "public sphere."[6]

Incorporating this notion of "place" allows for concretizing the categories of the civil-society construct so that the nature, range, and validity of rights claims advanced within the marginalized lived spaces of civil societies that have undergone the trans-formations entailed by globalization can be addressed and assessed. My contention is that arguments that seek to address the issue of citizenship within multicultural societies remain limited and incomplete as long as the constructs of the marginalized "others" they have adopted are relatively ungrounded. Claims to citizenship are not isolated phenomena; they always take place within a specific ensemble of relations that enable those claims. Forms of civic association that strengthen solidarity and trust in a community may not in themselves constitute citizenship claims, but they can be a vital enabling factor leading to the activities that do. Hence those forms of association that support the development of strong identities, enhance the degree of mutual trust and solidarity, and promote a stronger sense of participatory rights and responsibilities in traditionally nonpolitical spheres, while not themselves constituting citizenship claims, can nevertheless provide the necessary conditions for these to emerge. The point is that the discourse on citizenship is likely to be inadequate without grounding rights or citizenship claims within the associational contexts that enable them. Without incorporating this dimension, analysis of the normative parameters of citizenship will resonate only with the lives of those in communities that have already gained political visibility within the dominant cultural landscape, and cannot perceive, much less address, the needs and experiences of those that lie outside of that vision. The result, unfortunately and ironically, is that the partial and distorted image on which these analyses are based is likely to undermine the very notion of a just and democratic polity that these theories seek to promote.

Following this general perspective and emphasis in these works, I will focus on the specific institutional spaces in civil society where practices based on norms of mutuality, trust, and general reciprocity take place as part of the processes that mediate the relationship between the household and the institutions that control the primary resources of economic, political, and cultural power.

The set of relationships that I have outlined here can be represented in the schematic presented in figure 1, which lays out the sets of relationships between three levels of analyses that allow us to trace how the operations of the larger institutions of power affect individuals and households at the level of everyday life, and to see how power is reproduced within the institutions of civil society, which is where we carry out the routines of daily life. The institutional sites of civil society in effect mediate between the micro-level household and the macro-level of power institutions. It is within these sites that we live out the consequences of macro-level policies and trends. All of us live in households and participate in different institutional sites of civil society, continuously going from household to worksite, to educational sites, interaction with media, etc. So we are affected directly by what goes on in these institutions, and our identities, our opportunities, our experiences are based on the particular way that we interact with these institutions. These are also the sites that provide the basis for the networks that individuals establish and enter into as part of the quotidian practices that are the foundation of their engagement with the larger society. Because these are sites where the relations of power are reproduced, they are never neutral. One of Gramsci's major insights was to demonstrate that civil society is where the structure of hegemonic relations is reproduced, but never in a stable and

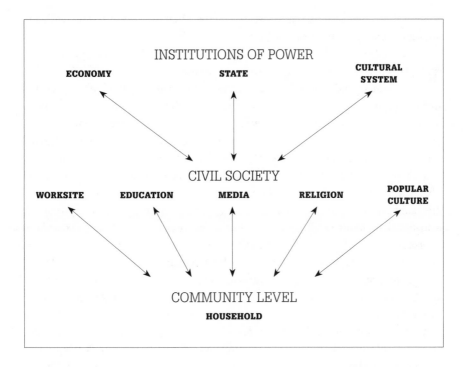

permanent way. So the meaning of ideologies, of perception, and the interpretation of experiences more generally, is always contested and either serves to reinforce the status quo or provides alternative optics that challenge privilege and hierarchy.

The framework I adopt here draws on a similar model developed by Louise Lamphere (1992) in her ethnographic study of immigration. She offers a general approach that addresses the issue that I have focused on here: how to conceptualize and empirically examine the dynamic nature of the relationships between institutional, structural levels and the practices of everyday life. The framework reflects the premise that only a combination of macro-level data on the local political economy and micro-level qualitative observations can provide an adequate understanding of the nature of changes in local communities. The linkage between these two levels is made both theoretically and empirically by establishing and identifying "mediating institutions"—what I designate as civil society—as the specific sites of participation and practice of individuals and groups. The pattern of interrelations that constitute communities takes form and develops within these mediating institutions, some of which Lamphere identifies as the workplace, school system, housing complexes, community organizations—all of which connect macro-level processes with the household and household networks.

These sites are where the changes in the broader institutional arenas—for example, a particular economic sector—are translated into specific outcomes that affect individuals and groups who labor at these "worksites" at the everyday level of social relations and practices. These are the "sites" where the reality of the relations of race, class, gender, immigrant status, and so forth, are constructed, "lived" as the "particular, specific, and concrete ways of living in and through the city" that I proposed above. It is here that the relations of race, class, ethnicity, national origin, and immigrant status are formed as actual practices that establish "social location." This is where these categories and dimensions are realized, concretized as specific mechanisms by which structural inequalities of power and wealth are produced, distributed, maintained, altered, and where negotiation of social identity takes place. To use an example from Lamphere, large-scale economic changes may decrease the tax base for a community school system, which in turn may lead to hiring and wage policies that result in high teacher turnover, and which at a particular school may affect the type and nature of their programs. And the options for those decisions will surely be considered within the particular configuration of race, class, gender, and immigrant status. This is the "site," then, where the changes in "macro-level forces are brought to bear on micro-level relationships" (Lamphere 1992, 4). Within this framework, the link between the institutional and the everyday levels is established by tracing the processes of interaction, the patterns of relations, and the strategies and interpretation that form at these specific sites and levels of practice. I use this framework in the next chapter to study the processes by which a particular region in Los Angeles underwent a complete transformation from predominantly Anglo working-class neighborhoods to overwhelmingly Latino communities. It allows us to trace how members of these particular communities lived out and interpreted these changes, and what this means in terms of politics and public policy.

There are, however, several aspects of this construct of civil society that need to be clarified. First is that the emphasis here is on linkage between institutional power and the activities or practices that constitute civil society. It is the nature, type, and purpose of activities that constitute the mediating sites as civil society. However, in formulations such as Putnam's, for example, significantly different types and forms of associational behavior are treated as if they are equally valuable in contributing to democratic practices, so that networks like the Boys Scouts seem to be on the same level as more explicitly defined political forms of relationships. But since not all activities have the same public character or political significance, it is necessary to differentiate these activities. In order to focus on the different ways in which these activities of the associational sites might promote democratic citizenship, Iris

Young has proposed distinguishing between private association, civic association, and political association (Young 1999, 7). She uses these to focus on the levels of associational activities since it is often the case that the same site can enable different forms of association on different occasions, and in different circumstances. Private association refers to activity that constitutes the dimension of sociality of personal networks that focus on matters that sustain the individual on a personal level, such as the family, friends, and social clubs. Civic associational activity goes beyond the relatively exclusive nature of the private, and focuses on practices that are concerned with promoting and attending to the collective life of the larger group, be it a neighborhood, city, or region. Political association is distinct in that these activities self-consciously aim at forming networks to give voice to public issues; to promote particular interests, principles, and values; attempt to hold institutional decision makers accountable; and try to influence the direction and/or content of decisions that affect the well-being of a community. Her analysis also suggests that it is both the processual and substantive dimensions of the activities of civil society that are important in delineating the linkage to the claims to democratic citizenship. This is important because these claims always take place within a specific ensemble of relations that enable them, not as isolated phenomena. Thus, for example, forms of civic association that strengthen solidarity and trust in a community may not in themselves constitute citizenship claims, but they may be vital in leading to the activities that do.

Despite the advantages and insights that this and related conceptualizations of civil society might provide, there are clearly problems and difficulties that can lead to weak, distorted analysis or to romanticizing the political potential of civil society. One of the primary problems with promoting the development of the types of relations of trust and reciprocity in a given community as a means of fostering political inclusion, is that when placed in societal context, these strong ties and networks can easily deepen the divisions between communities and actually lead to greater political instability and social division. Putnam alerts us to this difficulty when he states the following: "Dense but segregated horizontal networks sustain cooperation within each group, but networks of civic engagement that cut across social cleavages nourish wider cooperation" (Putnam et al. 1993, 175). But this also points to another of the weaknesses of analyses like Putnam's that ultimately never really confront the necessary role of explicitly "political compromise, restraint, and accommodation necessary for reconciling competing interests in a peaceful and more or less orderly way" (Foley and Edwards 1996, 47). And as Alvarez points out, civil society is not unambiguously a positive force for democratization, but it "is also a terrain of struggle mined by sometimes undemocratic power relations and the enduring problems of racism, hetero/sexism, environmental destruction, and other forms of exclusion" (Alvarez et al. 1998, 17). Mindful of these limitations, I am not proposing or assuming that the kinds of practices that deepen and/or thicken the networks of civil society are unproblematic, nor that they inevitably lead to a broadening of democratic inclusion. Rather, I argue that these practices incorporate the potential for political empowerment and collective action that are necessary but insufficient conditions for expanding the basis of rights claims and the boundaries of citizenship.

Rights Claims, Civil Society, and Institutional Context

Since the focus of my analysis is on the emergence of rights claims by marginalized communities, I need to address the question of what is involved when these types of claims are advanced. The foundational assumptions of long-standing conceptions of the nature of rights, as well as the relation between the modern "subject" and the "subject of rights," have been challenged on different grounds by the recent works of rights scholars.[7] I want to focus on the work of Margaret Somers in particular because I believe her framework offers a way to connect the strands of my argument to this point. Because I draw extensively on her work, I will lay out her argument and quote her work in some detail. In a number of earlier essays and in her more recent book *Genealogies of Citizenship*, Somers focuses on the historical conjunction between rights and institutional conditions, and argues that the underlying basis of the conceptions of citizenship developed in most traditions tend to define citizenship as a status or attribute of a category of persons.[8] This leads to static analysis, which in turn makes it extremely difficult to understand the ways in which citizenship practices emerge and how they are dependent on the particular and historically specific articulation of several institutional relationships related to citizenship. She writes that "Instead, I propose that citizenship be defined as an 'instituted process,' i.e., citizenship is a set of institutionally embedded social practices" (Somers 1993, 589). Somers continues, arguing that

> Thus, citizenship is reconceptualized as the outcome of political, legal, and symbolic practices enacted through relational matrices of universal membership rules and legal institutions that are activated in combination with the particularistic political cultures of different types of civil societies. As such, citizenship practices are also a source of political identity—the translation of this identity into a rights-based positive citizenship identity depends entirely on the contexts of activation. There are also theoretical implications: Quasi-democratic citizenship rights can emerge only in certain institution-specific relational settings and only in the context of particular social practices, namely practices that

support popular public spheres. Popular public spheres must be infused by participation from members of active civil societies. They must also mediate between civil society and the towering forces of nation-states and national markets. Thus, theories of citizenship and social class can no longer be confined to the opposition between the state and the economy. Such a dichotomy masks the centrality to macro-analytic analysis of nonstate forms of political participation and discourse (public spheres), and of such social institutions as family, community, voluntary organizations, and other aspects of civil society and associational life. Recognizable popular citizenship rights have only emerged historically in the participatory spaces of public spheres in tandem with "relationally-sturdy" civil societies. Theorizing about citizenship must expand beyond the relationship between the state and capitalism to include a sociology of public spheres and their relationships to the associational practices of civil societies. (Somers 1993, 589–90)

The institutional sites of civil society are most effectively construed, Somers contends, in terms of a "relational/network and institutional analysis," in which institutions are understood as "organizational and symbolic practices that operate within networks of rules, structural ties, public narratives, and binding relationships that are embedded in time and space. This relational approach disaggregates social categories and reconfigures them into institutional and relational clusters in which people, power, and organizations are positioned and connected" (Somers 1993, 595). Instead of using the concept of "society" to frame the issue of citizenship, Somers proposes the term "relational setting," which she defines as "a patterned matrix of institutional relationships among cultural, economic, social, and political practices. . . . A relational setting has no governing entity according to which the entire setting can be categorized; it can only be characterized by deciphering its spatial and network patterns and its temporal processes" (595).

This approach generates a different way of linking citizenship to the dimensions of subjectivity and agency. Instead of "categorical" attributes being the source of legal and political standing and action, "identity" becomes the axis for conceptualizing the source of political action.

In this usage, identities are not derived from attributes imputed from a stage of societal development (e.g., pre-industrial or modern) or a social category (e.g., traditional artisan, factory laborer, or working-class wife), but by actors' places in the multiple relationships in which they are embedded. It is no longer assumed that a group of people has any particular relationship to citizenship simply because one aspect of their identity is categorized as the "working class." "Social categories" presume internally stable properties such that, under normal conditions, entities within that category will act appropriately, whereas "identities" embed the actors within relationships and stories that shift over time and

> space. Social action thus loses its categorical stability, and class embeddedness becomes more important than class attributes. Thus, citizenship identities are investigated by looking at actors' places in their relational settings. (Somers 1993, 595)

Somers argues instead that rights claims must be understood within specific and local institutional relations, and that these relations mediate between the state and civil society, i.e., they constitute the articulations between state and civil society. As such, the framework provides a way to assess, at least in a general way, the degree to which various social and cultural practices—or, more specifically, "associational practices"—within civil society might be claims to rights. The forms and modalities of activities and practices that express claims to citizenship depend on the institutional mix of factors, so they allow for the possibility (and likelihood) that there are different forms and expressions of making these claims. Somers focuses primarily on the set of practices that constitute the "public sphere," understood as "a contested participatory site in which actors with overlapping identities as legal subjects, citizens, economic actors, and family and community members, form a public body and engage in negotiations and contestations over political and social life" (Somers 1993, 589). She thus establishes the theoretical basis for linking the various dimensions of civil society to the institutional axis of citizenship.

Like Somers, McClure argues that our understanding of, and discourses on, citizenship and civil society must be historically and institutionally grounded (McClure 1992). But her emphasis is more on historicizing the intersection of our notions of the "subject" who makes rights claims and the claims of sovereignty on which the state rests, and on situating this within the problematic of the "new" pluralism, more often known as multiculturalism. McClure argues that modern political theory since the rise of the nation-state has privileged both the "sovereign subject" as political agent, and the state as the legitimate locus of political action. What this obscures is the actual historical development of rights claims that is characterized by "the displacement of a range of diverse and contradictory localist and participatory constructs by centralized national and statist codifications of legal discourse." Thus the modern form of the "subject of rights" can itself be understood as an effect of the practical and discursive struggles of modern constitutionalism "under very specific historical and geopolitical conditions" (McClure 1992, 111).

Now the emergence of new social actors making political claims on the basis of race, gender, sexuality, and ethnicity in the current period has challenged established notions of the subject, identity, and agency.[9] In particular, the notion of a "sovereign subject" has been critiqued as a contingent construct masquerading as a universalist category, which then obviously undermines any universalist notion of a "subject of rights" or citizen. But these challenges do not necessarily signal the disappearance of the "subject of rights." Instead it is reinscribed in such a way that the issues and questions regarding political identity and agency are reconfigured. Thus, as McClure argues, "we might question rather than presume its [subject of rights] relation to contemporary assertions of rights on the terrain of 'differences' for these may themselves significantly transform or exceed the conventional figuration of the subject, especially as this has taken the formal character of individual citizenship in the modern state" (McClure 1992, 112). In historical situations where the emergence of these "differences" is closely related to non-national primary linkages and solidarities, what this calls into question is the degree to which existing discourses and practices of citizenship, limited by modernist conceptions that assume the coincidence of the boundaries of state, territory, nation, sovereignty, and citizenship, are capable of providing either theoretical or institutional spaces that can respond effectively to the new basis of rights claims.

How do the observations and suggestions I have advanced up to this point relate more directly to the question of the role of civil society in the politics of racial and ethnic diversity and its relationship to the notion of the public sphere? The following observation offered by Craig Calhoun a few years ago provides a point of departure to address these issues.

> Civil society and public sphere are not precisely equivalent concepts. Indeed, the importance of the concept of public sphere is largely to go beyond general appeals to the nature of civil society in attempts to explain the social foundations of democracy and to introduce discussion of the specific organization within civil society of social and cultural bases for the development of an effective rational-critical discourse aimed at the resolution of political disputes. (Craig Calhoun 1993, 269)

The critique in the first part of this book of both the Rawlsian and Habermasian frameworks coincides with Calhoun's second point. That is, while both theorists acknowledge that the validity of their formulations rests on the existence of particular kinds of qualitative social relationships, neither addresses nor accounts for the social mechanism that would produce these. My discussion here of relations of mutuality and social trust in Latino communities is intended to illustrate one such way by which realms of oppositional public spheres have been and can be created.[10]

However, as Calhoun cautions, not all associational relations in civil society constitute a public sphere. This has been the basis of some of the sharpest criticisms of Putnam's work on civil society. For example, in Jean Cohen's critique of Putnam, referred to earlier, she states that "the most glaring defect is the omission of the crucial category of the public sphere from Putnam's and most others' conceptualizations" (Jean Cohen 1999a, 56). She contends that, when combined with the discourse of civic and moral decline, the notion of civil society as equated with "traditional forms of voluntary associations" is likely to be used to undermine the oppositional politics of contestation of the disempowered, and

> blocks social justice and social solidarity instead of furthering them. Unless this model is corrected, the current revival of the discourse of civil society in the U.S. will play into the hands of social conservatives who aim to retraditionalize civic life and to substitute local "volunteerism" for the public services and redistributive efforts of the welfare state, as if these are the only options we have. . . . If civil society discourse is left in this form, we will not be able to articulate, much less resolve, the critical problems facing democratic politics in the coming century. My claim is that it matters very much, both politically and theoretically, *which* concept of civil society we use and seek to foster. (Jean Cohen 1999a, 56)

In a similar vein, Iris Young (1999) suggests that only certain types of associational relations and practices are likely to facilitate or constitute a democratic and just public sphere. Both Cohen and Young are suggesting that for those of us who aspire to a different, more inclusive, and just form of democratic politics, it is important to recognize that the sites of civil society are neither neutral nor apolitical. Gramsci made it clear long ago that without the transformation of these arenas of social relations, a popularly based democratic society was not likely to be achieved.

With this in mind, the theoretical positions I have discussed here suggest that while, under certain conditions, relations of reciprocity can prove to be an important mechanism for the development of social ties that are supportive of democratic forms of solidarity, they do not necessarily do so; nor are they the only form or type of mutuality that can establish the basis of social trust. Focusing only on relations of reciprocity as the sole mechanism for generating the social trust necessary to foster and sustain democratic politics limits the consideration of a broader range of possible sources that could do so. In chapter 6, I will take up the question of how to develop a more ample way of framing the issue of the role of trust, mutuality, and solidarity so as to promote a democratic politics capable of addressing the kind of deep diversity that now exists. But given the central role of rights claims in my analysis, I first want to clarify my adoption of a certain type of rights as the basis for my analysis.

Reconceiving Rights as Oppositional Political Strategies

While there are a variety of practices that Latinos engage in within the institutional sites of civil society that are politically salient, of particular importance for the issue of citizenship are what I have been referring to as rights claims. These surface as practices and beliefs that are intended to claim the right to certain benefits, practices, spaces—and more generally for greater and equal inclusion in the mainstream economic and political institutions. Chapter 5 will focus on detailing both the nature of the range of rights claims and the institutional sites and conditions from which they develop, but given the opposing views regarding the emancipatory nature of rights in both liberal and critical theory, I first want to lay out the groundwork for adopting a particular version of rights theory that coincides with my version of associative citizenship and the model of civil society I have described.

LIMITS AND TRANSFORMATIONAL SPACES

Somers and McClure provide a theoretical strategy for highlighting the political salience and valence of activities and actions that take place outside the formal, traditional, and especially electoral political spaces. This is a crucial step in being able to account for the ways that groups that have been marginalized and not had effective access to those established spaces have gone about seeking greater levels of inclusion. These marginalized spaces are often dealt with as if they were completely outside the existing institutional structure of power, and as if little action or behavior occurs there of any political significance. However, I think it is important to counter this view and see that the particular processes of marginalization are in fact constitutive of the existing power relations and the resulting structure of privilege and hierarchy. Strategies of containment of marginalized groups are developed and institutionalized as an integral part of the political process that is designed to maintain the status quo. How should we conceive then of the relationship between that political process and structures, and the kind of rights claims that I focus on here?

I believe that addressing this issue and advancing my reformulation of the relationship between citizenship and rights claims requires a more expansive conception of the kind of activity that falls within the category of "the political" adopted in more traditional views of "what is political" that limit its meaning to issues related primarily to governance. Critical theorist David Scott has made the argument that it is precisely the "political," in the sense of a strategic transformative potential and challenge, that is absent, or at least not the central concern in much of the work that has sought to study marginalized populations (D. Scott 1999, 13–14). It is precisely the transformative political dimension and potential that is the focus of a recent essay by Seshadri-Crooks suggesting the following as a way to frame this issue:

> We can conceive of margin/marginality in two ways. On the one hand, the margin can
> be conceived as the subject position—the excluded other that must be coaxed into the

center through incorporation, inversion, hybridization, revolution. On the other hand, the margin can be conceived as the irreducible remainder—that which is necessarily excluded by every regime of power/knowledge, including that of the discourse of rights. In other words, the margin can be conceived, not so much as that which is external to the power structure, but rather as its constitutive outside, an intimate alterity that marks the limit of power. (Seshadri-Crooks 2000, 12–13)

What both Scott and Seshadri-Cooks are suggesting is that conceiving of the margins, and those who are located there, as representing "an intimate alterity that marks the limit of power" provides a theoretical strategy for foregrounding and elaborating the transformative political dimension, and in particular, for how the "discourse of rights" can be refigured as an indispensable strategy of contestatory political struggle in the context of pluricultural liberal democracies. This notion of the marginalized sectors of society being constitutive of the dominant forms of power has also been explored by other prominent theorists, some of whom focus in particular on marginalized groups in postcolonial societies.

Homi Bhabha (1994), for example, offers a critique of binary conceptions of hegemonic power found in the work of the Southeast Asian subaltern studies group aimed at the historical recovery of the agency of marginalized populations. Instead of the domination-resistance binary couplet adopted in their studies, Bhabha develops the notion of hybridity to capture the complexity and instability of the mediations between the structures of domination and marginalized populations. Sustaining control over these populations is a constant challenge for elites, and reflects the fact that the relations between them and the marginalized is a space of hegemonic instability. While this unstable relationship clearly entails material domination, it also provides the opportunity for the marginalized to develop creative, innovative forms of political practices.

Spivak (1988a) also examines this space, but focuses more on the difficulties that scholars face in trying to adequately theorize and represent the voice and interests of marginalized communities. She problematizes the ability of theorists and researchers to articulate or "represent" the marginalized in a comprehensive and unmediated way.[11] In her introduction to a volume produced by the same Southeast Asian subaltern studies group, Spivak (1988b) views the condition of marginality as an inherently unstable location that is full of latent potential for resistance and opposition, an invisible yet present force that represents a challenge to scholars who tend to represent the existing conditions in a way that does not reveal that potential. What Spivak proposes is that the theorization of the space of marginalized politics must resonate with the destabilizing character of the latter, a project that another postcolonial theorist, John Beverly, describes as "a continuous displacement/deconstruction that subverts the constitutive binaries colonial/native, subaltern/dominant, inside/outside, modern/traditional" (Beverly 1999, 102). Spivak's conception of the inadequacy of representational efforts to capture the constantly vanishing presence of the marginalized, and the effort instead to illuminate the unstable, shifting ground of the subaltern, functions much like Bhabha's formulation, simultaneously constituting the visible and invisible limit of power.

POSSIBILITIES AND LIMITATIONS OF RIGHTS THEORY AND PRACTICE

While both Bhabha and Spivak clearly identify the spaces of marginalization as simultaneously the locus and the limit of hegemonic power, neither provides a way to situate this unstable power relationship within the structural and/or institutional analysis of societal relations. As a result, they are unable to provide much guidance on how strategic political elements can and do arise within institutional spheres.[12]

This limitation can be addressed by adopting a reformulated conception of traditional rights as mechanisms that can link transformative political practices to structural and institutional features. In order to do so, rights have to be reconceived in a way that enables us to discern their articulation with the lived experiences of marginalized communities as they take place within the spheres of both civil and political society. This reconstructive project has to engage the following questions: Can this notion of spaces of unstable marginalization help refigure the political positioning of rights in the context of marginalized populations? What do and can rights look like from the perspective of the racial and ethnic groups with a history of marginalization? What is the potential effectiveness of rights in the contested terrain of the public sphere from the political positioning of marginalization?

The development of rights is clearly one of the fundamental institutional features of liberal democratic societies. Rights are also considered by some political theorists to be a foundational component of liberal democratic discourse. However, there are a number of important critiques of the general notion of rights—particularly as they relate to their potential as a resource for political empowerment—that I believe can be engaged and refigured from the perspective of the subaltern limit. While there are a variety of critical arguments against the effectiveness or adequacy of rights as emancipatory resources, three of the most widely discussed have emerged from the perspective of critical legal studies, feminism, and cultural relativism, all of which have an affinity with the concerns of subaltern theory to the extent that both are concerned with political marginalization and forms of exclusion.

Emerging some twenty years ago, the field of critical legal studies encompasses a broad set of critiques of rights discourse and practice, but most studies seem to develop from a more general critique of liberalism.[13] Some take Marx's scathing critique of rights as a point of departure, while others depart from the basic positions articulated by the communitarian critique of liberalism. The former hold that rights claims emerged from a very specific set of political, economic, social, and cultural circumstances and patterns of development associated with the rise of capitalism, and while these claims attempt to secure civil and political freedoms, they completely ignore the fundamental reality of economic inequality. As a result, then, rights discourse simply obscures the fundamental causes of injustice, exploitation, and oppression, and thus diverts the energies of social struggle away from confronting the structural root of existing social conditions, including the multiple forms and patterns of societal exclusion. Other critical legal scholars have focused on the highly individualistic and abstract conceptions of the self that are fundamental in liberal thought and ideologies. The focus in liberalism is on the separation between the individual and community or groups, and it posits a conception of a "universalist" human nature that is incapable of providing any effective way of accounting for, or incorporating, forms of difference, and in effect results in rationalizing the particularistic interests of those in power. The concrete lived circumstances and conditions within which the self develops; the particular important, defining characteristics of individuals; the mutuality and mutual dependence constitutive of social relations—all of these are simply bracketed out of the rights discourse, and thus the real social nature of the self is completely occluded.

Feminist critiques of rights reflect the divergent perspectives and positions that characterize feminist theory more generally.[14] They range from those approaches that I would label "liberal feminist" at one end of the continuum, and which share many of the principles of traditional liberalism but focus on gender-based exclusionary theories of liberal societies and institutions, to more radical feminisms that reject the construction of the image of the liberal self as completely incapable of accounting for the differences based on gender and sexuality. The former concentrate on the various modes of discrimination that prevent women from gaining equal access to the traditional resources, positions, and general benefits of liberal societies, and so the emphasis is on equality of opportunity. The critique of rights discourse developed by this approach does not reject rights per se, but instead focuses on ways to make rights more inclusive and democratic. The latter perspective, however, sees rights as part of a set of institutions that are formalistic, hierarchical, and patriarchal, and as such, constitute a system of subordination based on gender and sexuality that reflects and privileges the male viewpoint and interests. Rights are part of this complex of ideology, practices, and institutions that rationalize and maintain the systematic subordination of women. One of the leading figures holding this view is Catherine MacKinnon, who summarizes as follows: "Abstract rights will authorize the male experience of the world" (MacKinnon 1983, 635). The problem with rights according to this approach, then, is not gender differences per se but rather male dominance. Although they differ substantially in basic assumptions and emphasis, what these feminist critiques share is that "they all ask the 'woman' question. Feminist theory examines the woman's condition in a male-dominated society from a woman's perspective" (Kim 1993, 55).

Another form of critique of rights also revolves around the issue of exclusion, but focuses instead on cultural inequalities. As is the case with feminism, the cultural relativists' perspective on rights is part of a more comprehensive critique.[15] The primary axis of this view is the rejection of cultural claims advanced during the modern period by Western societies as having universal validity and being culturally superior. These claims are considered to be a defining characteristic of cultural imperialism, taking the form of cultural essentialism that is interpreted by its critics as a strategy for rationalizing Western global hegemony, and for devaluing non-Western value systems, beliefs, and social practices.[16] As one recent essay discussing Western versus Islamic conceptions of human rights puts it, "Cultural relativists . . . reject universal human rights as a manifestation of Eurocentric arrogance or as an illusion doomed to collapse" (Bielefeldt 2000, 91). Rights are therefore viewed by cultural relativists as a product of the Western world and therefore reflecting the particular moral values, political principles, and historical experience foreign to most non-Western societies. While there are clearly those that reject the entire concept of rights, most of these critiques argue for reconceptualizing the discourses in a way that does not privilege Western cultural frameworks, and call for a renegotiation of both the theoretical underpinnings and the institutional structures and conventions through which the rights regimes are implemented.

What these critiques share is a varying level of skepticism that rights can in practice promote social change and emancipatory goals. However, while acknowledging the validity of many of the elements of these arguments, there are those committed to bring about social change and political empowerment in communities with histories of discrimination and political marginalization—i.e., the subaltern—who argue that some form of rights have been and continue to be crucial to achieving those goals. They point to the important role that rights claims have played in the struggles for inclusion and democratization waged by racial groups and women in the United States. For example, Patricia Williams writes: "For blacks in this country, politically effective action has occurred mainly in connection with asserting or extending rights" (P. Williams 1992, 57), and continues a few pages later arguing that "This country's worst historical moments have not been attributable to rights-assertion, but to a failure of rights-commitment" (P. Williams 1992, 61). And in his strong critique of the critical legal studies condemnation of liberalism, rights, and rights theory, law professor Robert Williams states: "For peoples of color, however, these icons mark trails along sacred ground. The attack by the Critical Legal Studies movement on rights and entitlement theory discourse can be seen as a counter crusade to the hard campaigns and long marches of minority peoples in this country. Minority people committed themselves to these struggles . . . [to attain] a seat in the front of the bus, repatriation of treaty-guaranteed sacred lands, or a union card to carry in the grape vineyards" (R. Williams 1987, 120).

What these debates illustrate is that both the theory and institutional practice of rights, like so many other societal institutions, have played a dual and contradictory role in societies. From a Gramscian perspective, they represent both the regulatory and empancipatory potential of civil society. On the one hand, they have clearly been used as mechanisms for excluding specific populations and providing judicial and even constitutional legitimation for doing so. On the other hand, as the previous quotes emphasize, rights claims have been crucial tools in the struggles to transform racist, sexist, and other forms of institutionalized exclusionary practices. While the critiques of rights theory and practice raise important issues that need to be addressed, emancipatory movements can ill afford to discard any resources, mechanisms, or strategies that may be of value in different phases of contestation. However, for rights claims to function in this way, the factors, discussed by their critics, that limit their effectiveness as a tool of empowerment need to be addressed. The question is whether there is an alternative way of conceptualizing and institutionalizing rights that can overcome these constraints. I believe there is, and in the next section, I want to outline some of the basic characteristics of this approach that proposes the need to engage the discourse and practice of rights in order to transform the static, male-centered, individualistic, abstract, and ethnocentric elements into an emancipatory political strategy.

RECONCEIVING RIGHTS AS POLITICAL STRATEGIES

While there are a number of different defenses of rights, many continue to rely on some of the same assumptions that have been the basis of the critiques discussed above. One approach, however, which shifts the basic frame of reference, is found in a number of essays that have attempted to develop a notion of rights that conceives of them as contested extensions of political struggles, and that seek to root them within the lived experiences of disempowered sectors of the society. Although not presented within the frame of the subaltern limit, these analyses can nevertheless be interpreted as addressing the spaces of marginality as the "constitutive outside," an "intimate alterity" that defines the limits of institutional, hegemonic power.

Let me begin by citing recent work by Jennifer Nedelsky that provides some grounding for reconfiguring rights at the location of intimate alterity. She correctly characterizes the way that rights function politically and legally within the United States as resting on a notion of autonomy or freedom as limiting rather than enabling. This construes rights as "barriers that protect the individual from intrusion by other individuals or by the state. Rights define boundaries others cannot cross, and it is those boundaries, enforced by law, that ensure individual freedom and autonomy. This image of rights fits well with the idea that the essence of autonomy is independence, which thus requires protection and separation from others" (Nedelsky 1996, 71). As long as rights are conceived of in terms of separating individuals from one another and the state, they are unlikely to be able to address the societal conditions that are the root cause of disempowerment. It is not separation but relationship, mutuality, and interdependence that characterize and define the horizon for action, and that provide the space for autonomy. This societal interdependence is the "precondition in the relationships—between parent and child, student and teacher, state and citizen—which provide the security, education, nurturing, and support that make the development of autonomy possible. . . . Interdependence becomes the central fact of political life, not an issue to be shunted to the periphery in the basic question of how to ensure individual autonomy in the inevitable face of collective power" (71).

Nedelsky spells out the implications of reconceiving rights as a political process. In this view, rights are not seen as "an effort to carve out a sphere into which the collective cannot intrude, but a means of structuring the relationship between individuals and the sources of collective power so that autonomy is fostered rather than undermined" (Nedelsky 1996, 72). So rights are conceived of as a particular type of mechanism whose function it is to "construct" relationships—"of power, of responsibility, of trust, of obligation" (75).

At first glance, this may seem to be simply a shift in perspective, but in fact there are several implications of this approach for the way that rights are incorporated into the political world. First, it emphasizes the fact that the meaning of rights varies historically as societies change and is always a function of the various forms of contestation by different sectors of the population. Second, it links rights to the issue of democratic accountability by focusing on the extent to which institutions structure relations that foster inclusion and access. Third, it stresses the inherent connection between social struggles, social movements, and rights claims. And finally, it allows us to understand rights as practices that take place within the networks of daily life located in the sites of civil society.[17] From this perspective, rights are conceived of as a particular type of political strategy, not a static and reified legal claim. As one activist legal scholar states regarding her experience in both the civil rights and feminist movements, "We asserted rights not simply to advance legal argument or to win a case, but to express the politics, vision, and demands of a social movement, and to assist in the political self-definition of that movement. We understood that winning legal rights would not be meaningful without political organizing to ensure enforcement of and education concerning those rights" (Schneider 1986, 605). Building on these views, I am proposing that rather than considering rights as moral claims that are unlikely to be persuasive against power, we should consider the history of the role of rights in promoting forms of social justice and full inclusion in democratic nation-states that are the final arbiters of such claims. This suggests that rights are better understood and more effective when they are considered and advanced as political strategies for empowerment linked to specific structural and institutional relations and contexts. These factors also imply that any assessment of the potential of particular rights as essential components of empowerment strategies must situate rights claims of particular groups within the specific societal position they occupy and the general societal conditions that exist at that particular time.

Conceiving rights in this way is facilitated by the perspective of the subaltern limit, because it foregrounds the complex, mediated, interdependent nature of the relation between the dominant and subaltern classes; that is, that the specific parameters of the former are to a significant extent constituted by the regime of exclusionary rights that it elaborates as mechanisms of political regulation. In other words, by exposing rights as they function at the limit of hegemonic power as a regulative institutional practice, their potential as destabilizing strategies of empowerment is also revealed.

CHAPTER 5

Grounded Rights Claims

Contesting Membership and Transforming Citizenship
in Latino Urban Communities

THE CONCEPTION OF CIVIL SOCIETY DEVELOPED IN THE PREVIOUS CHAPTER
provides a corrective to the limitations of the major approaches in political theory
that neither demonstrate how regulative, exclusionary practices function within
these sites, nor address the question of what institutional mechanisms can promote
a more inclusive and just democratic system in societies characterized by deep
diversity. They fail, in other words, to address the regulative and emancipatory
roles of civil society. In terms of the emancipatory dimension, this conception of
civil society is capable of linking what are clearly important normative theoretical
considerations relevant to groups with a history of marginalization, to a more
specific level of analysis of the complex institutional sites where the racial, ethnic,
and cultural disjunctions are actually engaged, and where the shifting parameters of
societal membership are negotiated. In this chapter, I attempt to demonstrate how
the four dimensions of citizenship have operated within the institutional sites of
civil society, by focusing on two cases in which Latinos have developed an array of
practices and rights claims in response to the effects of globalization, restructuring,
and transnationalization.

The first focuses on explaining how the processes that restructured what had been the Fordist center of industrial production in Southeast Los Angeles from the 1930s to the 1970s resulted in the development of new Latino communities and the emergence of forms of associative citizenship. Because I focus on the interaction between two levels of analysis—the macro-economic-political and household-based civil society—I develop the discussion to a much greater degree than the second case, which focuses on the immigrant rights movement and marches of 2006. I argue that the latter emerge from some of the changes brought about or extended by the restructuring process. But while the structural causes are similar at a general level, there are important differences that result from the changes in the post–9/11 political situation that have a separate effect and impact on the form of responses and rights claims. The discussion of the immigrant-rights mobilization will also allow me to focus on how differences between Latino immigrants and native-born Latinos play out politically, and what these mean for the notion of citizenship as a political strategy.

Drawing on the reframing of rights claims I have proposed, I argue that the kind of Latino rights claims that I will discuss here are rooted within the quotidian interstitial spaces of civil society, conditions within which the strategies of negotiating everyday life are developed. I focus on the specific characteristics of these institutional spaces, how they are constructed, and what it is in the lives of everyday Latinos that led them to advance rights claims as one of the most important responses to those conditions. This framework is relevant for understanding the situation of Latinos in the United States in at least two related ways. First, it provides a way of focusing on and linking the regulative processes of exclusion of Latinos to the broader discourse of democratization and social justice in political theory. And it also provides a way to understand the basis for the emergence of the particular configurations that alternative forms of political engagement and contestation in Latino communities have taken in the current period. These two aspects are related in a specific way, because the pattern of the current politics of contestation in Latino communities has been framed and shaped by modes of exclusion that were established during the period when the political, economic, and cultural dominance of the Southwest was being established by the new Anglo political elites and settlers. The initial cultural and ideological construction of the Mexican population in the region as "foreigners" has been a continuous thread in the historical relationship between Mexicans and the political and legal apparatus on the one hand, and between Mexicans and the general Anglo population that became the majority and dominant sector in the Southwest shortly after the Mexican-American War, on the other.[1] This initial racialized construction has served as the lens through which later-arriving Latino immigrants have been conceptualized.[2]

This view of Mexicans as inherently foreign was relied on to justify forms of exclusion and discrimination, resulting in a system of differential and unequal levels of access of Mexicans to institutionalized resources that determined the type and level of societal membership. This process of marginalization was not simply a byproduct of the process of social transformation in the Southwest. Histories of the nineteenth-century Southwest make it very clear that Mexican wage labor was a crucial element in the efforts to develop the economic base of the region. The development of agrarian capitalism required the creation of an infrastructure to deliver water to relatively semi-arid areas, and the building of a railroad system to transport agricultural goods to the markets in the Midwest and East, where the majority consumer base was located. And ranching and mining were key parts of the regional economy. In each of these sectors, Mexicans provided labor and knowledge without which the pattern of growth would have been impossible. So in addition to being considered perpetual foreigners, this was a population that had to be controlled and contained politically and socially while at the same time it was relied upon for its labor. This was accomplished through the combined forces of legal and political regulation and isolation, and the social mechanisms, practices, and ideologies of marginalization, including violence, that took place in the sphere of civil society. And while the particular factors that have had the greatest effect have varied over the last 150 years, the societal location of large sectors of Latino communities continues to be primarily determined by these twin processes, although the effects vary according to differences in class, immigrant status, racial profile, and gender.

Even while the sphere of civil society restricted their membership status in the larger society, Mexicans, and later other Latino groups, developed a range of strategies to confront these barriers—strategies that were rooted in the institutional sites of everyday life. Some of the most important social mechanisms that households and communities developed early on to survive and generally function in the new environment were relations and networks of social trust, reciprocity, and mutuality. Drawing on common but limited resources, providing services on an exchange basis, developing mutual aid associations, and improvising informal market relations, were common ways that these relations manifested themselves. While some of these included and emerged from relations of reciprocity, there were other forms of mutuality that contributed to the development of forms of social trust and coopera-tion that were the basis of the community's collective institutions.

While these practices were consolidated and incorporated in the networks of civil society in the nineteenth and early twentieth centuries, relations of this sort have continued to be a fundamental defining feature of marginalized Latino communities in particular. As the examples I will discuss in detail show, these networks of interaction and cooperation based on forms of social trust, reciprocity, and mutuality continue to be one of the major mechanisms of group adaptation, survival, and advancement, not only in Mexican-origin communities, but also among Central Americans, Dominicans, Colombians, Peruvians, Ecuadorans, and other Latin American groups. Through these relations of trust, households in these communities have individually and collectively found ways to accommodate, resist, circumvent, and engage the restrictive barriers that continue to affect them. My research found that in some instances these networks of mutuality and trust enabled the development of forms of collective action that contested policies or practices directly affecting these communities, and gave rise to the kinds of rights claims I discussed previously.

These are far from isolated instances, and in the last few years, while not necessarily approaching their research in terms of the framework of civil society, several studies of Latino communities have noted the important role of these kinds of networks in enabling various forms of collective activities designed to challenge patterns of exclusion and to gain access to spheres of decision making previously closed off to members of these communities. Studies of Latinos in Boston (Hardy-Fanta 1993), of Dominicans and other groups in New York (Jones-Correa 1998), of Central Americans in Los Angeles (Hamilton and Chinchilla 2001), and of a panethnic group of Latinas in Los Angeles (Hondagneu-Sotelo 2001) all reveal the central role of these types of networks in facilitating collective forms of action.[3] It is also clear that the salience of and reliance on these networks for political purposes vary significantly with class, immigrant status, and length of residence, in particular. Those few professionals I interviewed relied on their occupational networks and associations to promote their interests, while the middle-class respondents tended to see traditional electoral politics (including union membership) as the main mechanism for expressing their concerns in the political arena. It was primarily among working-class and immigrant Latino families and households that I found these informal networks of mutuality and reciprocity to be the most important in political terms. Clearly, then, there is a relationship between the socioeconomic and cultural positioning of the groups in these very diverse Latino communities and the relevance of the networking mode of political articulation. My sense is that, at least for the groups I studied, these forms of networks are most salient in terms of facilitating collective action among those who experience the more extreme levels of marginalization in their access to institutions of power and decision making.

As I discussed earlier, there is a substantial literature on civil society that focuses on the central role of reciprocity in establishing the level of trust required for an active, democratic society. Putnam directs his attention to this issue in the final chapter of his study of democracy in Italy, concluding that reciprocity is the most important norm that sustains trust, and that it "serves to reconcile self-interest and solidarity" (Putnam et al. 1993, 172). The relevance of this argument for the analysis of Latino communities in the United States is suggested by Putnam himself in his references to the central role of trust and reciprocity in the work of Vélez-Ibañez on Mexican rotating credit associations, which are widespread not only in Mexico but in Mexican communities throughout the United States. What I think Putnam misses, however, is that the centrality of these elements in Mexican society is not restricted to this specific form of practice. In a companion volume focusing on the politics of the development of civil society in a highly urbanized setting, Vélez-Ibañez builds on the work of the Mexican anthropologist Larissa Lomnitz, arguing that "for persons to take advantage of any resource in Mexico, relationships of confianza ('mutual trust') based on reciprocity within the same class must constantly be in operation. Based on kinship, fictive kinship, friendship, or 'fictive friendship,' such reciprocity within class layers forms the basis of social life in Mexico. Without it the individual finds living an extremely lonely proposition" (Vélez-Ibañez 1983b, 190). The major form that this dimension takes, however, is not simply trust (*confianza*) as such, but a more complex notion of "having trust in trust" (*tener confianza en confianza*). This is learned, according to Lomnitz and Vélez-Ibañez, from immersion in the model of thick networks of generalized reciprocal relationships basic to Mexican social life. But these relations are not simply a function of, or reducible to, the notion of exchange as currently understood. What I found in my fieldwork, and is also central in the analysis of Vélez-Ibañez, is that the form of social trust that emerged in these networks is a qualitatively more complex phenomenon. It has a number of not only cognitive but also emotive and psychological dimensions that enable and facilitate the cooperative linkages and practices that are central in those communities. This is one of the important informal institutional practices that generate the sense of belonging within the groups. "Reciprocity," as used currently, most often implies a utilitarian calculus of exchange, where this calculation determines how individuals enter into social relationships. From this perspective, social relationships become a question of the perceived advantage in entering into them. But mutual advantage does not exhaust the forms of mutuality, and so I prefer to use the latter term, rather than reciprocity, to refer to the various ways in which social trust can be generated. Reducing the complex and multidimensional qualities of all social relations of trust to the single dimension of exchange provides a limited understanding of what is entailed, and is unable to account for other important elements that may be involved in situations, for example, in which an individual has faith, confidence, or the expectation to be treated in a particular way. Trust can emerge from being extended recognition, respect, or care, for example. To construe relations established through these forms as being driven solely by a logic of exchange limits the ability to perceive or conceive of other logics of mutuality at work in them. For example, to say that one "exchanges" one's respect for an expected benefit at a later time precludes the possibility of considering that a different motivation or reason may provide the axial logic for the relationship thus established. While the logic of exchange is clearly one of the important bases of social networks and relationships, I suggest that this element of mutuality is more than a utilitarian and individualistic calculus used for exchange relationships, but is instead a general modality of establishing social bonds rooted in, and constitutive of, the practices of civil society, which then enables other forms of sociality—that is, it provides the conditions for other forms of sociality to function.

The relationships between civil society, rights claims, trust and reciprocity, and citizenship that I have put forth are not only theoretical abstractions but manifest themselves in the everyday life of Latinos. However, I have argued that perceiving the inherent relationships between these concepts and the quotidian experience is limited by the failure of traditional notions of citizenship to demonstrate how they arise from the institutional context within which they function. Tracing this latter process in the specific case of the Latinos I studied requires determining not only the nature of the rights claims they advance, but also what gives rise to these claims, how these claims are embedded within specific institutional sites of civil society, and the configuration of relationships that facilitated the emergence of prefigurative expressions of a new and different form of citizenship that I refer to as associative citizenship.

The extensive and profound changes of Latino communities in the United States during the last thirty years have been part of a broader national and international set of processes. Dramatic increases in the size and rate of growth of Latino populations have played a fundamental role in transforming the configuration of political, cultural, spatial, and economic characteristics and relations of virtually every region of the country. These are both cause and effect of a complex set of processes of restructuring, embodied in a broad variety of institutional strategies, policies, and practices at both the regional and international levels, that have been documented extensively in the literature on restructuring, globalization, and transnationalization.[4] As these developments have unfolded, the specific issues around which political and social divisions revolve have shifted considerably. As I have discussed in some detail, prominent among these is the reemergence of citizenship as a major focus of political and cultural relations, discourse, and policy agendas. This is to a great extent a direct consequence of the fact that the policies and practices that constitute economic restructuring have served as a catalyst to massive increases in the level of transnational migrations from Latin America, Africa, Asia, and the Caribbean. In particular, the demand for low-wage labor in the United States and Europe has acted as a magnet for immigrants from these regions seeking economic opportunity and progress. However, unlike European immigrants of the late nineteenth and early twentieth centuries, the majority of these new immigrants come from Third World societies, and thus their cultural, social, and particularly racial backgrounds and contexts are even more divergent and incongruous than those of the older generation of newcomers. These manifest themselves in fundamentally different values, perspectives, and cultural practices, all of which have been the source of conflict in cities and towns throughout the country. These divisions and resentments have resulted in basic political realignments that reflect a deepening of already tenuous racial cleavages and tensions. It is ironic that leftist theorists such as Wendy Brown critique "identity politics" as embodying a form of resentment while ignoring the obvious and glaring backlash among the white working class in particular. These shifting political and racial landscapes have resulted in clashes over the nature of the rights, responsibilities, obligations, entitlements, and other privileges of being a member of the national community. And these are precisely the factors that constitute and define the parameters and functional meaning of citizenship. What form the specific configuration of what are in essence elements of citizenship and belonging should take, has been one of the most contested terrains in the new politics and policy agendas both in the capitals of Europe and in virtually every region of the United States. The depth, divisiveness, and intensity surrounding this issue have been clearly evident in the campaigns in California to promote English-only amendments, to limit immigrant access to state-provided services, to abolish affirmative action, and in the intensive, repressive policies that Arizona enacted targeting Latinos. These types of debates have also found expression in recent works on rights and citizenship that attempt to account for the dramatic effects of the related processes of globalization and transnationalism on the complex relationship between the nation, identity, community, territory, and the state.[5] In particular, the rapid, large-scale migrations of people from Asia, Latin America, and Africa to European and U.S. megacities; their impact on cultural, economic, and political institutional relationships; and the construction, interpretation, and representation of these as perceived threats to the maintenance of the cultural ground of national identity, have given rise to the need to rethink the nature of citizenship within this multicultural context.[6] It is precisely this set of issues that led to the framework I am using here, and that I engage not only theoretically, but by demonstrating how a form of associative citizenship is being advanced by certain sectors of Latino communities in response to changes in the institutional context brought about by the forces of globalization and restructuring.

Latino Los Angeles: Reconstituting Borders/Boundaries

One of the areas where all of the dimensions involved in these changes have been clearly visible is the greater Los Angeles metropolitan region. Los Angeles has for many years had the largest concentration of Mexican-origin population outside of Mexico. In the late 1960s, however, immigrants from Central and South America as well as the Caribbean began to arrive in significant numbers, some blending into mixed neighborhoods, and others developing communities where the residents were predominantly from specific Latino groups. The breadth of these changes were reflected in the response of Robert Gonzalez to a question posed during an interview I conducted in 1993 regarding what he thought had changed most about Los Angeles during his lifetime.[7] Robert grew up during the 1950s in Belvedere, one of the oldest Mexican neighborhoods in East Los Angeles, and so had witnessed the dramatic changes he refers to here.

> I think that probably the biggest change is that now we are everywhere. When I was growing up in E.L.A. in the '50s, you knew where the Mexican areas were, and when you wandered out of those, you saw very few of us in places like Santa Monica and the westside. But now, it doesn't matter where I go in L.A., there we are. It feels so different now. When I was a kid sometimes my dad would take me with him on his deliveries over in Culver City, West L.A., Santa Monica, even Beverly Hills, and I would feel kind of funny, you know what I mean? I felt out of place; like I didn't belong. I wouldn't see any other Mexicans at all. But now, hell, I feel at home almost everywhere because I know there is going to be somebody that looks like me, that talks like me, no matter where I am.[8]

What Robert Gonzalez describes—the extensive growth in the size and location of Latino communities—is indeed one of the most basic features of the dramatic and rapid changes that have transformed Los Angeles during the last twenty-five years. As Robert recalls it, the Los Angeles of his youth was one where Mexican-origin communities had fairly clear spatial boundaries/borders, with all that is implied by this type of segregation. The established barrios in the Los Angeles area of the 1950s included communities like East Los Angeles, which consisted of neighborhoods such as Lincoln Park, Belvedere, and Maravilla. Other important Mexican communities were located in San Gabriel, San Fernando, Wilmington/San Pedro, and a small barrio in the Venice area. The pattern of labor-market segmentation, housing discrimination, and political marginalization that led to the restricted nature of these communities has been described in works by Acuña (1984) and Romo (1983).

However, this particular configuration of Mexican-community boundaries has been neither consistent nor even. Historian George Sanchez has shown that the type of segregation that formed part of Robert Gonzalez's experience existed in the late nineteenth century, but that between 1900 and 1940, Mexican residents were more widely dispersed throughout the Los Angeles area, with the exception of the Westside (Sanchez 1993). But between the early 1940s and the mid-1960s, the Mexican population once again found itself in relatively cohesive and segregated residential communities.

This is important to note because it reflects the fact that the development patterns of the Mexican communities in the area have been neither static nor linear, but have consistently been affected in fundamental ways by broader structural patterns and tendencies. Thus, in our effort to account for the dynamic of development underlying the creation of new Latino communities since the 1960s, it is necessary to frame the issues in terms of the contextual dimensions that provided the historical horizon for the specific strategies of adaptation, resistance, accommodation, and change adopted by the Latino population.

But first let me provide some sense of the size and characteristics of the different Latino communities of Los Angeles as it existed during the period of study, 1989 to 2000. The official estimate of the 1990 Census was that 3.3 million Latinos lived in Los Angeles County, 76 percent (roughly 2.5 million) of whom were of Mexican origin. The next largest group consisted of Central Americans, who numbered about 453,000, with over half being from El Salvador. However, the Mexican American Legal Defense Fund (MALDEF) estimates that nearly 430,000 Latinos in Los Angeles were missed in that census, and that it is a conservative estimate. So the figure is much more likely to be close to 4 million Latinos living in Los Angeles County. Among some of the other Latino groups, the official estimate is that there were nearly 100,000 South Americans, mostly from Colombia, Peru, Chile, Argentina, and another 90,000 Spanish-speaking people from the Caribbean. One of the important points underscored by these figures is the significant change in the composition of the Latino population since the late 1960s. Prior to that time, nearly all of the Spanish-speaking population in California were of Mexican origin. Since then, however, Latino communities have become more diverse. As the figures indicate, a large number of people from Central America, particularly El Salvador and Guatemala, now make Los Angeles home. And smaller but significant numbers have immigrated from Peru, Cuba, Colombia, Puerto Rico, and Argentina.

These figures reflect the dramatic change in the population base of the region. Between 1980 and 1990, the total population of Los Angeles County grew by 1.38 million residents, of which 1.24 million, or 89 percent, were Latinos. At the same time, 360,000 Anglo residents left the county, while the African American population increased by 20,000, and the Asian population grew by 490,000. These figures indicate that the majority of those new to the workforce, to the schools, the health-care system, those seeking to rent or buy homes and apartments, were likely to be Latinos. This influx of 1.24 million Latinos to the county is obviously one of the principal causes of the transformation of communities, of the dramatic increase in the number and location of neighborhoods with Latino majorities.[9]

But these data do not reveal where these populations established cohesive communities or neighborhoods that were integrated by a range of personal, economic, cultural, educational, service, and recreational networks. Both our ethnographic studies and a review of census tract data indicate that these populations were spread throughout the entire Los Angeles area. Entire neighborhoods were transformed into Latino communities, in some cases within a year. Latino communities with at least a minimal set of interactive networks developed in a large number of areas of Los Angeles that previously had a very small or no Latino presence. While some of these began to form during the mid to late 1960s, others developed in the 1980s and 1990s, and the process continues to this day.

One area where the early stages of the transition to a Latino majority were visible by the late 1960s was in Southeast Los Angeles, previously an area of predominantly white working-class residential neighborhoods. The rate of growth there accelerated quickly during the 1970s and 1980s, and by the time of our study, these communities were over 90 percent Latino. The largest concentrations of Latinos in that region were in the areas of Maywood, Huntington Park, Bell, Bell Gardens, South Gate, and Lynwood. A similar pattern of growth occurred in adjacent areas, such as Pico Rivera, Montebello, Commerce, San Gabriel, and Rosemead, to name but a few.

During the same period, relatively new Latino communities formed west of downtown, extending from the Pico-Union area to Santa Monica. An extensive barrio developed, for example, in the Culver City/Mar Vista area of West Los Angeles, concentrated in a corridor that runs from west Los Angeles to Westchester near LAX. The population of South Central Los Angeles, previously a predominantly African American community, grew to over 50 percent Latino. And the percentage of Latinos residing in and close to the city of Santa Monica increased dramatically. Whole areas of the San Fernando Valley were transformed into Latino communities, such as North Hollywood, Van Nuys, Canoga Park, adding to the older areas such as the city of San Fernando and surrounding Pacoima. Our ethnographic research also revealed that the dispersion and residential mobility of Latinos throughout Los Angeles was so great that many of their social networks overlapped in spatial terms. Thus, for example, while there were distinct Latino areas in Southeast Los Angeles such as Huntington Park, South Gate, Walnut Park, Vernon, Bell, and Bell Gardens, the social networks of many of the residents that constitute the basis of community linkages overlapped previously established spatial boundaries. Thus a high percentage of respondents from these communities indicated that their most significant relationships and networks were with households in sections of the San Fernando Valley, Hollywood, Orange County, and the San Gabriel Valley. So it is clear that the tendency to identify communities primarily, or only, in terms of physical, spatial boundaries is of limited value. It is rather cultural space that seems to form the basis of community networks that extend over considerable distances.

While the Mexican population continued to be the majority in most of these areas, there were particular neighborhoods where significant numbers of other Latino groups established integrated systems of social relations, networks, services, restaurants, stores, medical practitioners, cultural practices, etc. Thus Salvadorans and Nicaraguans established extensive networks in the Pico-Union area. Peruvians created close-knit economic, social, and recreational networks in both South Gate and Hawthorne. Some of the businesses whose clients were primarily Latinos were so successful that they branched out into three or four locations. One Peruvian restaurant, Pollo Inka, had locations in Hawthorne, Torrance, Orange County, San Fernando Valley, and Redondo Beach. A Cuban restaurant flourished in the otherwise higher-end Anglo community of Hermosa Beach, and yet the majority of customers were Latinos. Other businesses serving Latino customers developed throughout the city in areas that two years before had almost no Latinos. These businesses and service providers that catered to Latinos were one of the important measures that we used to identify the spatial location of new Latino communities. Significant numbers and networks of Cubans, some of which controlled access to the distribution of Latin American music to retail outlets in Los Angeles, established growing neighborhoods. Colombian organizations sponsored monthly dances and get-togethers that in reality served as a major mechanism for maintaining their social networks and also helped orient and incorporate recent arrivals into the new environment, very often by finding both temporary and permanent housing, furniture, jobs, etc. *Actualidad*, published by Peruvians, and *El Colombiano*, by Colombians, were regularly circulated throughout the region through Latin American restaurants, nightclubs, record shops, and travel agencies.

Many of these types of activities that were the basis of communities in formation had existed in older Mexican communities for decades. The publication of newspapers, a large network of voluntary and regional associations, cultural institutions, networks that provided food, clothing, shelter, and job information for recently arrived immigrants, were also part of the process of the growth pattern of Mexican communities going back more than a century in Los Angeles. In fact, many of the small communities of other Latino groups were located spatially within or adjacent to Mexican neighborhoods. The pattern of interaction between the Mexican population and the other Latino groups, however, was an uneven one, and in most cases that we examined were relatively limited. Culturally, Latino communities flourished and established associations to ensure that there would be continuity between the culture of origin and both the form and content of the social relations that were established there.

The development of these new communities, however, was not an isolated phenomenon. Their formation occurred as part of a process of transformation in the spatial and social landscape of the Los Angeles region (Soja 1989a, 1989b). Thus as Latino immigrants moved into areas with large concentrations of African Americans, such as South Central Los Angeles, Watts, and Compton, there was an outmigration of the latter group into areas further west, such as sections of Inglewood and Hawthorne, previously populated by a majority of whites. There was also substantial movement south to previously predominantly white neighborhoods in the Long Beach area. Thus Latino migration to areas such as these, as well as to communities that were primarily white before the mid-1970s or early 1980s—for example, Hollywood, Canoga Park, Van Nuys—resulted in many non-Latino residents moving to outlying areas. According to some of our non-Latino respondents, this was one of the factors that drove the development of new residential communities in relatively remote suburban areas such as Valencia, Saugus, and Newhall in the Santa Clarita Valley, as well as Simi Valley, Calabasas, and even as far as Oxnard.

What drove these processes of expansion and creation of new Latino communities? We can begin to answer this by returning to the observation made earlier that the development of new Latino communities in Los Angeles both transformed and were transformed by the broader changes occurring in Los Angeles, in fundamental ways. This was part of a process of restructuring that had occurred in the city since 1970 at several levels and along different axes, including economic, political, household, community, spatial and cultural relations, and patterns of practice.

INSTITUTIONAL CONTEXT: STRUCTURAL TRANSFORMATION, RESTRUCTURING, AND RIGHTS CLAIMS

I argued in the previous chapter for the need to situate the practices of citizenship within the institutional setting where they function. So I want to initially look at the forces and characteristics of the processes of transformation that led to the emergence of the type of rights claims that prefigure a conception of citizenship that differs from the existing mode. In the period since 1970, the dynamic that had the greatest influence in this sense were the related processes of globalization, restructuring, and transnationalization. I will describe how these processes developed in the Los Angeles region, the effects they had on certain sectors of several

Latino communities, and the kinds of rights claims that emerged from their efforts to cope with and negotiate those changes. These claims were a direct response to the circumstances and conditions that resulted from the large-scale structural change that occurred during this period. In order to demonstrate how citizenship practices are rooted within the institutional context in which they emerge, I will provide a detailed account of the various dimensions of these changes, both at a structural level and at the level of quotidian experience, which is of course lived out within the parameters set by the structural conditions. I am following here my previous argument that discussed the theoretical reasons for the need to establish the interaction between institutional contexts and the responses of marginalized populations to them. According to that position, the only way to illustrate the dynamic at work here is to provide a clear sense of what forces brought about the changes in these Latino communities, and to trace out how these influenced the lived realities of the individuals and households that formed these communities in such a way that the rights claims were a rational and meaningful response. These claims did not arise from some abstract theoretical formulation or from a highly elaborate political ideology. Instead, they were expressions of the sense of marginalization that derived from the conditions that these individuals confronted daily. The particular forms and dimensions of that marginalization were directly related to the processes of restructuring that were one of the major catalysts for the transformation of the region and these communities.

The basic dynamics of the economic restructuring process that occurred in the United States beginning in the early 1970s have been presented in great detail in general terms (Smith and Feagin 1987, Sassen 1988), and the specific form the process took in the Los Angeles area has also been investigated (Soja 1989a, 1989b; Scott 1996). One of the most apparent changes in Los Angeles after 1970 was the dramatic increase in the size of the Latino immigrant population. And this growth was a principal factor in promoting the pattern of Latino community formation beyond previously established Latino neighborhoods. What was not so apparent, but is nevertheless made clear by the literature on restructuring, is that there was a direct relationship between the basic forces of restructuring and the increase in immigration from Latin America and Asia. Of course the connection was not a one-dimensional or simple one, but was mediated through other factors as well. But studies of these processes showed that the restructuring mechanism was driven by policies adopted by international capital since the late 1960s to change its relationship to labor. Clearly, this was not a uniform process, but rather it took different forms and occurred in different ways in particular countries, and even different regions of the United States.

The detailed analysis of this relationship that Sassen carried out demonstrates that quite ironically, the economic policies pursued by the United States itself, particularly through its basic role in the International Monetary Fund and the World Bank, were actually one of the major reasons for the rapid growth of large Latino immigrant communities throughout the United States. As Sassen indicates:

> U.S efforts to open its own and other countries' economies to the flow of capital, goods, services and information created conditions that mobilized people for migration and formed linkages between the United States and other countries which subsequently served as bridges for migration. . . . Measures commonly thought to deter emigration—foreign investment, or the promotion of export-oriented agriculture and manufacturing in poor countries—have had precisely the opposite effect. Such investment contributes to massive displacement of small-scale agricultural and manufacturing enterprises, while simultaneously deepening the economic, cultural and ideological ties between the recipient countries and the United States. These factors encourage migration. (Sassen 1992, 14–15)

In addition to the displacement of traditional economic arrangements and the establishment of strong ties with the United States, it is also the case that the conversion to export-driven economies decimated the middle class and lowered the domestic standard of living in these countries, even as the overall economic output was increasing—most of it, however, targeted for external markets. This contributed to the migration during the 1980s of well-educated, skilled labor, particularly from Mexico and some South American countries such as Peru, Columbia, Chile, and Argentina. The same international economic policies and processes that were promoting investment and the expansion of manufacturing jobs in low-wage countries also directly altered the nature of the demand for labor in the domestic economy of the United States. The domestic traditional manufacturing sector went through a process of deindustrialization—reindustrialization that substantially downgraded (or "downsized," as the current corporate language calls it) labor demand, resulting in the growth of low-wage, semi-skilled or unskilled jobs. Coupled with the job growth in the high-technology sector and the great increase in subcontracting (including sweatshops and home work), what resulted was an economy characterized by very distinct and different labor markets for immigrant labor, for middle class, high-tech, and professional labor, as well as a highly polarized and fragmented social fabric. Thus, the long-standing popular anti-immigrant hysteria tapped into by the disclosures that Cabinet nominees hired undocumented immigrants, and which found political expression in Proposition 187 and aroused passionate divisions, was a situation set in motion by the United States itself. Although the economic dimensions and consequences of restructuring were fundamental in promoting migration from Latin America, in some cases there were other factors that played a significant role.

So that, for example, in the case of many immigrants from El Salvador, Nicaragua, and Guatemala, the conditions and dangers of the wars in their countries were a primary reason for leaving. Based on our interviews and ethnographic work, it appears, however, that the economic and political motivations were often intertwined. As some of the Central American respondents indicated, the civil wars ruined the economies in their countries and made economic survival even more problematic than before.

These structural processes transformed the Los Angeles of Robert Gonzalez's youth from a city with relatively segregated Mexican communities into one where Latino presence was pervasive.[10] However, the analysis of this transformation needs to go beyond the abstractions promoted by some multiculturalist approaches that simply note the coexistence of many different nationalities and racial and ethnic groups as context for the study of urban realities or for advancing theoretical perspectives. The dimensions of social location that are so often used to identify, to "place," or "situate" different groups in the city need to be construed as more than just conceptual categories or spatial metaphors. Instead, we need to view each "Los Angeles" as constituting a particular, specific, and concrete way of quotidian living in and through the city that is both bounded by and linked to other sectors by its particular configuration of factors such as race, class, gender, immigrant status, political access, and economic resources. Because these configurations were the result of dynamic processes and shifting tendencies, the growth in the Latino population in Los Angeles has to be seen as more than simply an increase in population statistics. Instead, these processes of change resulted in the emergence of new Latino communities and the transformation of older ones. Thus this process of Latino community formation needs to be situated within, and in interaction with, the pattern of changes in the broader structural and institutional context of the region.[11]

THE EFFECT OF ECONOMIC RESTRUCTURING ON LATINO LOS ANGELES

Los Angeles is one of the major centers where the processes of restructuring and the new forms of cultural and political relations emerged as defining characteristics of new institutional patterns of social formation. Its central role in the coordination of transnational corporate business operations transformed Los Angeles into one of the "command" megacities (Smith 1987). And like some of the other major urban regions, it became a "dual city" characterized by a regional economy that created a bipolar pattern of jobs, space, and access to goods and services—the growth of higher-wage technical, professional, and semi-professional occupations at one end, and low-wage, service, and industrial jobs at the other. And the cultural, ethnic, racial, gender, and spatial dimensions of this pattern of growth are evident in the statistics on income and occupation, as well as in the spatial distribution of the region's population and the nature of household relations. The high proportion of workers in the low-wage sector were Latino, Asian (many of whom were recent immigrants), and blacks, most of whom lived in concentrated central sections of the city, while the ranks of the higher-wage earners were disproportionately white and lived in the ever-expanding suburban boundary communities. As Sassen observes, "The corporate complex and the immigrant community today are probably two extreme modes in the formation and appropriation of urban space" (Sassen 1996a, 23). Although this "dual city" image can be interpreted in a simplistic way, it can nevertheless serve as a way to think about the broader implications of the specific changes that characterize the polarization that has occurred. Referring to the use of this metaphor in their study of New York, Mollenkopf and Castells argue the following:

> But the dual city metaphor which the city's income polarization suggests to observers is gravely flawed as an analytic approach. The "two cities" of New York are not separate and distinct, but rather deeply intertwined products of the same underlying processes. . . . But even if the dual city metaphor can be scientifically misleading and often rhetorical or ideological, it nevertheless challenges us to explore the dimensions of growing inequality and explain the sources of the tendencies toward polarization. (Mollenkopf and Castells 1991, 11)

Thus the analyses of the pattern of economic development in regions like Los Angeles emphasize the ways in which these polarized sectors of the city were mutually dependent on one another. It is here that the relationship between the pattern of economic change and Latino immigration is fundamental. For in this relationship lies one of the keys to explaining the nature of the diverse relationships between Latino communities and the broader society, as well as the pattern of Latino community development that has emerged during the last thirty years.

The studies of Los Angeles that proliferated in recent years provide a fairly clear view of the various elements that were involved in its transformation. It is evident that the forces of changes were regional in nature, affecting not only Los Angeles proper but also the adjoining San Bernardino, Ventura, and Orange counties. Until recently, Los Angeles was not thought of as a major manufacturing center. Despite this image, the fact is that the economic expansion that took place during and after the Second World War converted the region as a whole into the largest manufacturing center in the United States. The 1950s and 1960s were decades of unprecedented economic growth in the area, and Southeast Los Angeles was a key site of this expansion of jobs, income, and economic opportunity in general. There were several factors that affected the particular pattern of growth in the region from the end of the

Second World War. The flow of investment into capital-intensive Fordist industries (especially defense-related sectors) created relatively high-paying, stable jobs with good benefits that attracted migrant workers with average educations from other regions of the United States. And there were affordable, sparsely populated land areas to accommodate the new physical infrastructure required for growth, including suburban housing for workers. Manufacturing led the economic expansion, and by the late 1940s, Los Angeles had already developed what Soja describes as "the largest mass market automobile-glass-rubber type manufacturing complex outside the Midwest" (Soja 1989a). But the economic base of the region also developed the basis for the most extensive high-technology industrial complex in the nation, so that both Fordist and post-Fordist sectors were key to the area's growth.

During the period between the end of World War II and the late 1960s, the Los Angeles region experienced strong and steady economic growth characterized by expanding opportunities and greatly accelerated suburbanization. However, the pattern of economic activity that provided the basis for this relative prosperity began to shift. By the early 1970s, a number of downward trends became apparent, and this growth "machine" came to an end as the area was affected by the global restructuring process that began in the late 1960s. This was a long, sustained, and painful period of economic restructuring and adjustment in the area, changes that reverberated throughout, and ultimately transformed, every institutional sector of the region. This was the result of U.S. industrial corporations having initiated a series of strategies and policies in response to steadily declining profits and the loss of the competitive edge to the more efficient and productive emerging economies of countries such as West Germany and Japan. There were four interactive processes of restructuring in particular that constituted the local expressions of the forces of globalization, a relationship now often referred to as "glocalization" (Swyngedouw 1997; Robertson 1994, 1995). These were deindustrialization, reindustrialization, expansion of the service sector, and a shift in the role of the state. These processes were not peculiar to Southern California as we now know, but were part of a major reorganization of the international economy, and the Los Angeles region went through a series of stages in its adaptation to these processes of economic globalization.

The specific pattern of restructuring in the Los Angeles region included an initial phase that lasted until the early 1980s, and then there was a period of economic reconfiguration and growth between 1982 and 1990, which reached its peak in 1989. Between 1984 and early 1990, employment in the five-county region of Southern California grew by 22 percent. However, during both these periods, the effort to find lower-wage labor was a major goal of the restructuring policies and involved both developing technological advances that deskilled existing jobs and replacing higher-wage earners with a labor force willing to accept dramatically reduced wages.

Table 1. Employment by Sector, Los Angeles Region (percentage of total employment)

	1950	1970	1990
Manufacturing	23.9	27.9	20.5
Retail	19.0	17.3	16.7
Professional Services	10.4	19.0	22.5

Source: Scott 1996, 217–19.

As a result of this specific change in the labor demand, inexpensive immigrant labor became an essential component of the pattern of economic development. Immigrant labor worked not only for much lower wages but also without benefits, which represented a growing cost for capital. Table 1 shows that manufacturing, retail, and professional services have consistently been three important sectors in terms of employment for this population.

The data indicate that both professional services and manufacturing grew between 1950 and 1970, but that while the former continued its expansion between 1970 and 1990 by 18.4 percent, the latter declined by 26.5 percent. What the figures do not reflect, however, are the intra-sectoral shifts that reveal much more clearly why the nature of the changes resulted in a dramatic increase in immigrant labor.

These figures make clear that the leading growth sector in manufacturing was the high-technology industries, but that low-technology, labor-intensive industries also grew significantly during the restructuring period, a 62 percent increase. As Scott points out, this created a bipolar income pattern, with the higher-paying skilled, unionized jobs located in high-technology industries and lower-wage, non-benefit jobs concentrated in low-technology industries. This is where the Latino immigrant workforce in the manufacturing sector, which grew from 8.9 percent in 1970 to 30.8 percent in 1990 (a 247.2 percent increase), played such a crucial role (Scott 1996,

Table 2. Manufacturing Sectors in Los Angeles, 1950–1990 (percentage of total employment)

	1950	1970	1990
Low-Technology, Labor Intensive	29.0	16.3	26.4
High-Technology	19.7	34.2	31.9
Metallurgical and Machinery	18.7	17.5	16.1
Other	32.6	32.0	25.6
Total Manufacturing Employment	*459,115*	*1,102,000*	*1,350,375*

Source: Scott 1996, 215–44.

222). This bipolar pattern of job creation and wage distribution continued even during the worst recession, between 1990 and 1994, when the only two sectors of the local economy that grew were the high-tech motion pictures and multimedia, which produced the greatest number of jobs, and apparel and textiles at the low-tech end. In fact, the recovery was led by apparel production in the nondurable manufacturing sector (which increased by 26 percent between 1988 and 1996) and the motion-picture and multimedia industries, which produced the most significant job increase (87 percent, although the percentage of all L.A. County jobs in this area was still very small—about 2 percent). And the movie industry had the highest pay rates, about 180 percent of the average L.A. County pay, while the apparel and textiles sector pay was only 52 percent of the same figure, the lowest wage rate with the exception of the retail food-service sector (Dear 1996, 9).

As is clear, immigration played a defining role in these changes. In fact, it was immigration that accounted for the population growth in the Los Angeles region during the restructuring period. For every two residents that left the region, one immigrant arrived (Dear 1996, 11). The percentage of foreign-born residents in Los Angeles County increased from 11 to 32 percent between 1970 and 1990. And the number of Latino immigrants went from 398,200 in 1970 to 2,359,140 in 1990, an increase of 1,960,94, or 492 percent (Sabagh and Bozorgmehr 1996, 95). And the particular sectors of labor demand filled by Latino immigrants are clear from the following figures on occupational overrepresentation.

The data for Central American immigrants show the same pattern of concentration in low-wage jobs, such as childcare, domestic, and textiles work.

What this data documents clearly is that the economic foundation of Los Angeles created a dual city, with Latino immigrants living in poor, crowded, inner-city neighborhoods—or those plagued by crime near the inner city—working for

Table 3. Foreign-Born Mexican Immigrants in Overrepresented Occupations (percentage of total employment), 1990

Men		Women	
Textile Sewing Machine Operator	65.8	Farm Worker	70.7
Groundskeeper	50.8	Textile Sewing Machine Operator	53.1
Busboy, Kitchen Assistant	50.1	Assembler	39.6
Cook	44.8	Private Household Servant, Cleaner	30.8
Assembler	42.2	Janitor, Cleaner	30.4
Construction Laborer	39.1	Electrical Equipment Assembler	29.4

Source: Allen and Turner 1997, 211–15.

extremely low wages and without health benefits. At the other end are a majority of white professionals, in very high wage brackets, living in relatively expensive suburban housing, and whose affluent lifestyle generates some of the low-wage service jobs taken by Latino/a immigrants, such as domestics, gardeners, restaurant workers, etc.

LATINOS AND THE TRANSFORMATION OF THE "HUB" CITIES

The confluence of these processes was especially visible in the Southeast section of the area, a concentrated industrial zone that extended several miles directly south of downtown (Dear 1996, 12). Once known as the "rust belt," this area encompasses incorporated cities such as Bell, Bell Gardens, Cudahy Huntington Park, Maywood, South Gate, Vernon, as well as unincorporated areas such as Walnut Park and parts of Los Angeles that have been designated by the L.A. Department of City Planning as "South Central." This region played a pivotal role in the particular pattern of economic development of the Los Angeles metropolitan area. It was the principal site of the growth of Fordist manufacturing industrialization between the 1920s and the early 1970s, occupying a strategically key physical space that lies only a few miles south of the downtown center of Los Angeles. This was a result of decisions made during the 1920s by the economic and political leadership to extend the industrial base of Los Angeles through a process of suburbanization, promoting the growth of different industrial sectors in specific outlying areas. Thus the development of the aircraft industry was focused in the area extending about ten miles south along the coast from Santa Monica, while the growth of the movie industry took place primarily in Hollywood and parts of Burbank, and as Fulton describes it, "Cars and tires went to the lowlands, creating an industrial belt south and east of downtown, along the Los Angeles River and the major rail lines that followed the river from the rail yards south to the ports near Long Beach" (Fulton 1997, 72). The coherence of the Southeast region lies in the mutual dependence of these cities. Vernon, Cudahay, and Commerce developed as the actual physical sites of the industrial plants, with few residents. South Gate, Huntington Park, and, to a lesser degree, Maywood reflected a mixed pattern, having a significant number of industrial sites, but also having large residential areas and a strong commercial district. Bell and Bell Gardens were, and continue to be, primarily residential. The residential tracts throughout the area developed to house the new white working class that was migrating to the region, much like today's Latino immigrants, to fill the labor demand of the developing industries. Thus there was a clear pattern of coherence in the region that revolved around the configuration of housing, jobs, and commercial development—a pattern that continues in some form at least to the present day.

The local manifestations of the processes of restructuring were clearly visible in these cities, whose growth and development had been driven by their key role in sustaining the Fordist period of expansion. By the early 1980s, a significant number of firms in the large-scale manufacturing sectors of Los Angeles—particularly in durable goods such as steel, autos, rubber, and glass—closed and relocated either offshore or in other parts of the country. While closing of plants was one of the strategies of restructuring in the region, finding a source of cheaper labor for the new low-wage, low-technology small firms that were replacing them was another key strategy. The closing of the major Fordist manufacturing plants resulted in the loss of the primary job source for the residents of the area. In combination with other factors, this resulted in a rapid exodus of the mostly white working class, who were unwilling to accept lower-income jobs. This demand for low-wage manufacturing and service labor became a magnet drawing a rapidly expanding flow of immigrants from Latin America. Much as the white working class before them, they settled in the residential areas nearest the sites of the new low-wage growth industries, renting and buying in neighborhoods where housing costs had declined dramatically. Thus, by 1980, the local dynamic of globalization processes in Los Angeles had brought about a complete economic and cultural transformation of the region into an extensive network of Latino communities. The proliferation of low-wage jobs, the demographic transformation of the area, and the spatial clustering of Latino communities are all the result of the processes of restructuring, and at the same time, they define the new cultural and social matrix within which the networks of associational activities give rise to new patterns of interaction, different structures of needs, and distinct strategies of institutional articulation, all of which define a dramatically different terrain of civil society.

Because this region underwent one of the most rapid and extensive transformations as a result of restructuring, I selected it as the site to study how individuals and households responded to those conditions, focusing in particular on the emergence of rights claims. A preliminary indication of the extent of these changes is reflected in the fact that the Latino population in Huntington Park went from 4.5 percent in 1960 to 35.9 percent in 1970, 85 percent in 1986, 92 percent in 1990, and 95.6 percent in 2000. And these changes were clearly a function of the general restructuring process, which affected not only its economic profile, but its cultural, demographic, and political makeup as well. And because of the very rapid rate of change, it was not difficult to locate respondents who lived through these years. The degree of concentration of Latinos in this region is reflected in the following data for 1990.

While these figures indicate the high concentration of Latinos in these communities, the specific aspects of this process that propelled the transformation of this region were initially part of a more general closing of major manufacturing firms

Table 4. Population in Southeast Los Angeles Cities, 1990

City	Total Population	Latino	Percent Latino
Maywood	27,850	25,900	93
Huntington Park	56,065	51,579	92
Commerce	12,135	11,042	91
Cudahy	22,817	20,307	89
Bell Gardens	42,355	37,272	88
Bell	34,365	29,554	86
Pico Rivera	59,177	49,117	83
South Gate	86,284	71,616	83

Source: 1990 Census tract tables.

and loss of jobs in California. Thus, for example, in the short span of three years, 1980 to 1983, 157,000 manufacturing jobs were lost in the state of California, mostly in the steel, tires, civilian aircraft, and auto industries. In Southeast Los Angeles, the specific elements of the economic restructuring process were a mix of large and small closures and changes. For example, some 8,000 jobs left the city of South Gate in a four-year span early in the 1980s when General Motors, Firestone Tires, Weiser Lock, and Fed Mart closed. During roughly the same period, Chrysler Credit Corporation closed three new car dealerships—Dodge, Jeep Eagle, and an outlet for Chrysler/Plymouth/Hyundai. While the number of jobs lost, 175, was significant, it was relatively small compared to job loss when GM closed its plant. But another dimension of the effects of restructuring are illustrated in this case because the city of South Gate received 20 percent of its sales taxes from these three firms, nearly $5.6 million, and thus its ability to provide services and maintain its operations was considerably undermined.

Other plant closures and job losses included the shutdown in December 1982 of Bethlehem Steel, located in the city of Vernon. Over two thousand men and women lost their jobs that Christmas, and the main union of steelworkers, Local 1845 in nearby Huntington Park, became a food bank to help workers get through that period. In 1989, Dial Corporation discontinued its production of household liquid bleach at its Purex plant in South Gate, and later, in December 1991, it closed all of its operations there. Oscar Mayer was another major employer located in Vernon that shut down, firing its entire workforce, most of whom had been with the company for at least ten years or more. Some of these industrial sites had played a major role in the development of the region over a long period of time, and had established important social ties with the cities, so that for example, the Dial Corporation had been in the same plant for fifty years and GM had opened its plant in 1936. Despite this, there was virtually no consideration by management of the impact these closures would have on these host cities and communities.

But it was not only job loss that was involved here. The nature of the labor market and labor demand was also transformed. The jobs that were lost in this process were primarily unionized, higher-wage employment with good health, retirement, and other benefit packages. Yet during the very same period when the region was losing these high-paying, unionized jobs, other sectors were developing that employed low-wage, nonunionized, semiskilled Latino immigrant labor. Thus, although the city of Vernon lost a great number of jobs, its low-wage sector expanded by eight to ten thousand, primarily in the garment industry. In the mid-1990s, it had more than one hundred garment plants, many with sweatshop conditions and all with a high percentage of immigrant female employees.

The restructuring scenario in Southeast Los Angeles was clearly driven by the dramatic change in economic profile. The closing of major plants, and the loss of jobs and revenue that resulted set in motion a process of rapid and complete transformation of the region that included demographic, cultural, political, and household restructuring. While table 4 provides an indication of the high concentration of Latinos in the area, what is not reflected in these data is the high percentage of immigrant Latinos. Although it varies by city, the immigrant population in the Southeast Los Angeles region is estimated to average close to 50 percent. This is a region that in the 1960s was primarily Anglo. While the restructuring process did not determine the specific processes of community transition and formation, it did, however, create the conditions for these. Latino immigrants came to this Los Angeles region during the period between 1970 and 1990, driven not only by the economic structural changes we described, but also by some of the consequences of these changes on other factors. Thus, for example, one of the major reasons for the dramatic increase of Latinos in this specific region of Southeast Los Angeles had to do with the decrease in property values that resulted from the loss of jobs and revenues. The Anglo working class that was economically displaced by the forces of restructuring left the area. Home prices and rents dropped dramatically, and since newly arriving, economically strapped Latino immigrants had to seek out low-rent areas, they gravitated toward Southeast Los Angeles. Once established as a Latino community, of course, then the area further attracted immigrants on the basis of cultural familiarity. Small commercial and retail businesses to service these new communities soon followed. In fact, it was this transition that revitalized the economic base of the region. Thus, for example, in the vital commercial strip along Pacific Boulevard in Huntington Park, nearly 50 percent of the business sites were vacant in the mid-1970s. These were businesses that were oriented both culturally and in class terms to higher-wage working-class and middle-class Anglo tastes. When that population left, the businesses collapsed. Businesses that responded to the needs and tastes of the immigrant Latino grew rapidly, and by the early 1980s, the strip was a thriving commercial zone with virtually no vacancies, and became an important site for economic, social, and cultural activity.

Transforming the Public Sphere: The Development of Associative Citizenship

I have proposed that rights claims emerged from a series of networks formed within and between households and civil society to negotiate the effects of restructuring, and that these enabled the development of certain types of rights claims. Understanding the process of the emergence of these rights claims requires tracing the relationship between changes in the macro-level institutions, especially the processes of restructuring, and the quotidian spaces of everyday life within civil society and the household. The Latinos who replaced white working-class folks created a new, vibrant, and quite distinct series of institutional sites of civil society characterized by multiple levels of both thin and thick social networks based on reciprocity and mutuality.[12] Specific rights claims emerged in response to the specific conditions that I have laid out. While the latter provide the institutional context, they do not reveal how the changes in these conditions transformed the lives of Latinos who had to develop strategies for negotiating these and the challenges of maintaining continuity in their identities.[13]

The following discussion will rely on life-history interviews with fifty-one Mexican households who lived in this region, and twenty households from other Latino groups. These were carried out in Los Angeles between 1990 and 1998.[14] But before drawing from the analysis of the interviews, ethnographies, and life histories that document this process of negotiation and development of rights claims, let me summarize some of the key features of the institutional context that I described in the first section of this chapter.

The region of Southeast Los Angeles went through a basic economic, cultural, and demographic change between 1970 and 1990. It went from a majority white working-class area to one with an overwhelmingly Latino population. Between World War II and 1970, the Fordist industries that were located throughout the region produced relatively high-wage, unionized jobs, with extensive single-family neighborhoods, and several midscale commercial areas. Once these plants closed as a result of the regional restructuring process, a majority of the white population left the area and the local economy nearly collapsed. Commercial areas slowly reopened, and even small-scale manufacturing developed throughout the region. But as a result of the type of economic units that replaced the former plants, the labor market changed dramatically. The new jobs were primarily low-wage, nonunion positions with little or no benefits. These jobs were filled overwhelmingly by Latino working-class and immigrant labor with low skill levels, low levels of education, and relatively low incomes, transforming the area into a zone with a high percentage of working poor. A small percentage of residents did secure higher-wage jobs in other sections of the city, and this was reflected in some higher-valued properties scattered throughout the area.

The socioeconomic figures and processes I have detailed so far make clear that most of those who were part of study 1 were working-class Latinos; about two-thirds of these were immigrants, and about 20 percent of them were unauthorized. Economic hardship and even survival was a daily challenge for most of the respondents, the quality of schools in the area was poor, work conditions for many were difficult and tenuous, and most were aware of the anti-Latino movements and sentiments that were clearly evident not only in the media; many experienced firsthand what were essentially racial micro-aggressions and slights in their work, and sometimes in social environments. The effects of restructuring and of transnational linkages were inscribed in the physical spaces of commerce and industry, the cultural sites of sociality, and the spheres of commercial and economic interaction. But to understand how and why these conditions gave rise to the development of rights claims by some of the residents, we need to know how those affected by these processes made sense of these experiences and changes, what meaning they ascribed to them, and how they responded to the effects on themselves.

In the following, I argue that an integral and constitutive dimension of the social and economic configurations that resulted from the transformation that took place in the region was the range of associational practices that developed within civil society, and that some of these activities formed the basis of claims about rights to inclusion, access, or to goods and services in various dimensions of collective life. These were claims that emerged from the specific economic, cultural, and political changes that resulted from the particular ways in which the processes of globalization and restructuring manifested themselves in this region. They arose from, and were rooted in, the strategies developed by households to deal with their particular circumstances or the impact of these changes on its members. It is at this level that we can uncover what the structural changes that we have reviewed and that have transformed these areas mean for those who live in these communities, and thereby get a sense of how this section of Los Angeles is lived in and experienced by Latinos. It is through their stories of the strategies of adaptation, resistance, and accommodation to the processes of restructuring that we see how they created and lived in, and through, the "mediating institutions or sites" of schools, workplaces, households, churches, and how one of those "multiple Los Angeles" has become what it is.

The nature of these rights claims and the processes that give rise to them are reflected in the interviews that focused on the associational practices that took place across a variety of distinct mediating sites in civil society that included informal economy networks, workplace networks, schools, churches, soccer associations, social clubs, women's household networks, various restaurants and clubs, commercial businesses, and swap meets. Despite the differences in these sites, they all were locations where the types of quotidian experiences and networks that enabled rights claims that form the basis of a form of associative citizenship took place. I will discuss the various scenarios to illustrate this process, drawing on the ethnographies, participant observations, and life histories of men and women who lived or had lived in Southeast Los Angeles and other Latino communities, families and households that were interviewed between 1990 and 1998.[15] They reveal some key insights about the process of creating a new community; the multiple ways in which the restructuring processes affected Latinos—some benefiting, some losing everything; about the struggle, full of contradictions, to both engage and resist popular U.S. culture; and finally about what led to the emergence of rights claims.

During that eight-year period, over 90 percent of the residents were Mexican origin, with small pockets throughout the area of Central Americans, Peruvians, Colombians, and Cubans, some of which established small communities of their own, and others that were spread throughout the area. My discussion will rely on life-history interviews with fifty-one Mexican households who lived in this region, and sixteen households from other Latino groups. But in addition to obtaining these life histories, our nine-member research team spent hundreds of hours with different families and household members, accompanying them as they went through different aspects of their daily or weekly routines, including sharing meals; attending weddings, baptisms, funerals, dances, parties, quinceañeras; shopping with them at different markets and commercial sites; eating at many of the small restaurants and food stands in the area; attending meetings of various cultural organizations as well as rotating credit and burial insurance organizations, PTA meetings, and meetings of a Spanish-speaking parents' organization; and making visits to hospitals and doctors' offices, and employment as well as welfare offices.

I review some of the results of this research in two different ways. First I will provide a brief summary of some of the basic general themes that are related to the effect of the restructuring on peoples' lives. While this provides an overview of the range of concerns and perspectives that characterize respondents in these communities, I also present a more in-depth analysis of a range of sites where I conducted extended interviews and ethnographic studies, and that illustrate the qualitative texture of experiences of those Latinos I interviewed, and some of the ways those experiences affected and were affected by broader institutional contexts, and how their rights claims were one of the responses to those conditions.

Thematic Structures

We discovered that while the respondents discussed a broad range of topics and issues in the open-ended dialogues, there were nevertheless certain common themes/concerns that arose out of, and in response to, some of their interactions and activities in specific institutional sites. These themes included immigration experience, education, language, family cohesion, intra-Latino cultural and class divisions, the work ethic, and discrimination. However, while there was a common preoccupation with these themes and issues, there were clear differences on these issues along the dimensions of class, gender, country of origin, length of residence, and generation here. What became apparent to us quickly was the extraordinarily heterogeneous nature of these Latino communities, despite similar economic location. Thus, for example, although it is often assumed that the immigrant experience is probably the same for most Latinos, we found that this was simply not the case.

With regard to that immigrant experience, many different stories were told, but there was in all of them the notion of a break, a disjunction, and shock that resulted from coming to the United States. Even those who had adopted a patriotic stance toward the United States recounted having encountered difficulty with the transition at several levels. Several of them spoke about how they felt that simply because they were Latinos, they had been slighted or discriminated against by non-Latinos; the theme of not feeling like they completely "belonged" was a consistent one. And even native-born Latinos who were critical of immigrants who did not want to assimilate to the new culture still felt a much closer sense of commonality with them and had much more interaction with them than with non-Latinos. And, of course, we found some families, both immigrant and longer-term residents, who were very nationalistic. The form that this nationalism took differed on the basis of immigrant status. Thus, for example, the nationalism of second- and third-generation Latinos tended to rest on a selective version and interpretation of what it means to be Mexican or Cuban or Puerto Rican that normally coincided with memories, often idealized, from a particular period in the past. So we found, for example, some third-generation Mexican-origin residents who complained of Mexico having become so different from what they identified as central to being "Mexican." The practices and symbols that they continued to engage in as an expression of their

Mexican or other Latino identity were often those associated with a previous period. Thus for the generation of those who arrived before 1970, "Mexican" music meant mariachis and trios, not rock or classical. The same occurred with popular culture, courtship practices, and other areas of cultural identification. Yet, there was a basic and common self-identification as Mexican or Latino. Within the household and families, the difference in gender roles was a common and major concern and was key in determining the pattern of responsibilities, rights, and privileges. In some households where the gender relations were defined in traditional male-centric patterns, privileging males in terms of power and rights, the women nevertheless were critical of that practice—although in most cases, they did not express that in front of their male partners. But in most instances, and particularly when women worked outside the home, the assertion of certain claims and expectations about their male partners' responsibilities had clearly been incorporated into the relationship. And they all agreed that the immigrant experience itself, of the women often being alone and having to care for themselves and their children, of being out in the workplace, had changed the gender relations in Latino communities.

The work ethic and education were themes that were often linked and discussed in terms of the requirements for upward mobility. For most of the households we interviewed, the work ethic was simply assumed as a necessity; the identification with this varied in nature according to class differences, but it was a constant for most. Work is seen primarily in instrumental terms. Even the few professionals we interviewed who talked about this, while they tended to feel more pride in their positions, nevertheless mostly shared this instrumental view. And education was clearly linked to a better job. Most families with children emphasized education for their offspring as the key to a better life. Most of the immigrant households felt that they had to sacrifice to ensure that their children would be educated. And they clearly saw the need for education as a means to respond to the changing economic situation and the change in labor demand.

Last, we found a considerable difference and some divisions according to both class and country of origin. The life histories made it clear that there is very little structured and organized interaction between the different Latino groups. And many of those interviewed talked about negative images that some of the groups had of each other. These seem to be rooted not only in the fact that the countries they come from have different histories and traditions, but also in the way their engagement with the United States is viewed. Thus, for example, among the Mexican households, we often found that some respondents saw other Latino groups as "latecomers" who were now reaping the benefits of the struggles of Mexican immigrants to gain access to jobs and to establish new communities, services, etc. On the other hand, Latinos from other countries, but particularly some of the Central Americans, felt that the

Mexicans acted as if they were superior and discriminated against their groups in both subtle and obvious ways. Several argued that this was particularly evident in the workplace, where Mexican foremen, floor leaders, jobbers clearly treated Mexican workers in a preferential way in job assignments, responsiveness to requests and suggestions, and in social interaction. They complained that the Mexicans were clannish, treated members of other groups rudely and disrespectfully. Even those Central Americans who did not share this view were nevertheless very aware of this tension between the two groups.

Some of the families from South America, however, reflected a different view. They seemed much more inclined to view both Mexican and Central American immigrants more in terms of social distance and class standing, or at least self-perception of class standing. Even some who were clearly struggling economically nevertheless tended to think of these groups as being primarily below them in terms of class. But the interesting thing here is that class was not primarily construed in economic terms, but rather reflected a conception based on factors such as social manners, education, and moral values. These South American immigrants reflected the idea that one can be poor but be superior in "class" terms to those with higher economic standing. Several of the respondents talked about "una persona educada," i.e., an educated person. But these references were not to formal education; rather, they alluded to a person who knows how to respect others, fulfills his or her obligations, does not intrude or impose on others, and has both the desire and intellect to *superarse*, to better him- or herself.

These views informed the range of strategies that residents in this region adopted to deal with the conditions that resulted from the processes of restructuring. For each of the groups, these serve as a kind of cultural and networking prism through which the thematic concerns were interpreted and responded to. The variations in class, country of origin, and cultural practices were essentially the resources that each group drew on to develop their particular "common sense" interpretations of their conditions. That is not to say that there was consensus within each group, but rather that the discursive field for each group was shaped by the different types of experiences that I discussed earlier.

Now the rights claims that emerged, and that I will focus on below, developed in a way that drew on the respective discursive fields of each group. That is, the rights claims of each group were articulated using different modes of expression and conceptual framing. Yet the underlying themes are very similar. In each of the following cases, I organize the discussion of these rights claims according to the four dimensions of citizenship that I argued for: membership, inclusion/exclusion, belonging, and racialization. I identify and discuss the thematic(s) that served as the focus of the rights claims, and review the conditions or experiences within specific institutional sites that led to them. But I am not positing that any one factor alone led to the rights claims, but instead that these arose from a constellation of factors in the quotidian location that converged around specific thematics. Reductive, one-dimensional explanations cannot capture this convergence, so instead I identify the interactive situational aspects that result in the rights claims. I will situate each respondent within their set of networks and conditions, and then trace what combination of these factors led to and/or enabled the rights claims.

MODES OF EXCLUSIONARY INCLUSION: SOCIETAL MEMBERSHIP, POLITICAL EXCLUSION, AND RACIALIZED BELONGING

Many of the interviews and observations carried out as part of the fieldwork addressed several of the four components of associative citizenship that I summarized above, but did so in a way that often combined these themes. So there is considerable overlap in the discussions below in terms of the relationships, networks and practices, and sites of civil society that were the basis of the development of rights claims around each dimension. As a result it is difficult to discuss separately the various ways in which the four components of associative citizenship were advanced in the conversations and interviews we were part of. But it is clear that the views, opinions, and perspectives advanced by the respondents and participants in the interviews and conversation converged around the master theme of what I have labeled "exclusionary inclusion." It was also clear that most of them were aware that the experiences and conditions that they confronted were directly related to the process of economic and demographic change that I described earlier in this chapter.

This is reflected in one of the case studies based on participatory research that we carried out in late 1989 and early 1990 in one of the residential communities adjacent to a major section of the principal commercial area of Huntington Park. Over a period of six months, a group of women had extended, ongoing conversations with each other while they waited for their children in front of the grammar school, and among many other topics, discussed issues of lack of access (exclusion), what they perceived as anti-immigrant and anti-Latino political rhetoric and proposed legislation (membership). A common theme was the sense of being made to feel like they were not "Americans," and thus dealt with the issue of not being full members (membership). While they did not focus specifically on racialization, they had several discussions about "whites" who were biased and discriminated against Latinos because of their darker skins and language differences. The link to the restructuring of the region was also clear to several of the women who had been longtime residents of Huntington Park. This is evident in the comments of Florencia, a forty-one-year-old woman who had migrated from El Salvador in 1979. "Since I moved into this neighborhood, things have gotten really bad economically. My cousin, Mauricio, worked with a big plumber company and they paid him pretty good wages. But all of a sudden, they closed the shop and I think they went to Texas. I don't know why but all I know is that he has been out of work since then. He picks up jobs here and there, you know, gardening, construction, but nothing steady. It's almost like the whites (*los blancos*) don't want us to do well, don't want us to be part of their city except to take care of their kids, wash dishes in restaurants, clean buildings, you know?" In the follow-up discussion I had with her, Florencia said that she had applied for citizenship, and although she was aware of the long wait, in her view, even when she became a citizen, that would not change the opinion that whites had of her, or of any of her Latina friends who might become citizens. "I think that they will continue to see us as foreigners no matter what we do, and that they will never think we are like the real Americans." When I asked her why she believed that to be the case, she responded: "Look, you know, I worked in several big houses on the Westside (of Los Angeles) and it was always the same thing. They say sweet things to you, but treat you like a dog, like you are not a person, like you don't have any value (*valor*) as a person. And because they thought I didn't understand English very well, sometimes when I was in one room cleaning, they would be in another and I could hear what they said about the Hispanos—that we were like another race, you know, that we didn't have the same value as human beings as white people. They don't care about us really, they just want people who will work for cheap wages and so they will put up with us being in their houses because of that. But what can you do?—for women like me, those jobs are the only ones we can find."

We see here some of the themes that I have identified as being key elements that manifest themselves in the notion of associative citizenship, and that these are developed in the context of, and in response to, conditions that are a direct result of the pattern of job creation that restructuring caused. In Florencia's view, she and the other women who worked as domestics would always be considered outsiders, never to be accepted as full and equal members of society, even if they became citizens formally. She attributed this in large part to the views that whites had of Latinos as racially and culturally inferior. Attaining full membership was not likely for Latina/os in Florencia's opinion, and the prospect of feeling like they truly belonged to society here was remote as well. But Florencia's views also included an awareness of class differences. She said that although the whites "were the worst" in terms of their views, that many "upper class" ("gente con plata"—people with money) Latinos she had encountered shared similar views of Latino immigrants as inferior.

> They're not much better. They have good jobs, live in nice neighborhoods, and so they think they are better than those of us who can only get the low-paying jobs. But what

they don't realize is that the whites think the same things about them. They think that the whites accept them and think they are as American as the whites, but the truth is that they are fooling themselves. It doesn't matter how much money they have or where they live or that they have good jobs—lawyers, doctors, professionals—they are still not considered good enough. This is wrong—all of it is wrong—we're [Latina/os] here, we work hard, and yes, there are some bad ones among us like in any group, but most of us just want to make a decent living and hope our children can get ahead. So I think we should be accepted for what we add to the country, and that we should be given all the rights like everyone else. When I was in El Salvador, that's what I thought the United States stood for—equal rights and dignity—but once I got here, I realized that was not really the case.

This is clearly the kind of rights claims that is based on the marginalized position that Florencia and her friends occupy.

The conversations the women had eventually led to the creation of an informal network that varied between twenty and twenty-five women. The majority of these women were Latina immigrants from Mexico, with a smaller number from Peru, El Salvador, and Nicaragua. About 25 percent of the women were born and raised in the United States, with several of these being from second-generation families. However, despite their differences, the great majority of all the women had lived in the area for several years, and those in the smaller group that began to meet in their homes on a more regular basis, and to establish stronger linkages, had all known each other for between two and ten years. Their neighborhood activities overlapped considerably—having children in the same schools, attending the same church, frequenting the same park and local restaurants, shopping at the same nearby stores for staple goods—and several visited the same medical clinic that bordered their neighborhood. These women, in other words, shared common experiences that led to the development of ties or bonds of reciprocity, exchanging childcare, washing and ironing, and clothing, especially for growing children; they also shared strategies for coping with low incomes, medical treatments, and securing information about primarily part-time employment. Thus these became fairly thick networks of exchange and reciprocity based on mutuality, familiarity, shared experiences, and a sense of solidarity.

Since the group gatherings originated as social occasions that led to the development of these relations of reciprocity, part of the discourse naturally incorporated themes and issues regarding problems they tended to have in common, either in the present or that they had experienced in the past. These issues clearly were related to their status in low-wage jobs that were created by the specific pattern of economic restructuring I described, and they included such matters as childcare; low income, temporary jobs; household management and budgets; drug- and gang-related problems; poor education; and a consistent concern about the inadequacy of the health care available in the area. And through these discussions, there emerged a shared sense of their economic and political marginalization, which in turn led to critiques, but also to expressions that they were entitled to certain basic rights. These included social rights, but there were also much more direct claims about the right to participate in, or at least have an impact on, the decisions that affected them, their families, and their local communities. And these were directly connected with a sense of not being full and equal members of the society (membership), of a pattern they saw that excluded them and their children from certain types of opportunities and resources (exclusion).

It was clear that their sense of exclusion and disempowerment led them to believe they had the right to make certain claims on the society and political institutions, although obviously not expressed in the formal language of universal human or political rights, and it was the networks of reciprocity and the associative activity that enabled this consciousness to emerge. Expressions of this were found in their efforts, for example, to develop a set of proposals (handwritten as a guide and not a formal document) that they argued for in PTA meetings in their local schools. At one of their gatherings, one of the women indicated that she had read an article in the local newspaper that described proposed redevelopment plans for the area; she pointed out that these did not include any provision for improving local health care, and she was severely critical of the city council for only responding to the interests of the local merchants and economy and not being concerned with addressing the needs of the residents. This led to a relatively short-term but organized campaign to gather support to confront the city council on the matter, which they did at two council meetings. Although they were unsuccessful in their effort to have the health-care issue incorporated in the immediate plans, the visibility of the issue increased among the residents of other neighborhoods and was addressed in a number of church and school-related meetings.

There are three aspects of this case of informal associational activities and networks, which led to what were in effect rights claims about citizenship, that I believe illustrate the relationship between restructuring, civil society, and household-based activities. The processes, practices, and activities that led to the citizenship claims were based on the following characteristics: First, the women organized and became active on a situational basis to improve conditions for their families and their community that were directly a result of the transformation of the region into one of low-wage jobs with no benefits, a falling standard of living, and lower quality of life. Secondly, the participation in the more public and political activities was based on already existing relationships of familiarity, friendship, mutual trust, and solidarity rather than on membership in a formal, organized group. Third, these networks were not based on individualistic contract types of linkages, but instead on the basis of relations of reciprocity that included a network of exchanges of information, labor, various goods and services, food, and emotional and psychological support. The exchanges were not made with the goal of immediate benefits based on reciprocity. Instead the general expectation was that when the reciprocal support was needed, it would be available and be provided.

EDUCATION, EXCLUSION, AND UNEQUAL MEMBERSHIP

Another case in the same general area focused more on the specifics of exclusion and unequal membership that manifested themselves around the theme of education. By the mid-1980s, the school population in this area was overwhelmingly Latino, and most attended severely overcrowded schools. One of the grammar schools had a parents' organization that formed in the mid-1970s and was very active in working with administrators and teachers to address the problems of meeting student needs in a severely limited fiscal situation. Part of this was due to declining tax revenues, but also to the fact that the number of students had grown very significantly and rapidly with no corresponding increase in funds and resources. This increase in student population was a direct result of the pattern of settlement of immigrants in particular that was part of the process of restructuring in the region. Most of the leadership of the association had been elected by the early 1980s and consisted of a number of second- and third-generation Latinas and several Anglo men and women who had been relatively long-term residents of the area. By 1989, there had been no turnover in the leadership in several years, and quite a few continued to be active despite the fact that some of these individuals no longer had students in that school.

As I described earlier, one of the results of the restructuring in this area was a rapid and extensive growth in the Latino immigrant population. Indeed, Huntington Park underwent one of the most dramatic demographic transformations in California between 1970 and 1990. Many of these immigrants were either monolingual Spanish speakers or had difficulty in expressing themselves effectively in English. A group of them had attended the monthly meetings for more than six months despite the fact that they understood only a fraction of the discussions and usually relied on acquaintances to provide them with brief summaries. Since several of the parents already knew each other and had established some overlapping networks, including attending the same churches, using the same recreational spaces, shopping in the same local commercial district, and having regular social functions in their homes, the subject of the poor quality of their children's education came up during these informal gatherings. And they talked about what might be the best strategies for conveying their concerns to the leadership and to school officials, and for facilitating

---

greater participation on their part. During one of these discussions, someone suggested that they make a request that a brief summary of the proceedings be made in Spanish during the meetings so that the Spanish-speaking parents could understand the issues and be able to respond. They subsequently made that request from the audience at the next meeting of the organization, and the response was not only negative, but abusive as well. A number of the board members were indignant that such a request was made at all, and told the petitioners that they had no right even to make this suggestion, adding the none-too-novel opinion that they were in "America" now and needed to learn English, and if they were not so inclined, that they should "go back to where you came from." Only one member of the board, the only male Anglo member of the leadership, suggested that the request had some merit, and indicated that they needed the support of all the parents, and that if this measure promoted that goal, perhaps it should be considered. For over an hour, there was an emotional debate that was joined by the normally passive parents, and there was a clear split in opinions. The measure was finally moved as a formal proposal and rejected by an eight to one vote.

Immediately after that meeting, about a dozen or so of the Spanish-speaking parents met informally in the parking lot and agreed to organize a meeting to discuss how to respond to this situation. About two weeks later, a group of some thirty or so parents met for the first time in one of their homes for what was to be a series of meetings over the next month. Through these dialogues, they concluded that rather than try to fight the board of the existing association, they should form their own organization of Spanish-speaking parents, which they called Padres para la Promoción de Educación (Parents for the Promotion of Education). Within a year, their meetings, which moved to one of the small meeting rooms at the school, were regularly attended by more than thirty parents, a considerably larger group than those who attended the meetings of the original association. And as a result of a series of meetings with school officials and teachers, they were able to participate much more effectively in the education of their children.

As was the case with the informal associational activity of the women's group discussed earlier, the activities that at least the leaders of this group engaged in, to address the type and quality of education of their children, emerged from informal associational relations that already existed. Networks were based on the same factors of trust, friendship, common experiences, and exchange relations, although the particular configuration and content of these were different from those of the women's group. Some of the men had worked together, others were members of a soccer association, and several spent time helping each other with household projects or repairs. And several of the families knew each other through their common membership in a patriotic cultural association of individuals from the state of

Michoacán in Mexico, which sponsored a variety of activities, such as dances and parties, fundraisers, citizenship-qualifying courses, and counseling on amnesty and other immigration-related issues. In the course of their meeting to form this alternative association, the discussions clearly revolved around the assertion of their having certain rights despite the fact that most were not formal citizens. This was a theme that was consistently reiterated in different ways and registers, but the main rationale, although not articulated in these terms, was that they had a stake in their communities, and their welfare, and particularly that of their children, required their participation in those decisions that affected them collectively. The underlying concern was essentially what I have called "exclusionary belonging"—they were allowed to attend the meetings, but not allowed to participate based on the normative criteria of language. They were clearly aware that a majority of the leadership of the association did not consider them to be full and equal members. One of the women summarized the kinds of citizenship claims that emerged from this sense of marginalization in the following statement made at one of the initial meetings.

> All of us came to this country to work for a better life for ourselves and our children. And we do work, I have never asked for welfare or any help from the government and I know that is true of most of you as well. So I don't see why we were told to go back to Mexico. This is our community, we work here, we keep their business going because we buy from them, so I am not a foreigner here. We keep this community alive, it depends on us, without us to do their work and to pay rent and buy houses, what would happen to them? And I believe that because we are the community, we have every right to make sure that our desires are considered by these people who are making decisions about not only our children's education but about so many other things as well. I may not be a citizen but as long as I don't ask anything from anyone and don't harm or bother anyone else, I don't deserve the insults we heard at that meeting. I'm proud of what my husband and I have accomplished here, and no matter what, we are human beings who deserve respect and that we have a right to be part of the decisions that affect us.

These two examples illustrate the existence in Latino communities of precisely the kind of associational practices, activities, and values, located within the sites of civil society, that are concerned with the welfare of the entire community, and thus constitute a community public sphere based on the notion of rights claims. And in both cases, those informal associational practices and networks were the enabling conditions for the development of these rights claims. The deliberations that characterized the kinds of gatherings and meetings I have described fit the criteria proposed by those that argue for the need for revitalizing the public sphere. These activities were a coming together of members of a community to discuss and debate what constitutes the collective "good" for them, and they did so not primarily on the basis of narrow self-interest, but based on a concern with the quality of life for the entire community. They were, in other words, engaged in promoting collective democratic participation as a means to consider what was in the collective interest. But even more importantly, for the argument I am making here, there are social preconditions that existed that allowed these activities and the rights claims to emerge. Without the networks based on mutuality, common experience, reciprocal relations, solidarity, and friendship that already existed, it is unlikely that the kind of public action and the new claims to citizenship would have emerged. These qualitative relations in effect served an enabling function for the assertion of these rights claims and practices of an emerging type of citizenship.

ON THE STREET/IN THE "HOUSE": CONTEXT, NETWORKS OF MUTUALITY, AND RIGHTS CLAIMS

It was not only within the kinds of formats that I have described above that the enabling function of associational networks based on mutuality, reciprocity, and trust was evident. Rights claims that were advanced in interviews and ethnographic studies across a range of other sites of civil society were also enabled by these networks. Despite the differences in context and type of site, the common factor in these rights claims was that they were grounded in the interactional pattern with others in these networks that reflected the conditions of exclusion, unequal membership, racialization, and a sense of not belonging to the dominant society. And all of these networks were formed in response to conditions created by restructuring. The activities that took place at swap meets, restaurants, pool halls, soccer games, commercial areas, recreational sites, all were part of strategies of survival and adaptation that individuals, families, and households developed to negotiate the conditions created by low wages, poor infrastructure, lack of or inferior social services, limited health care, and ineffective education. In the following, I discuss some of the themes, networks, and rights claims that surfaced from conversations and interviews that were more spontaneous and took place in sites where individuals, families, and groups of friends engaged in the activities of everyday life.

Swap meets are one of the sites in Latino communities, particularly those with large immigrant communities, where larger numbers of residents congregate to shop for bargains. But trips to these places have also become something of a social event, involving affirmation of friendship ties, collaborative commercial purchases, eating traditional Latino foods, extensive discussions, and playful exchanges. Some of the youth also pursue their romantic interests while engaging in a range of activities. Our research team visited a number of these events within the cities we studied a number of times, and I continued to do so for a few years after we completed the formal fieldwork. This was part of our ethnographic work intended to discover how the conditions created by the restructuring were being lived by the residents. In the course of these studies, we engaged numerous merchants and shoppers and had extensive conversations with many of them. While I would not categorize these as equivalent to the more formal interviews we carried out in offices, homes, and other locales, they nevertheless provided a vibrant sense of what the residents' daily lives were like, how they negotiated their economic-margin status, as well as what the nature of their associational networks were like. One merchant, Francisco, had been setting up shop most weekends for several years in the swap meet in Huntington Park and sold a variety of household goods, garments, and some small furnishings. He was from originally from Manzanillo, a port city on the Pacific Coast of Mexico. He came to the United States without papers in 1976, at the age of eighteen, but was in the process of trying to obtain documents and hoped to eventually become a U.S. citizen. I had several extended discussions with Francisco at the swap meet over a period of four months, and eventually he agreed to an interview with us; we met in his home on three different occasions. He had completed a dozen or so classes at El Camino, a community college nearby, and was particularly interested in politics, history, and sociology. In addition to his own experience, he provided a range of insights about the concerns of many of the merchants that he had worked with for some time. He talked about the informal networks that they had, and indicated that they developed strategies and practices for coordinating some business efforts that relied heavily on mutuality, trust, and reciprocity. Although the merchants initially joined these networks because of economic self-interest, they quickly found the groups to be a resource beyond that concern. I was fortunate to attend six of these social gatherings, where an average of about a dozen of Francisco's fellow merchants gathered for socializing, but also engaged in discussions of community and political issues that they all had some interest in. These were apparently ongoing discussions and reflected some of the personal experiences that seemed to have had a strong effect on their ideological perspectives. They had been meeting for a little over three years, with attendance varying each time. The group expressed considerable interest in the research project, and I found them to be most eager to share their views on a range of themes and topics. After I described the general purpose of the research project, and the four dimensions that eventually became the basis of the notions of associative citizenship (although at that time I had not yet begun to call it that), they discussed their views regarding each of those elements while eating, drinking, and telling stories. These were not structured interviews and were much more a dialogical engagement with a good deal of give and take. But they understood that I was interested in their stories as part of my research project, and that the focus centered on the broad issues of citizenship and marginalization. There was a range of views, some reflecting the fact that a majority of them were immigrants, primarily from Mexico; but there were also several native-born participants, as well as two individuals from El Salvador, one from Honduras, and another from Nicaragua. The issues of citizenship and belonging were particularly prominent themes in these discussions. Most of the merchants believed that the United States provided much better economic opportunities than their countries of origin, but that it exacted a heavy personal price from those who migrated to take advantage of those. In response to a question I asked about what they believed their prospects were to become integrated into U.S. society, Mauricio, who sold linens and rugs, said the following:

> I have been here seventeen years, have lived in several cities, but they might as well all have been the same. Everywhere I've lived, whenever I worked with or had other dealings with "Americanos" [by which he meant most native-born residents], they always made me feel like an outsider, like I really didn't belong here. I've had some gringos tell me that to my face. And it has to be because we look different, we're darker and they don't care for people like us. I stay because I am able to make enough money to take care of my family and help my kids go to school so that they will have a better life later. But I see that even they don't seem to be accepted very much. And look at the news—every day you hear about anti-Latino stories. The only thing you can conclude is that racism against Latinos is very strong here. I don't think that we will ever be accepted as being true Americans—even the ones born here are always going to be thought of as foreigners. Yes, I'm trying to get my citizenship, but that's just for practical reasons—not because I think I'll be accepted any better.

I asked the others what they thought about Mauricio's view. One of the women in the group, Elsie, who sold Mexican food at the swap meet and was born in El Paso, said:

> Unfortunately, I think Maurie is right—I've lived here most of my life and have never felt at home [belonging]. Only when I lived on the border in El Paso as a child did I feel like I was part of the community. Well, of course, it was mostly Mexicans who lived there anyhow. I guess that's why. But once I left, in a lot of places it was like being a stranger in my own country. I've worked cleaning buildings, and in a restaurant on the Westside, and I think because I'm very light, customers don't think I'm Mexican, so they sometimes say things I don't think they would say if they knew. I hear them talk about us like we don't belong here; they even think the ones born here are below them. I hear some of our people talk about rights—but I don't think we have them the same way whites have them. It makes me very angry that we don't have those rights even though we deserve

them; if you work hard, don't get into trouble, pay taxes, and obey the laws, we deserve those rights—but we won't get them unless we fight for them.

In this case, although they did not engage in political action, they nevertheless were asserting rights claims based on a sense of marginalization, on not feeling as if they were accepted as "true" Americans, and on their belief that it was white racism, if not supremacy, that was the primary cause of what they perceived as "anti-Latino" beliefs and practices. What is key to note here, however, is that with the exception of Francisco, none of the other merchants had really formed clear views of these issues before the informal gatherings that eventually led to the discussions. Although I joined the group after they had been meeting for nearly three years, the members recounted over several meetings how they got together and how the tenor of the gatherings had changed, as well as some of the changes they each had undergone as a result of the engagements with each other. They described the development of bonds of trust and mutuality, and then reciprocity that was incorporated in their activities—including the lending of small amounts of money when cash was short, creating a basic rotating credit arrangement, and providing labor for one another as need be. This reciprocity eventually evolved to include personal relationships and activities, such as birthdays, funerals, weddings, etc. It became clear both from the recounting of the past and from the interaction I witnessed that Francisco was the catalyst for the development of a more critical set of political views among the group members. Although this situation does not exactly fit the Freirian model of consciousness-raising, Francisco's role seemed to parallel that of the facilitator in the Freirian approach. He continuously raised questions about issues that the group members had to engage in their daily pursuits, proposed critical perspectives and interpretations, and encouraged the others to share their views and opinions.

In this case, the networks of relations based on mutuality, trust, and reciprocity enabled the development of the kind of discourse about public affairs and current political issues, about collective concerns that affected the entire community, that works on the public sphere discuss theoretically. These ongoing sessions were in effect "schools of democratic discourse" through which each of the members came to develop a fairly critical political perspective. In their informal gatherings, there were consistent references and spontaneous discussions and debates regarding specific matters that were ultimately related to the elements of associative citizenship: membership, belonging, and racialization. Over a period of several months, it became apparent that much of this discourse converged around the theme of exclusionary inclusion or belonging, and that various forms of rights claims emerged as strategies for confronting the many ways in which this pattern was maintained.

Without the enabling social relations established through these networks, it is unlikely that any of these merchants would have come to see their world and experiences in the critical political way that was reflected in their exchanges. Much of the theoretical work on democratic theory and the role of associations in the public sphere focuses on the discursive interaction within formal associations or formats, and completely ignores the role of the kinds of relations and networks described here, which enable the development of politically salient views and beliefs among marginalized populations. These instances should alert us to the fact that there is a great deal of the kind of political education that is often cited as necessary for democratic societies that takes place within these informal associational relations and networks, and that can illuminate much about the processes involved in the development of politicized critical consciousness.

"HOUSE" MATTERS

The working of similar processes, and the central role of informal relations and networks of mutuality and reciprocity in the emergence of prefigurative rights claims, can be found at the level of analysis that focuses on the household. To illustrate how this occurs, I will discuss the specific experiences of one of the households that gave rise to those practices and claims. I focus on how members of this family, and several of those in their networks, became aware that conditions that are initially often experienced as personal were in fact public, collectively shared challenges and led them to assert rights claims, and that this process was enabled by networks of mutuality and reciprocity.

The first household was a Mexican immigrant extended family of seven that at the time of our study included a married couple, Mario Najera (forty-three) and Lucia (thirty-six); three daughters, Maria Luisa (fifteen), Isabel (thirteen), and Nancy (three); a son, Daniel (nine); and Lucia's aunt, Gloria (forty-eight), who had been part of the household for four years. They lived in Huntington Park for ten years, and before that in South Central Los Angeles for three years. Mario and Lucia married in 1974 in Uruapan in the state of Morelia, Mexico. At the time of their marriage, Mario was twenty-three and Lucia was sixteen. In 1977, Lucia secured a work permit with the help of a businessman in Los Angeles who had been a boyhood friend of her father. She came to Los Angeles in late 1977 and stayed with the family of a man from her neighborhood who had immigrated to the United States in 1971 and at that time lived in Norwalk. His wife helped find Lucia a job as a domestic, and she later went to work in a garment factory in downtown Los Angeles. Mario crossed the border illegally in 1978 and joined Lucia. He found work in a small neighborhood market in South Central Los Angeles, and they rented their own apartment there later that year. Since Mario had worked for several years as a butcher in Mexico, in 1985 he was able to secure a fairly high-wage job in a small but busy meat-processing plant in an area close to Huntington Park. Although Lucia stopped working at the factory several times during her pregnancies, she nevertheless continued to work at home, taking in washing and ironing, and at one point she sewed clothes for neighbors and friends. With their combined incomes, Mario and Lucia were able to save enough to purchase a small home in Huntington Park in 1984.

However, in 1990, a national meat-processing plant, reflecting a trend of the process of restructuring, bought out the firm where Mario worked and restructured the business. Meat was no longer prepared and cut at the facility, which instead served primarily as a retail outlet. The butcher positions were eliminated, and of a twenty-six-member work crew, only eight were offered a position with the new firm. The primary work was now the packaging of meat that was cut and prepared in a central plant in the San Fernando Valley. As a butcher, Mario had made nearly $15 per hour, with plenty of overtime, but his new position paid only $6.40 per hour and no overtime. His annual income was reduced by nearly two-thirds. Although angry at first, Mario came to consider himself fortunate to have been one of the workers who were kept on the job, especially since he was unable to find a job as a butcher anywhere else. This experience had a fundamental impact on the Najera household. Only a few weeks before the firm was sold, the husband of Lucia's aunt, Gloria, was killed, and she was left in Mexico without any means of support. The Najeras opened their home to her, and at the time they felt that her living with them would not impose any significant economic hardship. But with the reduction in Mario's income, an additional member in the household placed greater strain on an already difficult situation.

The Najeras had a difficult time meeting all of their financial obligations, and at one point had fallen behind in their house payment. As a result, they asked Gloria to find work so that she could contribute to the family income. She worked at several low-wage jobs, and even fifteen-year-old Maria Luisa took a part-time job in a card shop in Huntington Park. The family discussed the possibility of moving to either San Jose, California, or Las Vegas, Nevada, where friends living there indicated that better-paying work was available. But they were reluctant to leave the life they had established during the previous fifteen or so years. Despite the impact the reduced income had on the household, the Najeras nevertheless maintained the network of social and cultural activities and practices they had established during their time in Los Angeles. In addition to family friends, both Mario and Lucia had separate networks organized around their activities outside the household. For Mario, this revolved around his membership in a soccer club, which he helped organize in 1982. At least twice a week, and often more, he attended practices, games, meetings, or just "hung out" with club members. In the late 1980s, Mario, alone, began to attend dances sponsored by the civic club of "Morelia" in Huntington Park.

Lucia's activities outside the home centered on her involvement since 1989 in a Spanish-speaking parents' association that was organized to promote greater involvement of Latino parents in educational issues. A general meeting was held once a month, but Lucia attended more informal neighborhood meetings held in homes two or three times a month. The Najeras' story illustrates many of the realities that restructuring promoted, and their pattern of experiences and activities revealed aspects of other sectors of Latino Los Angeles. For example, both of the jobs that Mario held were created by firms who serviced the expanding Latino population in the area. The higher-wage job with a larger firm was atypical of the type of positions normally created during the deindustrialization of the area. Eventually, however, that job too succumbed to the same logic of restructuring, albeit in a different sector. One of the explicit goals of the restructuring process was to develop strategies to replace higher-paying, unionized jobs with lower paying, nonunionized ones. This is exactly what dramatically altered the Najera household. His job as a butcher in a unionized plant provided Mario with a relatively high wage and health and unemployment benefits. However, the firm that took it over circumvented the union and offered no benefits whatsoever. So not only was Mario's direct wage cut by over half; when the value of the lost benefits is added, Mario's income was in effect reduced by nearly 75 percent.

The Najeras' decision to settle in Huntington Park was also directly related to the process of restructuring that transformed the region. The flight of both large- and small-scale firms and businesses, and the large-scale movement of established households that resulted, created a drop in property values that made homes in the region much more affordable than in most other residential areas of Los Angeles. In addition, by the time the Najeras decided to buy a home, the residents of this section of Southeast Los Angeles were predominantly immigrant Latinos, so that they felt that the social environment was a familiar one, offering a full range of services, stores, and commercial outlets staffed by predominantly Spanish-speaking Latinos.

Another dramatic difference brought about by the change in the family's economic position was apparent in the area of medical care. Before the buyout, Mario's company contributed $70 a month for a group medical-insurance plan with a Kaiser HMO. This program covered the entire family, except Gloria, and as a result the Najeras worried little about getting relatively good-quality, quick medical care for themselves, but most importantly for their children. With the loss of Mario's medical benefits and the significant decrease in family income, family illness required seeking medical care at Harbor General County Hospital, where charges for medical care were based on income. I accompanied Lucia and her young daughter, Nancy, on one of their visits there and discovered yet another dire reality that thousands of Latinos must confront daily. Nearly three-fourths of the patients in the visibly overcrowded waiting room were Latinos, a large proportion of them children. Informal discussions I initiated with hospital staff and other patients revealed that waiting periods of six hours were not uncommon, that the staff was understaffed by nearly 30 percent, that caseloads exceeded capacity by nearly 50 percent. In this particular instance, we arrived at 9:30 A.M., but Nancy, obviously in great discomfort from a serious bout with the flu, was not seen by a physician until nearly 1:30 that afternoon. By the time Nancy had some lab work done and was seen once again by the doctor, and then had a prescription filled at the hospital pharmacy, it was 3:45 P.M. This is apparently not uncommon. Both Lucia and other patients I spoke with indicated that they expected to spend most of the day at the hospital whenever they sought medical care there.

Another of Mario and Lucia's worries concerned their children's education. Until 1991, both their young daughters, Maria Luisa and Isabel, attended a nearby Catholic school. While the Najeras believed that the girls would receive a much better education there, their real concern seemed to be for their children not to be exposed to gangs, drugs, and violence at the overcrowded public schools in the area. However, they were forced to transfer their children from the Catholic school because they simply could no longer afford the tuition. This continued to be one of the more painful experiences for the Najera family. Both parents constantly worried about their children while they attended school, and Lucia, in particular, was quite bitter about the situation. The considerable time I spent accompanying the adult members of the household as they went about their various activities revealed a great deal about the social and cultural life that the emerging Latino communities in the area had established. Since many of those in the area worked on Saturdays, Sunday was family day, and on several occasions, I was invited to go along with the Najeras. They indicated that their routine was fairly typical for other Mexican families in the area. And indeed, my work with other such households revealed that this seemed to be the case.

After breakfast, the family attended early Mass at a church where nearly all the other worshipers were Latinos. Then they would either visit friends or go shopping. Lucia indicated that before the change in the family's economic fortunes, they would have headed for the mile-long commercial shopping strip on Pacific Boulevard to buy clothing or small household items, etc. But on these days, they were much more likely to spend the next couple of hours at the nearby permanent swap meet in Vernon. The latter is extremely crowded, with mostly families, and resembles the *mercados*, or marketplaces, found in Mexico—much more than the traditional swap meet. Stalls are located both inside two warehouse-like buildings and on the grounds surrounding them. Nearly every type of conceivable item can be purchased here: plumbing supplies, tools, all sorts of clothing, auto parts, appliances, even car and life insurance. And the smells of homemade Mexican and Central American food from what seem to be dozens of food stands and stalls permeate the entire area. While Mario and the children seemed to enjoy these outings, Lucia constantly complained about the noise, the crowds, the disorder, the inferior quality of the merchandise, and frequently lamented not being able to afford to shop either on Pacific Boulevard or at the mall, as she used to. And while a few years back, they would have had lunch at one of the area's restaurants, they now eat at one of the much less expensive food stalls.

The networks and pattern of activities that were a fundamental aspect of the quotidian reality of the Najeras played a vital role in the development of strategies to negotiate the change in the their economic status brought about by restructuring. They also became the medium through which they began to develop a more coherent and clear sense of political ideology that eventually resulted in a form of rights claims. Mario recounted over a series of interviews that he had never had even the slightest interest in anything political until he lost his job and there was a dramatic change in his family's economic well-being. While he occasionally read *La Opinion*, the major Spanish-language newspaper in Southern California, and watched the *noticieros* (Spanish-language news programs) in the evenings, his attention was primarily on social and sports news. However, several of his associates, in both the soccer league and the hometown association that were part of his network, had also experienced loss of jobs or reduction in wages, and a general downturn in their economic status. In 1994, I accompanied Mario to several of his gatherings with these associates and had the opportunity to engage in a number of open-ended, unstructured conversations with a group that varied from six to twelve participants. They were aware that I was engaged in research on the community and knew that I had spent considerable time with Mario at soccer games, Sunday afternoon *carne asadas* (BBQ), and visits to events sponsored by the hometown association. So I was able to raise direct questions about their views on a range of politically salient issues, and on how they coped with the challenges in their lives that were related directly to the consequences of difficult economic situations. They indicated that many of their views had both developed and changed as a result of the many discussions they had as part of their social gatherings, over the previous two years in particular. It was evident that an essential part of the bond they had developed had resulted not only from these social get-togethers, but also because they had established relations of reciprocity in a number of areas. They shared considerable time helping each other in house and car-related repairs; they lent or traded various household and work-related items, and even lent each other money on occasion.

This level of familiarity and trust was a key element that led to their willingness to take each other's views seriously, and to engage each other in a semi-dialogical exchange of perspectives and opinions. And once I opened up the theme of how they saw themselves within the structure of U.S. society, many of their views were quite critical of the degree to which they believed they and their children could gain equal membership and standing in this society. One of the participants, Felipe, reviewed his path to coming to the United States and indicated that in his case, he had been motivated not only by the prospect of economic benefits, but also by his disgust with what he saw as a corrupt Mexican political system. He initially believed that the United States was different and that there would be great levels of equality and "justice" here. However, he said that after living in the U.S. for nearly thirteen years, his experiences here had led to great disillusionment, and he believed that the only way for Latinos to make progress was to "fight for fairness and justice." Others in the group articulated similar positions, all of which had emerged through the long-term discussions that they had engaged in for quite some time. What emerged were themes that touched on each of the four components of associative citizenship. On one occasion, the following was related by Tiburcio, who had lost a job in a local factory, was surviving as a day laborer, and was indignant over the fact that his wife, who had a green card, had recently been detained in an immigration raid at the shop where she worked.

> I thought that if we worked hard, obeyed the law, and respected our neighbors, that we would become part of the American dream. But look at what happened to my wife—all she was doing was working, and working very hard—and still they took her and treated her like a criminal just because she is Mexican. When she told one of the agents carrying out the raid that she had papers, she said that he told her that it didn't matter because they were probably fake. Now is that an example of the famous "American justice" that they claim exists? Clearly no. I have worked many jobs in houses in the best parts of L.A., like Beverly Hills, Pacific Palisades, you know, where all those people look to me like they are rich. And you should see the way they treat Latino workers. I was talking one day with a Mexicana that cleaned houses up there and she told me that she despised the people she worked for because she heard them say so many terrible things about us. So I don't think that Hispanos will ever be accepted by the "gringos." I know that some Mexicans born here now have money and good jobs, but I doubt that they are accepted as equals by their white co-workers. Why? Because they are basically racist against Latin Americans. The darker you are, the worse they treat you. I hear groups talking about human rights all over the world, but they should look at the lack of human rights right here in the United States. For many of us, even if you have papers, and even some who

are born here, if you are Latin American, you don't have the same rights—you're always made to feel like you are more foreign than other immigrants.

In the follow-up discussion, I asked Tiburcio when he came to hold these views. He indicated that while he had found some of what he considered negative behavior and beliefs offensive, he initially saw it as being a function of ill manners (*mal edu-cados*). However, once he began noticing that nearly all of his coworkers and friends had similar experiences, and shared some of his own reactions, he started to think that something more basic was involved, that the problem might be "the system" (*el sistema*). And he stated that those views became much clearer and coherent through the discussions he had engaged in with the group that was the central aspect of his personal networks. He and the others now shared a more generalized view that at least as far as Latinos were concerned, there was a fundamental problem of injustice and unfairness in U.S. society. The group clearly saw racialization that led to a sense of superiority as one of the major causes.

As mentioned before, Lucia had her own network of associates drawn from both her workplace and the parent organization at the school where her children were enrolled. The role that gender issues played in the development of Lucia's political views was clearly evident both in beliefs and network activities. The two sets of experiences that had the greatest influence on her were the harsh conditions involved in her work, both as a domestic and garment-factory worker, and her experience with school administrators as a member of a parent group. During three different lengthy interviews with Lucia, it was clear that her overriding concern was with both the immediate and long-term welfare of her children, and that she saw education as the key to the latter in particular. She indicated that her political views, and particularly her willingness to speak out in the parents' organization, evolved over a period of several years, and that her network of coworkers and friends had played a basic role in the formation of those views. The core of Lucia's perspective was the belief that the educational system in the United States was very unequal and was designed primarily for the benefit of the wealthy and more privileged families, particularly whites. But the groundwork for her view that the U.S. had a "double standard" for whites and Latinos developed initially in her experiences as a domestic. Lucia stated that

> In almost every house I cleaned, the owners treated me as if I didn't exist, like the only value I had for them was like I was a machine that cleaned their house. I didn't know before then that Mexicans were treated so poorly here. I thought that the U.S. was a place where equality was valued, but it is not. On our long bus ride from here to the other side

of town, my companions said that there were a few people that treated them well, but mostly the people they worked for had no respect for them and that they just didn't like Mexicans at all. They don't seem to realize that we don't do this work because we like it, but only because the low-paying jobs are the only ones that they will give us. That's why I want my kids to go to college, so that they will be able to get better jobs.

This concern led Lucia to begin attending parent group meetings at the grammar school where one of her daughters was enrolled. She established close relationships with a small group of women who were also active for basically the same reason, at first primarily social and economic. As was the case with her husband, these relationships were based on mutuality and reciprocity, with the women exchanging a variety of things, from baby clothes to household and food items; eventually this became a basic part of their way of negotiating their low-income status. They had begun to meet informally in their homes for social gatherings, but the main topic of discussion in most cases was what they considered the poor quality of the education their children were receiving. They believed that the best teachers, the best materials, and the best resources were to be found in the schools where the wealthy lived. Through their discussions and conversations, where each recounted various stories of schools they had seen in other parts of town, or that they heard about from others, they came to the conclusion that the inequality was not an accident. They felt that schools in wealthier areas were designed to prepare those children for college and better jobs, while the schools in their area were primarily meant to provide inferior education, since children in these areas were expected to become low-wage workers and so did not need the better resources. Lucia said:

That's why I have to fight for my children's education. The three girls are going to have even a greater challenge because they are girls, and from what I've seen, the better paying jobs go to men. And, you know, my girls are very dark so that's even a bigger problem since the whites don't like dark people. I have to make sure that we claim the right to a good education as a right that everyone who wants their children to advance can have. Talking with my friends, and seeing how the administrators only make excuses for poor education, makes me realize that we have to *claim these rights*, that they will not give them to us unless we struggle for them. This way, our children will have an equal chance to become a real part of the United States. They [whites] have to change their view of us because we are going to be the ones they depend on in the future; they have to begin to see that we are just as good as they are, that we are Americans too.

While I have reviewed only a few conversations in different venues where various types of rights claims developed, there were many more instances of similar stories and responses that we found in the study of dozens of households, and in many of the more impromptu conversations and discussions carried out during the ethnographic studies.[16] The four elements of associative citizenship were not referred to in all these instances, and in many cases, only one of those themes was touched on. Nevertheless, in the majority of cases, the views and beliefs that led to the articulation of the rights claims were forged within the network of relations based on mutuality, trust, and reciprocity that they relied on to meet the conditions of economic marginality. Those networks, in other words, were the key element in enabling the development of rights claims. While the samples of Latino life in Los Angeles presented here reveal a limited range of the experience of residents of these new communities, they nevertheless are not unique to these particular households. Similar patterns of economic strategies, and of cultural and social practices, were found in other households included in studies one and two described in the appendix. These summaries have been presented to illustrate how some of the larger-scale structural changes are incorporated in the texture of everyday life of those who struggle with the impact of decisions and processes they have little control over—and who, despite this fact, nevertheless devise strategies to realize their hopes and aspirations.

The Immigrant Rights Movement and Latino Politics Post–9/11

The parameters within which Latino citizenship is viewed completely changed after the events of 9/11. Despite the fact that no Latinos were implicated, nor was the border with Mexico involved, the issue of Latino immigration was reconfigured as the primary field of contestation regarding the citizenship status of Latinos. The study of Southeast Los Angeles in the first section of this chapter occurred during the 1990s, before the emergence of the "war on terror" that has reframed the issue of immigration as one of national security. This had a profound effect on Latino immigrants, but also had an important impact on Latinos more generally. As a result, this new context shifted the parameters for the discourses regarding issues of citizenship, and has affected the form and extent of practices and policies of marginalization and exclusion, as well as the political terrain and the nature of contesting these new parameters. However, although the political context changed substantially after 9/11, many of the practices that fall within the notion of associative citizenship, as I detailed in the studies of Southeast Los Angeles and other sites throughout the region, were central to the mobilizations that led to the immigrant-rights marches that took place in the spring of 2006.

How is it that immigration came to be linked to the issue of national security in a way that led to draconian measures against Latino immigrants? When the attacks of 9/11 occurred, the issue of Latino immigration was already a central aspect of the national political discourse, and there was clear and intense polarization around the issue. The debates and divisions over the amnesty bill of 1986 brought the issue of Latino immigration to the political forefront, and ever since, it has been a divisive and contested political battleground. What 9/11 did was to provide a political rationale to justify a shift toward much harsher measures and treatment of Latino immigrants by linking the issue to one of national security. This shift manifested itself in a variety of ways, but clearly the issue of "border security" became a linchpin in the strategy of the anti-immigration forces that has been used time and again to undermine serious efforts at fair and just immigration reform.

Let me recall the reasons that Latino immigration initially became a major factor in reshaping the racial composition of the nation. The tremendous growth of Latino communities that transformed the Los Angeles region after 1970 was due in large measure to the increase in Mexican immigration, one of the consequences of the restructuring policies adopted throughout the economic sector. The two related restructuring strategies that had the most direct effects were, first, the closing of large industrial manufacturing plants throughout the region, but particularly in Southeast Los Angeles, and second, the efforts to replace high-wage, unionized labor with low-wage workers. Together, these created a shift in the labor market, and job creation was heavily skewed toward nonskilled and semiskilled low-wage labor. The domestic labor force initially refused to settle for these jobs, and so in effect a labor shortage was created. The availability of these positions was one of the primary catalysts for rapid and large-scale migration of Mexican and later Central American wage laborers to the area. Immigrants initially moved into the existing Mexican communities in the region, but these were unable to accommodate the large numbers that arrived in such a short period of time. Thus began the steady transformation of neighborhoods and communities from white working-class and African American residents into predominantly Mexican and Central American enclaves, with the Latino population increasing dramatically. This pattern of transformation was soon repeated throughout the country, including areas where no Latino communities had ever existed. All this brought about dramatic changes in the economic realities and the social and cultural base of the entire Los Angeles region and the state of California. The processes of restructuring and the pattern of dynamic growth of Latino communities throughout the Los Angeles region not only transformed the region's social and cultural landscapes, but also completely reconfigured the political and policy agenda. The growth of Latino communities was largely driven by immigration, and it was the latter that became the focal point of new tensions, divisions, and conflicts that transformed the political landscape.

While many of the divisions and conflicts still reflected more traditional economic and political differences, it was really the cultural "foreignness" apparent in the changing faces of Los Angeles that aroused the most passionate hostilities, and that manifested itself in some of the issues that define the new political agenda. Although he was addressing a different specific concern, Mike Davis nevertheless outlined what I believe are the central issues that developed at the core of the new politics of Los Angeles (Davis 1992). Each of these has evolved from the consequences of the type of structural changes described throughout this chapter, but all revolve around the issue of immigration and the growth in Latino communities. Even those issues that appear to be more traditional political concerns, such as taxes, crime, electoral responsiveness, etc., are mediated and framed in a way that is related to the impact of immigration. Every election since the 1986 immigrant amnesty bill was adopted has simply served to confirm this.

The first issue, the growth in the number of working poor, arises from the impact of restructuring on lower-income working-class communities and the growth in the Latino immigrant population. While this has not affected Latinos exclusively, they have been disproportionately impacted because of the large percentage of them who work in the very low-wage jobs, with no health-care benefits, created by the restructuring process in the service and manufacturing sectors of the local economy. And the majority of adult Latinos do work. About 81.7 percent of Latino males and 56.3 percent of Latina females participate in the labor force. Nevertheless, a majority of the households we interviewed had an annual income of less than $20,000, despite the fact that in 75 percent of them, two or more individuals worked. While not officially poor according to the federal government's standards, households that fall in this category are clearly struggling economically.[17] The political significance of this increase in the numbers of Latino working poor was made clear in the comments of several of our respondents who fell into this category. They indicated that when an entire household works and still has difficulty affording the basics of housing, food, clothing, and health care, they have little reason to believe that they can achieve any economic or social mobility, or feel any loyalty to, or stake in, the existing system. And the kind of cuts in social, educational, and health services that have characterized state and local programs for the last few years will simply exacerbate this perception.

The second issue is the intensification of racial and ethnic hostility and conflict. If there were any doubts about whether this had any significance for politics or the policy agenda, the campaigns that were waged for and against Proposition 187 surely should serve to dispel them. Despite denials from proponents of the measure, it was perceived by the majority of Latinos as a racially motivated proposal. Several of our respondents pointed out that it was not Canadians, Russians, or Middle Easterners illegally in this country that were the object of hostility. Rather, they argued, it is precisely the phenomena we have examined here, the dramatic growth in the number of Latinos and their pervasive presence throughout the region, that prompted the support for the measure. The proposition provided the opportunity and mechanism to tap into a level of resentment that had been building for some time. Although the measure was overturned by the courts, it nevertheless revealed that immigration was a political lightning rod and was an indication that the political agenda would become even more racially polarized.

The last issue, however, is what I believe is the crux of the matter. It concerns the very meaning of citizenship and community. While the proponents of anti-immigrant measures presented their arguments in terms of economics, jobs, and the costs of social services, what was really at stake was what it means to be a member of a community, which is what citizenship is intended to define. As I pointed out in chapter 3, the literature on citizenship reveals that there are different and competing ideas of how to conceptualize membership. In the context of considering the impact of newly arrived immigrants, it was clear that anti-immigrant groups sought to frame the issue in terms of a strictly legalistic concept of citizenship. In their view, rights and responsibilities embodied in citizenship are a function of, and are defined by, legal criteria. However, my review of democratic citizenship, and the idea of associative citizenship that I have proposed indicate a very different alternative notion of the relationship between societal and political membership, one that is reflected in the activities that led to the mobilization of immigrants that came together in the spring of 2006.

These, then, are some of the key political issues that emerged as a result of Latino immigration and framed the political context within which the contestation of forms of marginalization that I refer to as associative citizenship developed. As I argued earlier, citizenship claims and practices only make sense if they are viewed as a response to a specific set of contextual factors. In my analysis of Southeast Los Angeles, it was primarily the economic and demographic dimensions that had the greatest impact on the formation of prefigurative rights claims. In the case of the immigrant rights movement and protest mobilizations, it is the political dimension and factors that are most significant in understanding the role that rights claims played as a response to them.

After 9/11, the intensification of racial conflict and the centrality of the notion of "what it means to be an American" became even more pronounced aspects of the politics of immigration as the discursive boundaries of efforts at immigration reform were completely altered. But while legalization, amnesty, deportation were specific issues that animated the marches, it was the latter concern—the nature of belonging and membership in the society, in effect proxies for an expanded notion of citizenship—that was the real focus of the mobilizations. These marches reflected a normative standard that holds that even unauthorized immigrants deserve to be treated with a measure of justice and dignity. Indeed, many of the posters and chants reflected this generalized normative principle.

But what were the specific measures, ideologies, and practices that brought more people onto the streets than any other of these demonstrations in U.S. history? The issue of immigration from Mexico was clearly not a new one and has always been linked with labor needs in the United States. There is a long history of permitting, and in some cases recruiting, Mexican workers to fill in periodic labor shortages.[18] When cheap Asian labor was restricted by law in the early twentieth century, Mexican immigrant workers filled that void, and their numbers increased substantially during the First World War, when labor demand increased significantly because domestic workers were entering the military and Mexican contract workers were recruited. This was the first guest-worker program and it laid the foundation for future patterns. The same occurred during World War II when farm workers were scarce, and both legal and illegal Mexican laborers filled that need. That morphed into the Bracero program, a guest-labor program that saw 4.6 million temporary worker visas issued to Mexicans between 1942 and 1964. The program ended the following year, but only after thousands of Mexicans stayed on as permanent residents. During the restructuring period that began in the early 1970s, once again the need for low-wage unskilled and semiskilled labor served as a magnet for Mexican and Central American workers to migrate to the United States in large numbers. It was during this period that there was significant growth in the number of unauthorized immigrants from Mexico, a situation that was one of the unintended consequences of the provisions of the Immigration and Nationality Act passed by Congress in 1965; it emphasized preferences for family unification as the basis for granting visas, but provided limited access based on U.S. labor-market needs, which had shifted to creating a large number of low-wage jobs in agriculture, service, and manufacturing sectors. As a result, large numbers of unauthorized workers from Mexico in particular continued to migrate to fill these positions. This occurred during a period of economic displacement of thousands of middle- and higher-wage occupations and the loss of incomes for millions of citizens. Resentment toward unauthorized immigrants steadily grew over the next decade and led to increasing political pressure on Congress to address the issue of illegal immigration; Congress finally acted in 1986 and passed the Immigration Reform and Control Act (IRCA). This included a legalization program for those in the country prior to 1982, and a number of other provisions that focused on border security and employer penalties. Table 5 reflects the very significant increase in undocumented immigrants between 1980 and 2010.

While IRCA was intended to address the political conflicts surrounding the issue of immigration, anger over the amnesty provision and the continued rapid

Table 5. Illegal Immigrants in the United States

1980	3,000,000	2000	8,600,000
1990	3,500,000	2010	11,400,000

Sources: "Illegal Immigration, Population Estimates in the United States, 1969 to 2011," Immigration.ProCon.org; Passel, Cohn, and Gonzalez-Barrera (2013).

Note: This table reflects the very significant increase in undocumented immigrants after 1970, when the number of undocumented immigrants in the United States was less than one million.

growth in the number of immigrants after IRCA resulted in increased divisions and tensions between immigrant advocates and critics. This continuing political conflict led Congress to pass additional legislation in 1990 and 1996. A recent study of Latino immigrant trends indicates that "Despite U.S. enforcement efforts after 1986, Mexico-U.S. migration increased steadily in the 25 years after IRCA, with the total Mexico-born population growing from about 2.8 million in 1979 to about 11.5 million in 2009. Unauthorized migrants accounted for about 60% of the increase" (Marc Rosenblum 2011, 11). Together with immigrants from the Northern Triangle of Central America (El Salvador, Guatemala, and Honduras), the total number rose from less than 1 million in 1970 to 14 million in 2009 (Marc Rosenblum 2011, 22). The growth in undocumented immigrants was particularly controversial and fueled the conflict up to the recent period. According to figures from the Department of Homeland Security reproduced online by ProCon.org, in 2008 there were 11.6 million unauthorized immigrants in the United States. About 61 percent were from Mexico and 14 percent were from Central and South America.[19]

Despite the considerable political conflict and divisions over these issues, in early 2001 President Bush and Mexican President Fox laid out an immigration reform package that appeared to have some bipartisan support. But the political calculus changed after the 9/11 attacks, and the emphasis shifted dramatically to focus on security and immigration control; this was evident in the fact that responsibility for immigration policy and enforcement was put under the control of the newly created Department of Homeland Security. Driven more by ideology than rational policy considerations, immigration was thus directly linked with the war on terror, and immigrants, particularly immigrants of color, immediately became seen as potential threats to national security. Using the rationale of security concerns, what followed was an escalation of enforcement measures directed against immigrants of color. The war on terror morphed into the war on immigrants. A net of wide-ranging tactics of intimidation, harassment, etc., resulted in a resurgence of the "Latino as foreigner" trope that had been part of the ideological construction of

Latinos since the annexation of large sectors of Mexico, and brought the question of whether Latinos were "real Americans" back into the center of political discourse, particularly in the realm of popular culture. The treatment of Latino immigrants and the violation of their rights made it plain that the issue of the "right to belong" was once again in play and led to the outrage that manifested itself in the mobilization of millions of Latinos.

Immigrant Rights Claims

While the protest marches of 2006 have been extensively studied from a variety of perspectives, I focus here primarily on those aspects that are directly related to understanding the fundamental role that rights claims and the networks that enabled them played in developing support for the mobilizations.[20] A sense of the importance of these claims was already evident in the response of diverse sectors of Latino communities to the passage of Proposition 187 in California in 1994, a measure intended to essentially establish a statewide citizenship screening system and prohibit illegal immigrants from using education, health care, or other social services. The measure was declared unconstitutional in 1997 after opposition to it led to significant political mobilization of both legal and illegal Latino immigrants, as well as native-born Latinos. Many of the participants in and organizers of the 2006 marches had been active in the campaign against Proposition 187, but the later protests mobilized thousands of new participants and actors. While the specific details of that initiative were different from the local and statewide and federal immigrant-control legislation that had been proposed after 9/11, what was common to many of the organizers and participants in both political actions was the sense that these measures were not just about controlling undocumented immigrations, but they were based on, and a manifestation of, a more generalized anti-Latino political ideology and political agenda. This is key, since research has shown a consistent divide in the way political interests are perceived by native-born and immigrant Latinos.

In several of the interviews that I carried out as part of my study of Southeast Los Angeles and other sites described in the appendix during the period that Proposition 187 was covered by the media (1993–1995) several Latino immigrant and native-born respondents indicated that they initially supported the measure because they interpreted the measure as being primarily about undocumented immigrants. But once they were exposed to the efforts of Spanish-language media to educate Latino communities about the realities of the measure, and witnessed, and in some cases experienced, anti-Latino behaviors and actions, they shifted their views and came to reinterpret the measure as an expression of anti-Latino sentiment and politics. So despite that division, when the anti-immigrant politics was seen more broadly as an anti-Latino agenda, individuals from both sectors engaged in common collective action.

Previous, similar anti-immigrant legislative measures, and the much more repressive enforcement actions taken throughout the country against Latinos, led many of the participants in the 2006 marches to become active for the first time. Despite the many new and different participants in these mobilizations, the marches need to be understood as a continuation and extension of long-developing grievances and claims based on a sense that the anti-immigrant and anti-Latino agenda violated normative principles of equality, justice, and rights, and provoked varying levels of fear, indignation, and anger. Individual participants reflected different mixtures of motivations and views, but most converged around issues connected to the constellations of these normative and emotive factors. This is reflected in several of the studies of participants found in the secondary literature as well as in a series of interviews I carried out between September 2007 and July 2008.[21] In the following section, I review examples from both sources that illustrate and emphasize the key role of associational networks that are the basis of the kind of rights claims that constitute the prefigurative dimension of the alternative conception of associative citizenship that I have argued for.

There is substantial agreement in the studies of the 2006 marches that there was a wide array of participants with different ideologies, perspectives, and political interests, and that more generally, their characteristics crossed class lines, they had different immigrant status, and they came from a variety of Latin American countries. Because of the extremely diverse backgrounds of the participants, one of the central questions raised in many of the articles on the marches has to do with understanding what brought them all together in common collective action. One approach to this has been to examine the connection between ethnic identity and solidarity among Latinos from different backgrounds. In her study of the marches in Colorado, Lisa Martinez (2008) offers a helpful review of some of the literature on that relationship, and draws on it to support her findings that participation in the marches helped to establish some level of solidarity across differences in background and experiences. This is supported generally by several other studies (Barreto et al. 2009), but the issue of how these solidarities form is not a primary concern of these works. However, other studies do probe this question and provide a sense of what was involved in the formation of these solidarities. For example, Pallares and Flores-González (2010) frame their examination of the nature of the issues and networks that led to the participation of some of the youth by first observing that the mobilizations "combined the efforts of more traditional community and immigrant organizations with those of loose political and social networks of groups

and individuals" (Pallares and Flores-González 2010, 161). They add that there was
no set of shared ideologies, political beliefs, or meanings that were the basis of
protests. Instead they argue that the conceptual framework for the mobilizations
"is best characterized as a set of common referents provided by the lived experience
of communities of immigrants, their nonimmigrant family members, and Latinos
at large. These common referents are informing their political identifications and
visions and enabling certain *coyunturas*, or coming together for specific purposes"
(161). Key here is that it was not necessarily the political ideologies as traditionally
conceptualized that established the connection between these participants, but
instead specific "common referents" that served to overcome the differences there
might have been. For the particular set of respondents and protest participants in
their study, the comment referent was a specific politically constructed notion of
the family. In the case of the two groups that were the focus of the research, Pallares
and Flores-González concluded that "family is a common referent and common
conduit through which questions of citizenship and democracy become publicly
articulated, ultimately informing the goals and political strategies pursued" (165).
So the participants' views about Latino societal membership, denied or restricted
institutional access, and forms of inequality converged and were filtered through
perceived common lived experiences at the familial level. For example, 48 percent
of those that were interviewed were from mixed-status families; that is, some
members were legal and at least one member was in the country illegally. For these
respondents, the normative issues and views that led to participation in the marches
were formed on the basis of experience with family networks where the level of lived
experience is affected directly by the mixed status of the members. The visibility
and salience of the consequences of immigrant status becomes more pronounced in
these situations. State actions targeting undocumented Latino immigrants increased
the visibility and salience of immigrant status in the activities of these familial
and extended networks of friends and relatives. Policies and enforcement actions
increased deportations and family separations, and initiated harsher and stricter
border enforcement; even expedited removals became more common. The impact
of these on the families was the experience that established the common referent as
the basis of collective action despite other differences, such as class and nationality,
that might have existed between the participants. The authors conclude that as a
result of the increased visibility and salience for everyday lived experience of these
and other actions perceived to be anti-Latino, the "concept of family has become
politicized in new ways and has acquired political meaning for undocumented immigrants and their families, legal immigrants, and for the wider Latino communities
in which they reside" (164). In a different study of marches that took place in the Bay
Area, Bloemraad and Trost (2011) also emphasize that the impact of harsher policies

and actions on the family established common links between otherwise differently situated Latino youth participants in the marches. However, they place even greater emphasis on the notion of networks as the vital mechanism for establishing common referents. They observe that "a recurring theme in our interviews was the essential role played by social networks of friends, family, and acquaintances in mobilizing respondents to participate" (Bloemraad and Trost 2011, 186).

These studies suggest that networks based on mutuality and trust, particularly referential trust,[22] can play a crucial role in establishing the common referents that initiate collective action. This is supported by other research on the marches that studied different sites within civil society, such as schools, religious congregations, hometown associations, where networks of mutuality were key in developing what Pallares and Flores-González referred to as *coyunturas*—instances where despite the existence of differences of background, belief, and the experiences of family, friends and relatives with immigration issues served as a common referent. The study by Bloemraad and Trost (2011) examines examples of youth being recruited and mobilized through school-based associational networks of friends and classmates. They report that many were convinced to participate in the marches after being exposed to discussions about what some youth described to others as wrongs that different members of their families or family friends had experienced. They quote one teenage participant who was persuaded to join the marches by others in her school networks: "At first I had no clue what was going on, but then all my friends were like, 'Yeah, the immigrants. . . . They're trying to kick everybody out. Like, if they find someone that is an immigrant, they're going to kick them out. I was like, 'Oh that's not fair,' so they told us what days [the protests would be] through text messages on the phone and stuff" (186). Other sites within civil society reflected similar processes of mobilization. For example, Heredia's study of the role of the Catholic Church in the mobilizations shows that associational religious networks led to members participating in the marches. Members of organizations visited and provided information highlighting the abuses of immigrants, but more importantly activists "framed" the issue in terms of Christian values, social justice, fairness, etc. (Heredia 2011, 192–93). This led many of the nonimmigrant Latino members of the churches to identify with the plight of immigrants, and it appears that despite differences, the common referent here was not only the vulnerability of family but also the common frame of reference that membership in the church provided. Yet another important site within civil society that was important in mobilizing large numbers of Latino immigrants was the network of hometown associations. Fox and Bada studied the relationship between civic and political engagement and membership in these associations and found the same important role played by associational networks through which members were exposed and alerted to the anti-immigrant policies that had been enacted, and to the punitive effect that proposed federal legislation would have on Latinos; they were also provided examples of harassment and harsh treatment of even legal immigrants (Fox and Bada 2011, 148–52).

While all of these studies suggest the importance of social networks, the primary focus was on their functionality in encouraging participation in the marches, and not on the nature of the networks themselves. What was it about these networks that made them effective mediums for political mobilization? What was it about the nature of those networks that established the commonality that led them to participate in the protest marches? This is an issue I addressed as part of a broader study of the role that networks play in promoting various forms of civic and political engagement among Latinos. One section focused on the immigrant-rights movement and participants in the mobilization. Between May 2007 and June 2008, I interviewed twenty-three individuals who had participated in one or more of the marches. I recruited several of them through contacts with a few Latino organizations, including a number of hometown associations with whom I had already carried out research, and others through Latino immigrant-rights organizers and activists who knew some of the nonimmigrant participants in the mobilizations. The major research question I focused on was what led these individuals to participate in the marches. I asked in particular about their most important networks of interaction, and the extent, if any, to which these networks influenced both their decision to be part of the protests and their views about immigration, citizenship, political justice, and the relationship between these.

The group I interviewed included seven native-born individuals of Mexican origin, one native-born person of Salvadoran origin, three individuals born in Mexico who had attained U.S. citizenship, eight Mexican immigrants, three Salvadoran immigrants, and one Honduran immigrant. Seventeen of the twenty-three respondents indicated that their views and participation in the marches were greatly influenced by at least one of their important social or work-related networks; four said that they had been moderately influenced, and two stated that they had developed their own views on these issues. So at least for the majority of these individuals (74 percent), their views and decision to join the marches were based to a significant degree on their interaction within their everyday networks. In some cases, these networks were related to their jobs, where they engaged in ongoing discussions with their peers about immigration-related matters. This led several of them to begin to watch Spanish-language news coverage of these issues. For several others, it was their participation in hometown association networks that had the most important effect on their views. These had all attended meetings of the HTAs where the main item of discussion was the impact of anti-immigrant policies and practices on friends and relatives of members of the association. According to these respondents, a major theme in these discussions was the sense of injustice of these events; they indicated that speakers would say things like "No es justo" (It is not just), "No hay razones" (There are no acceptable reasons or justification), or "No hay perdón" (These are unforgivable). Yet another group of respondents were most influenced by networks of family members, relatives, and friends. In these cases, among those who were immigrants and those who were undocumented, there was a fair amount of consistent discussion in these networks and their various gatherings about the issue of immigrant status, questions of amnesty, the deaths that resulted from border-enforcement policies, and the incredibly laborious process and difficulty of attaining citizenship status. Despite the different types of networks located in different sites of civil society, for all those who indicated the strong influence of these on their views and behavior, it was the visibility and salience of the negative consequences of the harsher treatment of immigrants that had the greatest effect on their own opinions, feelings, views, and behavior. They were influenced by experiences of those they knew, or the narration of stories by individuals they knew about harsh consequences endured by other immigrants, and even empathy with those they did not know but whose experiences of deportation, family separation, incarceration, or long-term detention they learned about from the news or stories they heard from persons in their networks.

I also asked about the respondents' views of citizenship and rights, and how these related to their experiences and/or opinions about immigration. I posed a series of questions about whether they thought citizenship should be defined only in legal terms—i.e., being born here or "having papers"—whether they thought immigrants should have the same rights as citizens, and if they believed that governments had the right to control who enters and lives in the country. The details of their responses of course varied, but the majority of respondents believed that citizenship had to be more inclusive; some mentioned that people who came here to work and decided to stay, who paid taxes and raised children, who participated in community affairs—that these people were good for "los Estados Unidos." Most agreed that immigrants who committed crimes and who otherwise were "bad for the community" should not be allowed to stay and certainly not allowed to become citizens. But those immigrants who contributed to the society through work, by raising decent children, through military service—these have "earned" the right to have rights, to use Arendt's well-known phrase. So most of these participants in the marches implied in their responses to these particular issues that there were alternative bases for citizenship, or at least for being an accepted member of the community and society.

And finally I asked them to talk about what it was about the networks that they were part of that had influenced them. While there were a series of different substantive references, i.e., specific things that these networks provided for them and for the rest of the members of those networks, what most impressed me about these responses was the view that they trusted the people who were part of these networks—"Se puede confiar en ellos" (They are people who can be trusted), as one middle-aged Salvadoran immigrant put it. They also expressed a sense of mutuality—having similar concerns, experiences, struggles that they shared—which I believe functions much like the notion of common referents that Pallares and Flores-González found in their studies. And this resembles Vélez-Ibañez's analysis of the centrality of "confianza en confianza"—trust in trust—in establishing and maintaining networks of mutuality. It is this dimension—trust in trust—that appears to be the characteristic of the networks that enable the process of using a common referent as the basis for joining in the type of collective action represented by the marches.

These are the kinds of ties individuals had with those they accepted information from, whose narrative and stories framed the issues they came to share common views of, and that established at least a temporary form of solidarity. It may have been the substance of the information or the relating of narratives that established the commonality between members of the networks, sharing the identification of a common referent, but what made this possible were the preexisting or newly established relations of trust and mutuality within those specific networks. These are the same characteristics within sites of civil society that I have argued are capable of enabling the kind of rights claims that imply an alternative conception of associative citizenship, as I have proposed.

CHAPTER 6

Critical Theory and the Politics of Solidarity

Contradictions, Tensions, and Potentiality

ONE OF THE MAJOR CLAIMS I HAVE MADE IS THAT AN INCIPIENT OR PREFIGURATIVE stage of an alternative notion of associative citizenship has been advanced in certain sectors of Latino communities. The rights claims emerging out of experiences rooted in everyday life are types of prefigurative, existential expressions of, and strategies for, negotiating the conditions of marginalization—rights claims that I believe are the empirical expression of associative citizenship. While I believe the informal rights claims are a viable option for the most marginalized sectors of Latino communities, they do not necessarily function in the same way for other sectors of Latino communities. As with most ethnic and racial groupings, the level of incorporation and inclusion in the dominant institutions, including economic, political, and civil society, vary by a number of factors, including class differences (income, occupation, education) and immigrant status. So the feasibility of political strategies that can be used effectively will vary accordingly.

The double challenge presented in the effort to overcome Latinos' history of exclusionary belonging is how to balance the need for societal cohesion with the need to develop strategies of political cohesion or solidarity among Latinos. This challenge is implied in the way that James Cohen summarized the choices that the

United States as a society will have to make because of what he calls the Latinization of major parts of the country (James Cohen 2005, 169). My claim throughout this book is that a politics built around the notion of Latino citizenship may provide a way to balance these two seemingly opposite goals. This is because a strong, normative sense of inclusiveness and full membership as an organizing principle has the potential to cut across some of the differences that separate Latino groups from others, providing a means of mobilization that strengthens the internal connections between different Latino groups by demonstrating, through strategies of praxis, the commonalities that these different groups share in the new context of the United States. At the same time, it is possible to promote a level of cohesion with the larger society based on a form of inclusion founded on normative principles of justice, equality, and tolerance. While there may be very substantial differences between different Latino groups, the one thing they have in common is a history of being ideologically constructed and represented in relatively similar terms. Given the long history of being homogenized, the politics of citizenship can build on combating that reductionist perception—internally different, externally the same—a variation of the "difference as sameness" theme. However, developing this type of common political agenda is a challenge that often involves opposing tendencies because of the differences within Latino groups on the one hand, and between Latino communities and the white majority on the other.

The focus of my discussion here, then, is to delineate what is involved in this dual tension, and to explore ways to balance them. First I want to examine the political significance of the intra-Latino group differences and deal with the possibilities of establishing common political agendas, and then follow with a discussion of what this common political solidarity implies for the issue of societal cohesion. The first aspect of this challenge results from the all-too-common tendency in the political discourse of the last two decades to assume that Latinos are a relatively homogeneous group with similar interests, values, and perspectives. So, for example, speculation about the potential of Latinos to affect local, state, and even national elections has become a staple feature of each electoral season for the past two decades. Politicians, academics, and media analysts have created a discursive field that includes a number of often competing and even contradictory themes. Some commentators focus on the increasing significance of the "Latino" vote, while others note the low turnout rate of Latino voters; studies argue that the demographic changes of the last thirty years have positioned Latino voters to play a broker role, while others point to a legacy of continued marginalization. What often seems to underlie otherwise differing interpretations is an unproblematized assumption that "Latino" refers to an empirically identifiable, unified group. One finds the same kind of assumption operative in the ways that "Latino" is deployed in marketing strategies and campaigns

(Dávila 2001). But an increasing number of scholars have critiqued and contested this very idea.[1]

The contemporary politicized notions of Latino identity emerged from the Puerto Rican and Chicano movements of the 1960s and 1970s. While often framed as referring to an existing type of commonality, these labels were in fact normative affirmations of the need for political unity or solidarity as simultaneously a condition of, and the goal for Latino empowerment politics; that is, these constructs of the affirmation of Latinidad on the one hand were a declaration of Latino solidarity, but on the other hand urged the need to create this solidarity. The same tendency to define Latinos in terms of commonality was promoted by the federal government anxious to simplify ways of responding to pressures from a variety of Latino groups, by marketers interested in developing strategies based on the broadest appeals, and by Latino political brokers who wanted to convince policymakers of the existence of a large and unified Latino population. While each of these tendencies to homogenize Latinos was driven by very different logics and rationales, they all constructed the imagery of Latinos as a relatively unified "group" defined by a certain type of commonality and therefore either explicitly or implicitly embracing the notion of Latino solidarity.

Many of the issues surrounding both the politically and theoretically contested terrain of Latino unity and solidarity are addressed in Beltrán's *The Trouble with Unity* (2010) and Barvosa's *Wealth of Selves* (2008); they resonate at both a theoretical and political level with the challenges to the differential levels of societal and political membership of Latinos represented not only by and through the immigrant-rights movement, but also by a range of political actions initiated by community-based organizations, traditional party activists, civil rights groups, and a host of coalitional groups. I read Beltrán as offering a nuanced theoretical interrogation, explication, and critique of the problematic nature of tensions that characterized Latino political development extending from the Chicano and Puerto Rican movements of the 1960s and 1970s to the present, and she advances this analysis using the discursive parameters of political theory, and more specifically a position that relies heavily on a version of agonistic democratic theory. So Beltrán's framing of the analysis focuses on delineating the types of differences that any strategy of building cultural and/ or ideological solidarity would have to address and engage. In the interpretations she develops, Beltrán draws heavily on a conception of multiple identities and goes on to argue that a conception of Latino politics based on a notion of an assumed unity misconstrues the nature of Latino identity, and that such a politics would thus most likely be based on the assumption of a consensual model of democracy that is incapable of creating the kind of political space needed in a society characterized by deep forms of diversity. While the work provides a persuasive argument regarding the need to understand and incorporate the highly diverse, heterogeneous nature of Latino populations in political analysis, there are a number of issues and problems that are left unresolved, and in particular the question of Latino solidarity, which I believe that from the standpoint of political mobilization and action, represented by the types of groups mentioned above, is the other side of the theoretical coin Beltrán engages. Despite the many differences that exist, there have been and continue to be, as Beltrán's work also demonstrates, political actions that are able to overcome them and form some basis of political unity or solidarity, even if these are often transient or fleeting in nature. So while it is clearly the case that deep and fundamental differences divide Latinos along a number of competing and interacting axes, the question remains whether, or to what extent, the possibility of a form of Latino solidarity has any conceptual, theoretical, or political traction. While it is likely that some notion of solidarity will continue to be adopted and advanced at the ideological level by groups across the political and marketing spectrum, does it make sense to pursue the issue of Latino solidarity from a theoretical and conceptual perspective?

What I want to explore here are some of the problems that are raised by how different formulations of solidarity are framed, and to suggest that in particular, these concerns tend to converge around the issue of commensurability, which for the most part is left unaddressed in these various positions. By framing, I mean the configuration of underlying assumptions that define the discursive theoretical field and the concepts mobilized to elaborate the analysis. Nancy Fraser's (2009) recent discussion of justice focusing on the meta-level of framing provides an example of how this approach not only can help clarify how a particular theoretical framework both enables and limits the direction of the derivative analysis, but also facilitates our ability to assess the comparative strengths and weaknesses of the different constructs. By juxtaposing these different framing strategies of the concept of solidarity, and identifying the different meanings and dimensions of solidarity, we can trace both the theoretical and political implications of these constructs for a Latino politics that has the potential to negotiate the dual tensions I have indicated.

Dimensions of Solidarity

One of the things that becomes immediately clear in reviewing the various discussions of solidarity is that the term is used to refer to quite different phenomena. So I first want to delineate some of these varying conceptions in order to be clear about what we are in fact referring to when we talk of Latino solidarity. In his important but underappreciated book on solidarity, Hauke Brunkhorst argues that the modern framing of the issue of solidarity is rooted in the motto "liberty, equality, and fraternity," advanced to symbolize the normative foundation of the French Revolution that is traditionally thought of by democratic advocates as embodying the hallmark of democratic citizenship (Brunkhorst 2005, 5). Brunkhorst traces the process by which the qualitative dimensions of social relationships that the notion of fraternity was meant to capture eventually transformed into the idea of solidarity. The important point for my analysis, however, is that there was a recognition not only that the qualitative aspects of social relationships had a direct bearing on the democratizing of society, but that democracy in fact required the existence of a certain type of connectedness between citizens. Yet even a casual survey of the history of political theory in the last two centuries reveals quite clearly that while liberty and equality have been predominant concerns and themes of much of modern political theory, attention to fraternity, or more generally the political significance of the qualitative nature of societal relations, has been scant to say the least.[2] In her essay on the relationship between fraternity and justice, Munoz-Dardé observes that one of the reasons that this concept has not received much consideration in the realm of political theory is that "fraternity does not sit comfortably in the logic of individual rights expressed by liberty and equality" (Munoz-Dardé 1999, 83). This lack of attention to the issue of fraternity may also reflect the effort among some political theorists to distinguish clearly between "the social" and "the political."[3]

Despite its neglect in the area of political philosophy, the issue of solidarity has not only been engaged but is central in many of the key works of social theory, such as Adam Smith's work on moral sentiments, Marx's theory of proletarian revolution, and analyses advanced by Tonnies and Durkheim distinguishing between different modalities of solidarity. But the more recent work on solidarity has developed in a context defined by the conflicts that have arisen from the transformation of the racial and ethnic composition of Western liberal democracies that has affected the framing of the analysis involved. So it is important to keep in mind that the general issues raised by the notion of Latino solidarity are not unique to that group, but arise within the broader context of the dilemmas and tensions that characterize modern pluralist democracies defined by deep cultural, ethnic, racial, and conflicted religious diversity—i.e., where group differences involve strongly held opposing beliefs and ways of life.

The conceptions and analysis of solidarity in the more recent literature reflect two broad dimensions around which particular analyses are organized and deployed. The first is related to the issue of social cohesion, and the second focuses on the question of political solidarity. While these have different centers of gravity, they nevertheless are inherently related. I will argue here that developing an effective strategy for the study of Latino solidarity can benefit from understanding how this intersection has been framed in a number of recent efforts to address questions focused on, or related to, the issue of solidarity more generally. First, I examine how the intersection between social and political solidarity is variously framed in approaches focused on two different substantive concerns—the first being how to incorporate different competing groups into a specific political community, and the second how to create a form of solidarity that can mobilize marginalized groups or sectors of a population to press for greater levels of incorporation. Second, I propose that while the framing strategies adopted in these approaches differ in substantial ways, they nevertheless rely on notions of mutual understanding and/or trust, and the communicative structures by which these can be created and maintained. Third, I suggest that a model for the study of Latino solidarity should be based on the notion of translation.

The Social and the Political in Framings of Solidarity

In the current context, several different framings of the problematic of solidarity can be identified; that is, each has different theoretical groundings and presuppositions, draws on and constructs different conceptual configurations, and applies them to different dimensions of the problematic. These framings can be discerned by identifying the primary concerns or questions that these analyses seek to address; grasping the major arguments advanced to answer these questions; determining the key concepts mobilized in developing that argument; and tracing the linkages between these concepts. I want to focus specifically on two distinct framings here, each of which engages the relationship between social and political solidarity.

The first approach is developed in works with different emphases and specific concerns that nevertheless share a similar framing of how to approach the question of solidarity. This framing is concerned with identifying how forms of solidarity that promote social cohesion are related to, yet differ from, the type of solidarity necessary for the viability of political community. For example, in her effort to develop a theory of political solidarity, Scholz argues that we need to distinguish three forms of solidarity: social, civil, and political. Social solidarity is the form of connectedness between persons that creates social cohesion and is concerned with the level of "interdependence among individuals within a group; primarily descriptive and secondarily normative, social solidarity pertains to group cohesiveness. . . . that entails some degree of shared consciousness, shared experience, or some other uniting feature among group members" (Scholz 2008, 21). This form of solidarity both generates and depends on social bonds characterized by specific patterns of moral obligations between the members of the group. While Scholz provides an extensive discussion of theorists that address these concerns, less well developed in her work is the issue of the tensions between group and societal cohesion, which is crucial for the study of highly diverse liberal democracies.

Social solidarity is then distinguished from both civic and political forms of solidarity. The first, civic solidarity, refers to the relationship between individual citizens and the primary political community, which in the modern period takes the form of the state. Scholz argues that the effective functioning of the state depends on the existence and acceptance of a form of collective responsibility that citizens must have for the well-being of their fellow members of the society. Unlike the kinds of bonds based on mutual dependence and group ties that characterize social and civic solidarities, political solidarity is primarily defined in moral and ethical terms that arise in response to acts or conditions of injustice or oppression, and "highlights individual conscience, commitment, group responsibility, and collective action" (Scholz 2008, 33). So it is clear that Scholz frames her problematic in a way that reserves the political valence of the dimension of solidarity for action that is undertaken with others to address what are perceived wrongs carried out against others in the society. Although Scholz does not develop the linkage between the societal and political community, it would be difficult to conceive of political solidarity developing without the existence of some level of social and civic forms of solidarity. The need for political actions or movements based on political solidarity arises only if there is breakdown not only in the primary function of the state, but also in the shared understanding of the mores and ethical conditions defining the political community.

The distinction between social and political dimensions of solidarity is also one of the key elements in the very different work of Brunkhorst. This is developed within a broader project of demonstrating that "solidarity coincides with the concept of democracy" (Brunkhorst 2005, xxiii). Brunkhorst makes it clear that he wants to preserve the notion of solidarity for the realm of the political, but unlike Scholz, he does not consider it either oppositional or consisting of a moral impulse to address forms of oppression or injustice. Instead, he conceives of it as the kind of bond or connection between public selves in a democratic system. In fact, modern solidarity as Brunkhorst conceives it is only possible in a democratic system, so it is more appropriate to consider this notion as democratic solidarity, a form that facilitates the functioning of pluralistic society characterized by significant degrees of difference. Modern democracy is the only form of solidarity that can provide the expression of, and foundation for, individual freedom in a highly differentiated and developed society. The irony, however, is that he traces the evolution of this notion of solidarity from its rootedness in the realm of the social. The main historical sources of the revolutionary concept of fraternity that evolved into the notions of solidarity of the later nineteenth century and that arose to address forms of exclusion, such as marginalization and "pauperization," were the classical idea of civic friendship and the Judeo-Christian notion of brotherhood. While friendship and brotherhood were located within the social realm, they nevertheless both pointed to the transcendence of that very space by going beyond bonds that were connected to kinship, family, and clan. In the contemporary period, solidarity cannot be rooted in the social realm, but it can be realized as a form of what the translator of the book refers to as "solidarity among strangers" (Brunkhorst 2005, viii). It is this insistence that democratic solidarity cannot be based on notions of "peoplehood" established by cultural, racial, ethnic, or historical ties that make this solidarity dependent on "communication, will, and action" (Brunkhorst 2005, x).

Despite the very different constructions of the notion of solidarity in Scholz and Brunkhorst, these nevertheless converge around the need for shared understandings and communication, and the indispensable role of the social in developing the bonds of solidarity.[4] These works focus on the concept of solidarity in a more generalized sense, and in the context of less specific notions of difference. But I now want to turn to how this more generalized notion of solidarity is affected when it is both situated and interrogated within racialized political communities; to engage the thematic framing of racial and racialized solidarity advanced in some recent, key works as a way to delineate what is both in play and at stake in introducing this dimension; and to extend their analyses by suggesting an alternative framing strategy.

Racialized Solidarities

A range of processes of racialization have been fundamental and constitutive in the formation of the parameters of political community from the earliest phases of U.S history. These phenomena have not only extended to and pervaded the formal sphere of governance, but represented a mode of subordination that incorporated mutually reinforcing social and political strategies, practices, and ideologies. This interface has been studied from a variety of perspectives, but I want to focus here on how race has affected the conceptualizing of the issue of solidarity reviewed above by distinguishing between three different framings of racialized solidarity: civic, nationalist, and agonistic. These are reflected in recent works on racialized solidarity advanced by Hooker, Shelby (resonates with Scholz), and Beltrán (resonates with Brunkhorst) that are representative of the kinds of issues and themes concerning solidarity that have been problematized and reformulated to provide a more accurate accounting of these issues and to provide strategies for incorporating this dimension (Shelby 2005, Hooker 2009, Beltrán 2010).

Although all three of these approaches frame the issue of solidarity around political considerations—i.e., they focus primarily on political solidarity—there is no neat and discrete separation possible between that dimension and the realm of social solidarity or the question of social cohesion in these approaches. This is because they recognize the inherent interdependent nature of the relationship between these two spheres, and that racialization processes have never functioned solely within the political realm alone, but have been enacted and sustained by the pattern of regulative social mechanisms that provide the sites of racialized performance and relations more broadly. One finds these patterns rooted within social arenas involved in employment and labor markets, housing accessibility, health care, education, transportation, and so on. So it would be difficult to somehow bracket these from the way that racialized patterns affect questions of political solidarity, and thus all three theorists engage the reciprocal interaction between political and social solidarity. The difference in emphasis, however, is clear.

CIVIC SOLIDARITY

Each of the framings of the issue of solidarity engage two different types of political solidarity, although the significance of each varies in the three approaches. The first involves the question of the issue of solidarity within racialized groups, and the other between groups and the broader public and political sphere. In developing a conception of *civic racialized solidarity*, Hooker makes clear that her primary concern is *political solidarity*, which she views as "the solidarity that exists—or should exist—between members of a political community" and "denotes the ability of individuals to engage in relations of trust and obligation with fellow members of a political community whom they may see as inherently 'other' in some fundamental way" (Hooker 2009, 21). The main conceptual pivot here, then, is the concern with the kinds and nature of bonds that tie members of a political community to one another and so reflect a focus on the grounds and conditions for establishing a set of viable civic relations. This requires interrogating how both juridical and societal processes at the same time frame and delimit the normative parameters and discursive field within which the construction of the identity of the "we" that is the basis of a political community takes place, and thus determines and legitimates its patterns of inclusion and exclusion.[5] Hooker's framing of the issue of political solidarity in terms of the civic dimension is reflected by her making clear that the specific context of political solidarity that she is concerned with is the same conceptual and theoretical terrain that theories of multiculturalism have defined, and by her statement that her analysis is "principally concerned with the place of race and political solidarity in theories of multiculturalism, a topic that has not yet received sufficient attention" (Hooker 2009, 15). Hooker's initial framing question, then, concerns what the nature of political membership must be in order for societies characterized by deep racial diversity to function effectively, and the criterion for the latter appears to be the standard of justice; she argues that "the racialization of solidarity is thus a key aspect of the question of justice in diverse societies, yet political theorists have not grappled with this issue" (11). While the latter issue of justice is not developed systematically, it is nevertheless clearly one of the thematic elements of the overall interpretative framework that both is the basis of and frames the analysis and argument.

We get a sense of how Hooker believes this racialized dimension affects the framing of the broader context of civic solidarity when she states that "In a racial-ized polity, the *social and affective* distance that accompanies race also produces different ethical-historical perspectives between whites and nonwhites" (Hooker 2009, 9 [my emphasis]). This clearly illustrates the inherent connection between social and political solidarity in Hooker's approach and reflects the point I stressed earlier that one cannot simply focus on political solidarity without seeing how it is linked to, facilitated by, and reflective of the nature and dimensions of social cohesion and solidarity. This is developed further by Hooker: "In order to agree to the creation of institutions that treat all fairly, democratic strangers must recognize that they have an obligation to live with others on terms of fairness, reciprocity and mutual respect" (Hooker 2009, 4). So the norms of reciprocity, mutual respect, and trust are rooted in the social realm of relations, yet are qualitative characteristics necessary for democratic governance to function effectively. This in turn requires the development of a form of civic solidarity that recognizes the central role of racialization in determining the differentiating contours of political community, and that engages the fundamental differences between white and nonwhite ethical-historical perspectives that embody both the quotidian and structural dimensions of those differentiations. But the crucial question that follows from this framing of the issue of the relationship between social and political solidarity, and which Hooker does not address in any systematic way, has to do with how these conditions of mutuality, reciprocity, and trust can be produced and maintained in such a way that the difference in ethical-historical perspectives can be engaged in a systematic and institutional way to promote racial justice. She provides neither an analysis of this issue nor a sense of how to address it in terms of political engagement between the racially divided groups.

PRAGMATIC RACIAL SOLIDARITY

Instead of making civic bonds and the way they are inflected by racial cleavages the primary theoretical focus of analysis, the nationalist framing of the challenge of solidarity instead concentrates on the issue of the degree to which the political valence of identity can establish the types of bonds and forms of connectedness necessary for grounding effective challenges to exclusionary forms of politics. The primary question here shifts to the terrain of political mobilizations and whether, or to what extent, commonalities of social and cultural identities can provide the cohesion within groups to act in a unified way in the political sphere and to establish a common agenda for action. Shelby's critical examination of this dynamic in *We Who Are Dark* helps to illustrate both the strengths and weaknesses of this approach in both understanding and establishing the complex interplay between the cultural, racial, and ethnic dimensions at stake in the effort to create solidarity along nationalist lines.

Rejecting what he considers essentialist conceptions of black identity, Shelby argues that his main concern is to respond to the question of whether there is a form of black solidarity that is feasible and effective in the post–civil rights era. Since he believes that the question of black solidarity has been framed largely by and within the discursive field established by black nationalisms, Shelby's approach is to engage and critique the notions of solidarity advanced by various strands of the latter, including "classical" black nationalism, Black Power ideology, and the notion of solidarity based on a common group identity. Instead, he formulates and advocates the notion of pragmatic black nationalism as the basis for black unity and political organization that coheres around the demands for racial justice and the normative ideal of racial equality. Much like Beltrán, Shelby argues that strategies of political empowerment have to come to terms with the wide divergence in the characteristics, experiences, and conditions of blacks. "Blackness" alone cannot provide the basis for a form of solidarity on which effective forms of politics can be developed to address the broad range of interests, ideologies, and class positions of blacks in the United States. Instead, Shelby states that "I defend a conception of solidarity based strictly on the shared experience of racial oppression and a joint commitment to resist it" (Shelby 2005, 11–12), and that "my concern is to explain and defend the role of black political unity in bringing about a just society" (12). Shelby advances the position, then, that it is not "blackness" itself, i.e., a type of group or collective identity, that can serve as the basis of black political unity or solidarity. Instead, a form of "pragmatic" solidarity can and should be based on the fact that "virtually all blacks are vulnerable to being victimized or disadvantaged by anti-Black racism and thus can identify with one another on that basis" (12–13). And, according to Shelby, this pragmatic black solidarity is completely compatible with, and can be accomplished within, the very parameters and "core values of liberalism" such as equal citizenship for all, individual autonomy, democratic rule of law, basic rights such as speech and association, tolerance and equal opportunity" (6). So the crux of Shelby's affirmative position seems to be that the common characteristic of blackness has been and continues to be the basis of the common experience of racial oppression, and that this should be sufficient to establish a form of black political unity.

However, what Shelby does not address, and what is left unclear, is why (and the extent to which) this commonality is likely to transcend the other multiple axes of differences that exist among blacks, which Shelby is attempting to provide a response to. What Shelby must assume for his position to be feasible is that the many forms of racism are experienced by all blacks similarly, or at least that these forms of racism will have the same impact or effect on all blacks regardless of class position and differences in gender, income, wealth, social status, residence, quality of life, etc. While it is clear that some forms of racism might indeed be experienced similarly across these fundamental differences, it is unlikely that the engagement with them and consequences suffered will affect all blacks the same in all spheres of experience regardless of differences in income, wealth, education, or occupation. So, for example, the lived experience and consequences of labor-market racial discrimination will be very different for an unemployed working-class black male with limited education living in a low-income poverty area than it will be for a black attorney in a large firm who has a fairly secure position. While the former may not even be able to find employment because of racism, the latter may not receive a promotion or a raise in income because of discrimination. The effects of racism on each, however, are qualitatively different and will be experienced as such. For the first, the result has to do with mere survival, while for the second it may be a matter of making $250,000 instead of $300,000, which makes it an issue of a more or less affluent lifestyle, but certainly not a threat to survival. The impact and meaning of racism is dramatically different in each case even though racial discrimination—or to use Shelby's term, racial oppression—is in play. The question is whether these two individuals are likely to see themselves as sharing the same "fate," and to share a similar conception of what constitutes racial justice in concrete political terms despite the very different impacts on their lives. Shelby offers little in the way of evidence to support this assumption. I would argue that bridging the differences in lived experience—i.e., how class and gender concretely affect the quality of life across the spectrum of black population in the United States—requires a more substantive basis for establishing unity of political purpose. For example, how would Shelby account for the rise of the black conservative movement? In their perception of racism, are they likely to be similar enough to liberal or poor blacks to make common cause with them? As Rousseau argued long ago, it is very unlikely that more privileged members of a community will understand the lives and struggles of those who are impoverished or marginalized societally. So Shelby's position does not really address this issue, and the challenge of communication and understanding across the kinds of differences that exist within black communities is likely to be very similar to the difficulty of establishing common points of mutual understanding between other kinds of groupings in a highly diverse society more generally.

AGONISTIC SOLIDARITY

Much like Shelby, Beltrán confronts directly the problematic of assuming or establishing unity, or what I would label solidarity, among Latinos. However, unlike Hooker's reliance on and engagement with the framing of the issue of solidarity in terms of the discursive theoretical parameters of multiculturalism, or Shelby's framing of black solidarity within the conceptual terrain defined by Rawlsian liberalism, Beltrán draws on a quite different configuration of theoretical premises drawn from Arendtian perspectives, radical democratic theory, postmodernism more generally, and agonistic theory more specifically, in her framing of the analysis.[6] Beltrán notes that the tendency toward claiming or assuming a Latino unity on the basis of a shared consciousness and identity continues to be the basis of how Latino politics is conceived of by politicians, grassroots organizers, and academics despite it being clearly a fiction. Since the idea of Latinidad is often mobilized to capture this sense of unity based on a common or shared identity, one of the common threads throughout Beltrán's analysis is the effort to destabilize and reconfigure the term. Beltrán asserts that she will "propose a new, more explicitly political understanding of Latino identity, in which political subjectivity is recognized as inescapably fragmented and where agonistic identities are understood as foundational to its democratic project" (Beltrán 2010, 19).

Drawing on Arendtian and radical democratic theoretical optics, Beltrán argues that such a notion of Latino political subjectivity has to be based on reconceptualizing Latinidad not as a quality or characteristic but rather as a verb, as a form of action and performance, and she offers a "reading of Latino politics" that "sharpens our appreciation of Latinidad as the effort to inaugurate a new political 'imaginary'" (Beltrán 2010, 70). This theoretical move is the key to the notion of solidarity that Beltrán seeks to replace the idea of Latino unity with, and serves, I believe, as the normative criteria underlying her detailed analysis and critique of the Chicano and Puerto Rican movements of the 1960s and 1970s, as well as her review of more traditional studies of Latino politics with their emphasis on electoral politics. Instead of a conception of Latino politics based on the fiction of unity, Beltrán argues that the differences this image ignores, obscures, or represses can be engaged and negotiated through the very action undertaken with others within the public realm. Here Beltrán, relying heavily on Arendt's view, incorporated and extended by Wolin's notion of fugitive democracy, seems to be saying that politics is fundamentally a performative practice that is the only means by which the open-ended nature of human experience can continue to be nurtured and incorporated into a democratic polity without the kinds of arbitrary closures and exclusions that lead to forms of oppression and intolerance. And this is the corrective to false notions of Latino unity, and the key to a notion of Latino solidarity that can serve as the basis of Latino collective action that neither represses dissent nor is arbitrarily exclusionary. The sense of Latino unity and Latino solidarity is not a fixed quality or characteristic, but can only be the product of the kinds of actions that are engaged in to create an open-ended democratic politics, a public realm. It is only through the discussions, the debating, the strategizing, and analysis involved in collective action that Latino solidarity can be created, constructed. "I show how the embodied action of Latinos does not simply reflect but actively constructs communities and solidarities within the public realm. Performance and the physical claiming of public space is capable of producing a shared sense of membership, particularly for those who have historically found the public realm to be a site of silence, alienation, and invisibility" (Beltrán 2010, 17). And while she does not dwell much on what provides guidance or direction to this form of solidarity, she appears to hold a position similar to Shelby's and Hooker's, that is, that a commitment to the political principles of justice and a nonracialized polity is key to this kind of action and can provide the element around which commonality of purpose can be created. As Beltrán puts it, "In this vision of politics, energy is directed at building majorities based on shared political visions of social justice rather than the solace . . . of equating political agreement with identity" (19). What is not addressed by Beltrán, however, is how this open-ended process of performative politics creates the kind of connectedness that both Hooker and Shelby assume to be necessary for their notions of solidarity to be viable.

While each of the conceptions and the analysis of the issue of solidarity that I have engaged here has a different emphasis and focus, and rests on alternative sets of both substantive and epistemological assumptions, there are nevertheless some important convergences that raise a different set of both political and theoretical questions. Each of these analyses of solidarity resolves their engagement with the issue of identity by shifting the theoretical and political ground from one based on unitary group identity to more general political principles as the basis for establishing solidarities and/or membership claims. But this seems to simply move the question of how the connections or bonds of solidarity can be formed down the theoretical road and does not provide any explanation of why it is that substituting more general principles for identity-based conceptions of solidarity is more likely to provide a basis for establishing a common ground for collective action. Earlier framings of this kind of disagreement or disjunction might posit that the former are understood as "universals" and the latter as "particularistic." But the attempt to organize and establish solidarities around generalized universal principles does not seem to have been much more successful than the attempt to organize those solidarities based on group identity.

Translation, Narrative, and Solidarity

I argued earlier that while there is a distinction between social forms of solidarity by which groups are incorporated into a set of functioning relationships that define societies, and political forms of solidarity that are capable of initiating and sustaining collective action, that they are nevertheless interdependent. Recall Brunkhorst's analysis that seeks to demonstrate that a key element in the notion of political solidarity is the qualitative dimension of social relationships, i.e., that there must be a certain kind of bonding or connection between people that the notion of fraternity was intended to describe. It is this dimension that I believe is undeveloped in the analyses of solidarity reviewed above. Each develops a concept of political solidarity that reflects a sense that there are practices of injustice or societal wrongs that need to be addressed and changed, yet none addresses what type, if any, of societal solidarity must exist as an enabling condition. How are the varying interpretations of these conceptions of injustices to be mutually understandable? How are the content and meaning of these transgressions to be understood across the many types of differences that the three theorists amply demonstrate exist within (as well as across) Latino and black populations? As I indicated earlier, Hooker argues that political solidarity requires relations of trust and obligation grounded on mutual understandings. Shelby assumes that the meaning of experiences of racial oppression transcend differences in economic class, gender, status, etc., and that there is a level of mutual understanding among blacks that makes solidarity possible. And Beltrán's notion of a politics that is based on the negotiation of differences requires a space that would allow for the mediation between the differences—a space that would promote and enable mutual understandings. So they all rely on some notion of communication and mutual understanding as either a condition or goal for their formulations of political solidarity to emerge. While the framing strategies adopted in these approaches differ in substantial ways, they nevertheless rely on notions of mutual understanding and/or trust and the communicative structures by which these can be created and maintained, which would constitute some level of social solidarity.

Despite the quite different nature of the problematic of solidarity reflected in the approaches I have focused on here, and in contemporary analysis of justice and democracy, they nevertheless share the common terrain and rely on this dimension of mutuality, which assumes the possibility of mutual communicative understandings. This has of course been a primary concern and component of the very extensive literature on, critiques of, and debates about deliberative democracy, as well as the work on communicative rationality initiated by Habermas. However, the issue of the nature and role of mutual understandings in establishing the kind of public realm that is key in the works on solidarity discussed here, is still highly contested despite having received extensive and thorough treatment. So I want to suggest that we might want to reframe the issue of political solidarity around the question of commensurability. This has not only been at the center of debates about deliberative democracy and Habermas's communicative democracy, but has also been a major concern of interpretive anthropological and sociological analysis. This work has made clear that any notions of communication and mutual understanding mobilized in the study of societies characterized by deep diversity must go well beyond the idea of rational discourse and incorporate a wide variety of other forms by which different groups communicate with one another and with others.

However, I do not believe that these positions go far enough in appreciating the significance of the depth of the distance between groups separated by differences of class, race, gender, and status—for example, in terms of establishing mutual understandings. Instead of extending the types of communicative and interpretive forms that should be allowed for in political intercourse, the challenge of com-mensurability, and the achievement of a level of mutual understanding necessary for creating political solidarity, and ultimately a democratic public realm, requires something more like a model of translation than simply deliberation. Recent works in translation theory appear to be confronting issues and problems very similar to the ones involved in trying to establish a politics of mutuality but make the issue of commensurability the primary organizing conceptual pivot.[7] The challenge in both arenas is to convey the meaning as understood within one societal or group context to others whose meaning structures are neither coincident nor resonant with those of the former. However, a major perspective in translation theory proposes that the goal must be to find ways to communicate the "quality" of experiences across differences, and not simply to try to find the equivalent word or symbol in another framework of meaning structures. So it is not just the "meaning of" but "meaning for" that has to be facilitated through the channels by which differently located groupings come to construct images of others. This aspect has found little traction and has not been a major concern in the relevant literature on political solidarity, but some work developed a few years ago in response to Habermas's construction of the relationship between justice and solidarity points to a kind of position consistent with this emphasis in translation theory.[8]

As I argued earlier, the foundational role of mutual recognition, reciprocity, and solidarity in the notion of the public sphere advanced by Habermas has been the focus of a number of works that provide the basis for an alternative way of conceptualizing the mechanisms of social trust in democratic polities. I want to frame this issue a bit differently than some of the literature and interpret the challenge involved as one similar to that of translation, since communication across deep differences is a shared concern. I indicated in chapter 2 that Habermas's notion of the public sphere establishes unrestricted communicative modes as a defining element, and that the form of mutuality on which this depends consists in mutual trust and reciprocity, which in turn require an intersubjective network of mutual recognition. What is crucial in these networks is the effectiveness of conveying the "meaning" of intentions, beliefs, and perspectives. Habermas develops his position through an analysis of the relationship between justice and solidarity. My focus here is a line of argument that extends and deepens the notion of mutual recognition in a way that can serve as an alternative theoretical basis for explaining the political role of social trust that depends on a mode of translating the meaning across difference.

Habermas's critical theory depends on the viability of his concept of the "ideal speech situation." In order for this notion to be effective in promoting the process of the resolution of conflicting values, there must first exist social bonds of mutual trust and reciprocity between those who engage in that public dialogue. And these in turn require an intersubjective network of mutual recognition, which Habermas sought to elaborate through his discussion of the relationship between justice and solidarity. Adapting and modifying the work of Kohlberg on moral development, Habermas argues that individuals can only take form "by growing into a speech community and thus into an intersubjectively shared lifeworld" (Habermas 1989b, 46). Therefore any norm that governs behavior cannot secure the integrity of the individual "without at the same time safeguarding the vitally necessary web of relationships of mutual recognition in which individuals can stabilize their fragile identities only mutually and simultaneously with the identity of their group" (47). Thus justice, which is the realm of promoting equal treatment and dignity for individuals, cannot be realized without solidarity, that is, without at the same time pursuing the welfare and wellbeing of the members of a community without which the individual could not exist as himself or herself. For Habermas, then, the grounding of the legitimacy claims of democracy rests and depends on the existence of these qualitative characteristics of the social relations between its members. Without bonds of respect, mutual recognition, and solidarity, the conditions for the realization of a just and democratic society would be absent.

Let me begin by reviewing the way in which Benhabib takes up the issue of solidarity and mutual recognition in her assessment of the debate between Kohlberg and Gilligan on moral theory (Benhabib 1996). As an adherent of a modified version of the model of deliberative democracy put forth by Habermas, Benhabib subscribes to the premise that claims to democratic legitimacy in such a model rest on general principles and moral "intuitions" based on the discourse model of ethics. Benhabib argues that the conception of the moral domain found in the contractarian tradition that Rawls represents is in fact a limited, partial, and exclusivist construct, whose validity is thereby seriously restricted. Benhabib develops this critique by introducing a distinction between two perspectives of the self-other relations, which are the basis of moral theorizing. The first she labels the "generalized other." It views self-other relations in terms of the norms of formal equality and reciprocity by which "each is entitled to expect and to assume from us what we can expect and assume from him or her" (Benhabib 1996, 159). This perspective rests on commonality and implies the need to institutionalize mechanisms to secure and guarantee the viability of mutual expectations. The moral categories entailed by this view are thus those having to do with rights, obligations, and entitlements, which require relatively formal and thin social bonds. While Benhabib clearly considers this dimension of the moral domain as necessary to establish democratic legitimacy, she argues, however, that it is not sufficient. What is absent is the standpoint of the "concrete other," which views individuals as rational beings with specific histories, needs, identities, and desires. Thus it is the individuality and uniqueness of the self that comes into play here. The logic of this perspective calls for moral norms that promote mutual recognition and affirmation, rather than expectations, and which, according to Benhabib, include friendship, love, and care. Benhabib refers to this ethical position that characterizes the domain of the concrete other as the "ethics of care." She proposes that moral positions based solely on the image of the "generalized other" are incapable of facilitating or establishing the grounds for an authentic engagement between the self and the "other," because the "other" in this view is an abstraction, or, as Benhabib describes it, a "disembedded and disembodied" being, which brackets out the "otherness" of the "other." Therefore, the principles that discourse ethics establish for the model of deliberative democracy can be valid only if they are based on the equality, dignity, and equal standing of each person, and on an open, dialogical process that promotes and facilitates the incorporation of the substantive or "concrete" otherness of the participants (171). By introducing the qualitative dimensions of personal bonds and care in the form of the "concrete other," Benhabib argues that the distinction and tension between a more formalistic "ethics of justice and right and one of care and responsibility" can be overcome (170). Again, in this formulation we find that the qualitative dimension is what enables the effectiveness of democratic pluralist membership.

While in general agreement with Benhabib's project of trying to establish and maintain a balance between the formation of individual identity and the collectivity, Nancy Fraser argues that there is a limitation that arises from the way that Benhabib construes the relationship between the qualitative dimension that underlies the discourse-based ethical position and the political sphere (Fraser 1986). Fraser notes that Benhabib's account of the "concrete other" is meant to emphasize the specificity, and provide for the affirmation, of the individual. Fraser refers to this position as the "individualized concrete other," but suggests an alternative formulation that she believes addresses the logic of political power more directly (Fraser 1986, 427). She calls this "the standpoint of the collective concrete other" and with it wants to stress the significance of group membership for understanding the connection between moral and political practice. In particular, Fraser wants to underscore the fact that the model of democratic legitimacy must be able to account for inequalities of power. These inequalities will in all likelihood be reflected in what she calls the "socio-cultural means of interpretation and communication," by which she means the vocabularies and narrative traditions and resources that are available "to individuals and groups for the construction of individual life-stories or group identities and solidarities" (428). Thus viable democratic public spheres must ensure that the discourses of the various groups have a real and meaningful space and presence. Without this, the dialogue that is supposed to be the means both for validating the discourse model of democracy and for mediating deep cultural and value differences would in fact be no dialogue at all.

Fraser argues that this emphasis on the collective dimension of democratic public space, on the "collective concrete other," requires a different sort of ethical foundation, one that reflects a different dimension of qualitative social bonds that facilitate effective participation in the public sphere. She suggests that this perspective or standpoint leads to an ethic of solidarity that "would require one to relate to people as members of collectivities or social groups with specific cultures, histories, social practices, values, habits, forms of life, vocabularies of self-interpretation and narrative traditions," and the ethical force of this orientation is that "we owe each other behavior such that each is confirmed as a being with specific collective identifications and solidarities" (Fraser 1986, 429). Thus the qualitative bonds that facilitate the emergence of effective democratic public spheres are based on networks of social practice that instantiate norms of mutual affirmation and collective solidarity. In Fraser's formulation, these bonds of social solidarity mediate between the ethic of care and the ethic of justice and rights, and therefore seem to function as the ethical domain that corresponds to the realm of civil society, and that bridges the institutional spaces of public and private relations. These are indeed modalities of reciprocity, but reciprocities of recognition and validation rather than of exchange or obligation.

This perspective is enhanced and further extended in an essay on toleration by Adeno Addis in which he argues that a distinction between negative (or paternalistic) and positive toleration must be incorporated in any analysis of marginalized communities (Addis 1997). Dominant institutions may allow the marginalized to participate within the polity, but only on its own terms, which are reflected in the fact that it is only in terms of the language, principles, values, beliefs, and narrative traditions of the majority embodied in the public institutions that legitimate public action can take place, thus in effect marginalizing the minority within the public sphere. This results in the paradoxical outcome that this form of toleration both includes and marginalizes at the same time. The public identity of the polity is in fact defined by majority culture, and so it is extremely unlikely in this situation that the minority culture can influence the "background framework within which sense is made of public deliberations about the terms and conditions of political life and institutional arrangements" (Addis 1997, 121). Addis argues that a public sphere that is based on the thin qualitative nature of social bonds under the conditions of paternalistic tolerance cannot establish any of the conditions of mutual recognition, reciprocity, solidarity, or respect that are necessary for dialogical deliberative democracy to effectively mediate the conflicts that arise from the type of deep differences that are characteristic of multicultural societies. Addis summarizes the likely consequences as follows:

> A society that acknowledges the fact of pluralism (and its normative desirability) without providing the institutional means through which the ethic of reciprocal empathy, respect, and inclusiveness are cultivated is a society which at best allows minorities to be tolerated as the marginal Other or, at worst, lays the ground for an endless and destructive conflict, where in most cases the minority will probably shoulder the greater cost. (Addis 1997, 126)

As an alternative to paternalistic toleration, Addis advances what he calls the notion of "pluralistic solidarity," a type of social bond that promotes a "partial and contingent . . . shared identity" between groups by fostering forms of communication between them that lead each to perceive and understand that their distinctiveness is "to a large degree defined in terms of its relationship with the Other" (Addis 1997, 127). This shared identity can only be created discursively through genuine dialogue that promotes an understanding of the substantive specificity of the culture of each "other". In this sense, Addis clearly accepts the deliberative model of democracy as the best approach to reconcile democracy and multiculturalism. But he makes a crucial addition to the model as typically articulated. He argues that if we are to come to understand what constitutes and defines the specificity of each "us" that coexists in these societies, then we need to get beyond the thin layer of engagement that characterizes paternalistic toleration. We need to address the process by which each "us" comes to form its image of each "other." Addis argues that it is through the institutions of the media, the law, and the educational system that the cultural imaging of each group is framed. Therefore the dialogical engagement must be situated within these institutional means by which those images of each "us" are constructed. It is only by creating institutional spaces that facilitate and foster mutual interrogation, a mode of institutional dialogue, that the process of "shared identity" or solidarity can function effectively, for it is within and through these structured spheres of interaction that we can in fact reveal who "we" are, "tell the stories about where we have been, what is important to us, how we relate to one another, and what and who the problems are, as well as possible solutions to those problems" (128). Pluralistic solidarity can only be forged through structures and processes that facilitate the telling and listening to each "other's" stories, where the exchange is framed in terms of narrative and existential categories so that the fullest dimensions of the lived experiences can be conveyed and understood. Formal requirements, procedures, and rules alone cannot promote the type of "partial and contingent" qualitative social bond that is necessary for this process to function and to establish the basis for a viable pluralistic democratic citizenship. Although Addis only does so in a schematic manner, he is thus one of the few scholars who suggest a way to think about the institutional forms that can promote this mutuality and solidarity, and in a way that links the analysis to the realm of civil society and the public sphere.

The formulations advanced by Benhabib, Fraser, and Addis are all based on the centrality of "mutuality as mutual recognition" as the necessary foundation for a democratic and just polity. I suggest that this is a fundamental modality by which the mechanisms of mutuality can be established, and as such provides an alternative to the notion of reciprocity as exchange as the primary means for doing so. These analyses provide an alternative as well to the position implicit in Putnam, Leonardi, and Nanetti's (1993) framework and those influenced by it, that the forms of social bonds that generate the social mutuality needed to facilitate democratic development are generated primarily by participation in formal voluntary associations.[9] Instead, this perspective conceives of other processes and institutional spheres, which are not only capable of generating the mutuality needed for democratic polities, but are vital to the process. It therefore leads us to a more "political" notion of civil society, one that foregrounds the process of conflict negotiation required by societies characterized by the level of racial and ethnic diversity that exists in the United States. And one that recognizes that the types of informal networks and spaces I discussed in chapter 5 are vital sites where relations of mutuality are developed in marginalized communities. From this perspective, social mutuality is seen as functioning on the basis of a different logic, a logic of recognition, where what has been constructed as "foreign" is translated into the familiar, into a form and frame of reference that has the potential to establish a bond or solidarity based on the qualitative dimensions of others, rather than on abstract constructions of them. But this recognition depends on the ability to create institutionally embedded narratives that illuminate and highlight the meaning structures of the different groups in the society. As I believe Beltrán's analysis of Latino heterogeneity implies, the goal should not be consensus, as positions such as Rawls's and Habermas's hold. The agonistic position that Beltrán, Fraser, and Addis subscribe to is based on the recognition that consensus is not likely to be realized across such great diversity, but that institutionally embedded narrative structures can at least maintain an ongoing process of continuously mutual exposure to the complex lived, quotidian realities that forge the beliefs that people hold of each "other." It provides a mechanism capable of creating the grounds for collective social solidarity that enables mutual interrogation, which can lead to the "partial and contingent" shared identity that Addis articulates. But, instead of pinning the prospect of a more democratic and just polity on the hope that individuals will join voluntary associations, this approach conceives of the generation of this form of social mutuality and solidarity as a political project to be struggled for by the creation of institutionalized public spheres to facilitate and promote a form of social and cultural engagement whose goal is explicitly that of mutual understanding of the substantive, qualitative specificity of each "other." However, adopting this approach would require the willingness to consider the real possibility that the very meaning of the concept of democracy as it has been elaborated for the last three centuries has to be transformed. My sense is that this kind of project would provide a concrete means for engaging and transforming the "common sense" that Gramsci saw as the "glue" that maintains hegemonic power. And I believe that organizing around the constellation of dimensions of associative citizenship can be a means to that end. It also addresses the dual nature of the challenge that Latino incorporation represents to both the larger society and to Latino communities. This is because the differences that have emerged among Latinos result in the same problem of incommensurability as the differences between Latino communities and the larger society. And so the model of translational politics that I have outlined here applies equally to both sets of relationships.

I believe this is consistent with the position that Alain Touraine (1997) proposed in his treatise on democracy. In summarizing his argument, Touraine states that "in the past, democracy struggled first for political freedom, and then for social justice. What struggle is it waging today? This book offers an answer: democracy's raison d'être is the recognition of the 'other'" (Touraine 1997, 190). He is not arguing that recognition alone can provide the foundation of democracy, but rather that, in the context of the diversity that now characterizes large-scale liberal democracies, mutual recognition must be one of the primary components. Nor does Touraine hold that we must abandon or minimize the need for rights and freedoms, but rather he insists that these should be construed as means to promote the mutuality that recognition both implies and requires. They are not subordinate to recognition, but are in fact constitutive of it. And this reconfiguring of democracy in terms of processes of recognition can only be achieved by the creation of institutional spaces in which the particularity of an "experience, a culture, or a memory can be reconciled with the universalism . . . of juridical and administrative organization" (191). These democratic spheres are places of "dialogue and communication" and the "politics of recognition makes possible and organizes a recomposition of the world, which must bring together that which has been separated" (191). In a position that parallels the one advanced by Addis, Touraine holds that, in this concept of democracy, "membership in the collectivity, the civic spirit, and therefore participation in collective actions and symbols must give way to as direct an encounter as possible with the other. The ability to listen and debate must replace mobilization toward a common goal" (192).[10] Touraine completes this argument with the following: "The criterion by which a democratic society is to be gauged is not the form of consensus or participation it has attained but the quality of the differences it recognizes and manages. It is the intensity and the depth of the dialogue between different personal experiences and cultures, which are so many particular and limited responses to the same general questions" (191).

In Touraine's view, the most extreme form of difference that this model of democratic engagement and recognition must confront is represented by the immigrant, whom he takes to be the "emblematic figure of modern society. An immigrant is at once integrated into the society in which he or she lives and foreign to it. The host society must recognize his or her experience and language. It must experience his or her presence, not as a threat but as the return of a part of human experience that the host society has been denied or has lost" (Touraine 1997, 191–192). Here, Touraine extends the line of argument, making mutual recognition and solidarity the centerpiece of democracy, to the conclusion that I contend is implied in its premises. It makes the eradication of the image of difference as "foreignness" the defining characteristic of democratic pluralistic citizenship. This is particularly salient for Latino politics because imagery of foreignness has been a fundamental and constitutive element of the role of Latinos in the national imaginary. What the transformational rearticulation of the meaning and purpose of democratic principles proposed by Touraine reveals are the intrinsic limitations of these constructs. The conclusion that must follow is that democratization in the context of deep diversity cannot be realized until the forms of engagement between "others" have been decoupled from the optic of difference as "foreignness." And only the type of institutional spaces that Addis articulated can provide forums of narrativity that allow for the mutual interrogation of the substantive specificity of the participants. Not until they are reconfigured in these reformulated parameters can the notions of mutual recognition and solidarity lead to the theoretical and institutional grounding of a democratic pluralistic citizenship that resonates with, and corresponds to, the fluid forms of social formations that define the contemporary world.

Finally, let me be clear that I am not arguing that the path to a more just, equitable, and inclusive system for Latinos will be achieved solely through the kind of politics of associative citizenship that I have argued for. This is not an end in itself but rather a means to an end. As my discussion of neoliberalism indicated, there are limits to what can be achieved through these kinds of inclusionary politics. Without fundamental changes in the market logic that pervades all spheres of U.S. society, the lives of marginalized communities will not change much. But there has to be a political first step in a direction different from traditional political approaches because the kind of structural change that is required is simply not, nor will it be, on the political agenda within traditional electoral politics. What I am proposing is a possible strategy that can provide an alternative basis for building the kind of counterhegemonic consciousness based on the grounded, material interests of not only Latino communities but the larger society as well. As James Cohen (2005) suggested, Latino politics can be a vehicle for societal transformation, and associative citizenship can be a crucial element of a more general set of transformational political strategies for promoting a more equal and just society.

Conclusion

THE LATTER PART OF THE BOOK HAS FOCUSED ON HOW CERTAIN TYPES OF networks of reciprocity and trust formed within the sites of Latino civil society can enable rights claims that are the basis of what I refer to as associative citizenship. This represents an alternative to existing frameworks and notions of citizenship and is intended to incorporate four dimensions that determine the level and type of social and political membership—that is, the nature and level of access to, and participation in, major societal institutions. This provides a more complete conception of Latino citizenship than other approaches and is based on T. H. Marshall's (1950) notion of citizenship as "full" membership in all of those institutions. It does so by incorporating the four factors that have had the greatest effect on the level of Latino membership and belonging in the United States: (1) the relationship between societal and political membership, (2) the pattern of inclusion and exclusion, (3) the sense of belonging, and (4) the effects of racialization.

This framework reflects my view that citizenship is not only a legal or political status, but is also a resource for a transformational politics, or a politics of empowerment, aimed at achieving the full social and political membership of Latinos. While my focus has been on developing this framework and illustrating the way that certain institutional conditions give rise to rights claims as the basis of associative citizenship, I have also emphasized that the emergence of rights claims cannot bring about social and political change without being converted into organized, collective political action. In most cases, this means having to rely on developing strategies and tactics outside the traditional boundaries of electoral politics. There are hundreds of examples of grassroots political groups and actions that were initiated in Latino communities dating back to the initial seizure of Mexican territories in what is now the U.S. Southwest. These have been organized around nearly every issue that affected their life opportunities and conditions, including health, education, voting rights, housing, and labor market access, among many others.

Although I proposed the conception of associative citizenship as a theoretical alternative, I want to conclude by once again pointing to the contemporary Latino immigrant-rights movement as an example of a form of political action that relies heavily on the types of rights claims based on associational networks that have been the focus of my argument. One of the major goals of that movement has in fact been to initiate a process of converting rights claims into effective political mobilization aimed at changing public policy. So, far from being an abstract formulation, practices and enactments of associative citizenship have been thrust into the public sphere as a strategy for challenging the various ways that large sectors of Latino communities are kept from achieving "full" societal and political membership.

The depth and scope of this movement gained national attention when within a three-month period during the spring of 2006, between 3.7 and 5 million people filled the streets in over 160 cities in forty-two states. In every region of the United States, immigrants and their allies contested the harsh anti-immigrant policies and practices that had gone on for nearly twenty years, and that culminated with Representative Sensenbrenner introducing and the House of Representatives passing HR 4437 in December 2005. While the media and much of the nation treated the mobilizations as a kind of short-term political spectacle, in fact the marches were the culmination of years of political organizing and planning involving hundreds of local and regional groups. Hometown associations, workers' organizations and unions, community-based groups, church groups, student organizations, and a host of others came together to organize the largest mass protests in the history of the United States. Participants were majority Latino, but many people from other groups joined the marches as well. And they included a wide array of backgrounds: professionals, immigrants, parents, children, grandparents, students—all became one voice demanding legislation that would finally respect the human rights of immigrants, with or without papers. While the immediate policy goal of the marches was the repeal of the Sensenbrenner bill and has since morphed into the demand for comprehensive immigration reform, the broader meaning and goal was best captured by the many placards and signs declaring that "Somos America"—"We are America." And many of the marches were labeled the "Somos Americanos" marches. This captures the fact that it was not simply the issue of legalization that was being challenged, and which brought millions into the streets. Instead this was a declaration of the demand for full membership as I have discussed it here, and is an indication that the protestors were advancing a new concept of what it means to be "an American." It was in fact about the need to expand the notion of "belonging" and citizenship to include those who have for so long been perceived and treated as lying outside the boundaries of the normative public imaginary of who is an American.

Since the marches, there has been a great deal of research and study of the various aspects of the mass mobilizations that I discussed in chapter 5 (Bada et al. 2006; Pallares and Flores-González 2010; Voss and Bloemraad 2011; Wang and Winn 2006). As I pointed out there, one of the consistent themes in these studies is that much of the discussion, debate, and interpretations that motivated people, many of whom had never participated in any form of political action, took place in the kind of institutional sites of civil society that I discussed in chapters 4 and 5. The specific themes that they discussed, listened to, and thought about were their experiences in work sites; encounters with schools, government agencies, and officials; and experiences of being slighted in encounters with non-Latinos in local parks, commercial shopping centers, restaurants, and other public spaces. There is a clear linkage between the emergence of what I call rights claims and the development of political views critical of the existing parameters that have defined citizenship and belonging in a way that has excluded them. This is what led them to join the marches.

Measured by the policy goal of comprehensive immigration reform, the marches and mass mobilizations have not yet been successful. But something more fundamental emerged from the coming together of millions of Latinos united in their views that existing notions of citizenship and belonging are incapable of incorporating Latinos as full and equal members in U.S. society. A more just, inclusive democracy in the United States cannot be realized until these are transformed—transforming citizenship—and the notion of associative citizenship I have argued for can be an element in that ongoing struggle.

Methodology

Case Studies, Life Histories, and Ethnographies

THE ORIGINAL INTENT OF THIS STUDY WAS TO FOCUS ON A SERIES OF CASE studies. However, during the initial review of the ethnographic reports, interviews, and life histories collected between 1990 and 1993, a number of issues and themes related to questions of citizenship, belonging, and democratic governance emerged as key elements in the narratives. In response, I began to link the findings with the literatures in political theory, social theory, and other disciplines that focus on the challenges of deep cultural and racial diversity in liberal democracies. Eventually I shifted the focus of the research entirely and made engagement with and critique of that literature and the advancement of the alternative notion of associative citizenship the central thrust of the investigation, drawing on the results of the fieldwork to illustrate the grounded nature of the analyses.

In the end, I abandoned a systematic review of the case studies and focused on extensive theoretical issues instead. As a result, the material in chapter 5 illustrates processes rather than provides a traditional case study. The following descriptions of the primary studies carried out between 1990 and 2008 are intended to help readers better understand the materials from which the examples provided in chapter 5 are derived.

Study 1. Restructuring and the Transformation of Latino Communities in Southeast Los Angeles, 1990–1993

This study was funded by a portion of a grant from the William and Flora Hewlett Foundation that was secured through the UCLA Chicano Studies Research Center in 1989. Our research was funded from 1990 through the end of 1993, and it included three principal faculty investigators: Richard Chabran (UCLA), Luis Rubalcava (CSU Northridge), and myself. We hired six graduate students who worked on the project for varying periods of time and whose training, which began a few months before the William and Flora Hewlett Foundation grant was available, was paid for using research funds secured primarily through small grant programs at UCLA. Our project was designed to study how the economic restructuring of the region led to the emergence of new Latino communities in the portion of the Southeast Los Angeles region once known as the Rust Belt, which includes incorporated cities such as Huntington Park, South Gate, Maywood, Bell, Bell Gardens, Vernon, and Cudahy; unincorporated areas such as Walnut Park; and parts of Los Angeles formerly designated by the Los Angeles Department of City Planning as South Central.

The project framework included three components and levels of analysis: (1) a structural analysis of the changes in the political economy of the region using economic data from the 1990 Census as well as several reports on economic development and decline in the Los Angeles area, (2) ethnographic studies of multiple sites of community activity, and (3) carrying out research on life histories of households and families. At the end of the project, a total of seventy-one life-history interviews were conducted with fifty-one Mexican and twenty other Latino families and households throughout this region. In addition to collecting these life histories, members of the research team spent more than two hundred and ten hours with different families and household members, accompanying them as they went through various aspects of their daily or weekly routines, including sharing meals; attending weddings, baptisms, funerals, dances, parties, quinceañeras; shopping at markets and commercial sites; eating at the small restaurants and food stands in the area; attending meetings of various cultural organizations, rotating credit and burial insurance organizations, the PTA, and a Latino parents' organization; and visiting hospitals and doctors' offices, as well as employment and welfare offices. Close to a third of our interviews were recorded, with the others documented in extensive field notes.

Study 2. Mapping Latino Lived Experience in Los Angeles, 1994–1998

Although the major grant for study 1 ended in December 1993, between October 1994 and the end of 1998 a modified version of the project was extended to include other sections of Los Angeles undergoing significant growth in Latino communities. While the initial team of researchers disbanded at the end of 1993, I and a number of both undergraduate and graduate students continued to carry out research based on the same framework adopted in study 1, but we focused primarily on ethnographic work and interviews with a range of subjects in different locations in the Southern California region. Ethnographic observations, interviews, and life histories were gathered over a four-year span in Southeast Los Angeles (Huntington Park, Southgate, Bell, and Vernon), and in a broad range of Latino communities in the Southern California region, including downtown Los Angeles, Venice, Gardena, Hawthorne, and Pacoima, among others. This research emphasized tracing the various strategies that individuals and households developed to negotiate the challenges of economic, political, and cultural forms of marginalization. Observations and interviews were carried out in sites that included work with a parents' group, Padres Unidos de South Gate Por Nuevas Escuelas; an informal economy network of street vendors in Huntington Park; a grammar school Latino parents' organization; soccer clubs and associations; a women's household network; and the Paramount Marketplace and Mercado del Pueblo swap meets. We also gathered thirty-one life histories from individuals who participated in these various groups and activities.

Study 3. Ethnographic Study and Interviews of Immigrant Rights Protesters, 2006–2008

I carried out this field work alone. I attended several of the pro-immigrant rallies and marches in Los Angeles in 2006–2007, and subsequently carried out interviews of approximately one and a half hours with march participants between September 2007 and July 2008. Eleven of the interviewees were members of either a Mexican or a Salvadoran hometown association. These subjects referred me to nine additional march participants who were not members of those associations. The primary focus of these interviews was to discover the extent to which social networks affected the participants' decisions to join the marches.

Notes

FOREWORD

1. Bini Adamczak, "The End of the End of History, and Why the Era of Revolutions Is Upon Us." *Popular Resistance*, July 13, 2013, http://www.popularresistance.org/the-end-of-history-and-why-the-era-of-revolutions-is-upon-us/.

INTRODUCTION

1. See, for example, Lewis (1966) on the "culture of poverty," and the critique in Leacock (1971).

2. See the assessment of this claim in Douglass (2012).

3. Although the category of exclusion has not been a key concept in the canonical tradition of political theory, there are a number of relatively recent works that make the argument that it should be. See, for example, Cole (2000), and Williams and Macedo (2005).

4. The essays in Gutiérrez (2004) provide an excellent overview of the scope of these changes.

5. This paraphrases slightly the notion of politics advanced by the noted historian of political ideas Mulford Q. Sibley (1970, 1).

6. I trace the historical development of the particular way that the concept of foreignness has been applied to Latinos in chapter 3, drawing on a small but important literature on the political valence and modes of deploying the notion of foreignness. See, in particular,

Behdad (2005), Booth (1997), Harman (1988). I have also been influenced by some works on the related notion of the "stranger." See Simmel (1950), Harman (1988), and Rundell (2004).

7. This has parallels and is suggested by the work of Paul Hirst (1994) on associative democracy, but focuses on the processes of membership and inclusion rather than Hirst's emphasis on self-regulatory processes of democracy.

8. Examples of these political forms of contestation can be found in the case studies in Alvarez, Dagnino, and Escobar (1998). The idea of prefigurative rights claims as a precursor to broader demands for citizenship is suggested by Somers (1993, 1995).

CHAPTER 1. FRAMING THE QUESTION OF CITIZENSHIP: MEMBERSHIP, EXCLUSIONARY INCLUSION, AND LATINOS IN THE NATIONAL POLITICAL IMAGINARY

1. The literature documenting the wide array of contestations is vast, but for some of the more useful and widely cited works, see Acuña (1984, 2000), Almaguer (1994), Barrera (1979), Chavez (2008), Coutin (2003), De Leon (2002), Gómez (2007), Haney-Lopez (1996), Morín (2005), G. Martinez (1997), Montejano (1987), Román (2000–01).

2. For a basic but detailed discussion of Gramsci's concept of hegemony and the role it plays in his overall theory, see Adamson (1980).

3. There is now an extensive literature on the development of new Latino communities throughout the country. For example, on the "new South," see Smith and Furuseth (2006), Odem and Lacy (2009), and Lippard and Gallagher (2011). On the expansion of Latino communities and the issues they face, see Martinez (2011), and Millard and Chapa (2004).

4. Latinos now make up a majority of California's public school students, with nearly 50.4 percent of students in the 2009–10 school year identifying themselves as Hispanic or Latino (*Los Angeles Times*, November 13, 2010).

5. See Acuña (2000) for an extensive history of the causes and consequences of these differences.

6. See Farley (1996) for a discussion of some of those changes through the 1990s. Since then, the trends he reviews regarding diversity, inequality, divisions, etc., have become even more pronounced.

7. Also see the essays in Craig Calhoun (1992) for a sense of the wide array of issues and interpretations that the idea of the public sphere has generated. It has had significant influence across many disciplines and literatures.

8. See Jean Cohen (1999a and 1999b) for another discussion that focuses on the distinction between the transformative and regulative roles of civil society.

9. The study of Latino electoral behavior is one of the mainstays of traditional approaches to Latino politics that replicate the set of assumptions that underlie mainstream studies of American politics within the field of political science. See the essays in de la Garza, DeSipio, and Leal (2010) for a representative sample of these types of studies.

10. See Kingfisher and Maskovsky (2008), and Collins et al. (2008) for discussions that focus on this linkage as being the goal of neoliberalism.

11. See the essays in Birch and Mykhnenko (2010) for a review of the characteristics and critiques of neoliberalism.

12. Fraser (2009). See especially chapters 1, 2, and 3 for applications of the framing analytic to different dimensions of political theory.

13. See Faist (2009) for a review and discussion of the various arguments on incorporation.

14. Fortunately this situation is being contested by a number of young Latina/o political theorists such as Cristina Beltrán (2010), Edwina Barvosa (2008), Anna Sampaio (2004), Inés Valdez (2012), and Diego von Vacano (2012).

15. These include Flores and Benmayor (1997), Oboler (2006), Coll (2010), Plascencia (2012). I will discuss these works in my analysis of Latino citizenship in chapter 3.

16. For a particularly insightful analysis of the more general issue of the theoretical and political dimensions that determine the parameters of the "we" that constitute and regulate which groups are included in the normative imaginary of political communities, see Balibar (2004).

17. See the following in particular for discussions of the expanding and wider-ranging literature on citizenship: Isin (2000, 2002), Isin and Turner (2002), Isin and Wood (1999), Beiner (1995a and 1995b), Shafir (1998).

18. See the essays by Walzer (1996) for a sense of how this issue has been framed by even ostensibly progressive theorists.

19. There are many works that attempt to provide an overview of the key approaches. See Faulks (2000), Delanty (2000), Heater (1990), Shafir (1998), Aleinikoff (2001), Kymlicka and Norman (2000) for representative discussions.

20. I adopt the notion of civil sphere from Alexander (2006) because it provides a reformulation of the way that civil society has been deployed in theoretical attempts to establish linkages between sites of everyday experience and the modes of democratic governance, and is better suited for the notion of associative citizenship that I will develop in later chapters. See also Alexander (1997), and Alexander and Smith (1993).

CHAPTER 2. POLITICAL THEORY AND CONSTRUCTS OF MEMBERSHIP: DIFFERENCE AND BELONGING IN LIBERAL DEMOCRACIES

1. Habermas (1998). Habermas has produced an enormous range of works in which he has developed an overall theory of society within which the model of deliberative politics dealt with here is situated. I focus only on that portion of Habermas's theory that addresses this directly.

2. For example, see the discussion by Baumeister (2000, 133–68).

3. For examples of the range of criticisms, see Blum (1994, 1998) and Bannerji (2000).

4. Although they do not focus on the theoretical dimensions of diversity as does Kymlicka, there are Latino scholars who frame the study of Latinos as an ethnic group, and who seem to have accepted the parameters of what amounts to an uncritical position that is ultimately configured around the question of assimilability rather than a recognition of the basic racialized foundation of exclusionary practices. An example of this kind of position is found in Hayes-Bautista (2004).

5. See also Walzer (1994, 1996, 1997).

6. It is important to note that Young does not attempt to develop an analysis that is valid and applicable universally. Instead, she insists that theories need to be grounded in the specific circumstances that they seek to engage and explain.

7. The political challenge of this level of diversity is explored in great detail by Beltrán (2010), who draws on particular debates in political theory not only to demonstrate the nature of these differences, but to examine the implications for democratic governance.

CHAPTER 3. RECONCEPTUALIZING CITIZENSHIP: MEMBERSHIP, BELONGING, AND THE POLITICS OF RACIALIZATION

1. In addition to the many books published during this time, the journal *Citizenship Studies* was founded in 1998 and publishes some of the most advanced discussions on a wide range of issues related to the theme. While there are many monographs and edited volumes on citizenship, I found Isin and Wood (1999) and Delanty (2000) to be particularly useful in providing an excellent overview of the many approaches that address the issues I focus on here.

2. While the debates between liberals, communitarians, and those advocating for civic republicanism are often considered passé and outmoded by some theorists, the fact is that these framings of citizenship continue to be the basis of the way that citizenship regimes are construed, adjudicated, and distributed in most liberal nation-states and thus must be engaged seriously by any efforts to move beyond their theoretical limitations. The pressures to develop new intellectual fashions as a means to career mobility within the academy often lead to the tendency to move to the next intellectual fad without prior theoretical disputes and differences being resolved.

3. For examples of approaches to citizenship that focus on the role and significance of "difference" in the political community, see Lister (1997), Werbner and Yuval-Davis (1999), and Isin and Wood (1999).

4. Isin and Wood (1999) label this approach as "radical citizenship," and Delanty (2000) describes it as "radical theories of democracy."

5. Both the research projects and the concept of citizenship developed by the group members are described in Flores and Benmayor (1997).

6. A number of feminist theorists have attempted to develop a notion of citizenship that is capable of incorporating and accounting for particularistic differences based on gender. These analyses generally attempt to demonstrate the way in which the normative construct of "who" is a citizen is based on a male-centered political imaginary. While these critiques of the traditional notions of citizenship provide a valuable corrective and alternative conceptions of political membership that is inclusive, the focus on gender does not address the configurations of racialization that affect groups like Latinos. These do, however, highlight the fact that Latinas have often been affected by gender bias in the citizen regime. Theories of intersectionality suggest that gender and race operate in conjunction with one another to produce a specific pattern of marginalization based on the particular historical experience of a group. The notion of citizenship I develop focuses on racial exclusions, but follows the example of many of the feminist works that seek to demonstrate how particularities such as gender need to be incorporated in theories of democratic citizenship that are based on addressing modes of exclusion and marginalization.

7. While I am not claiming that this is the only valid construction of citizenship, I would argue that studies of citizenship that do not address or incorporate these dimensions are incomplete.

8. These issues related to membership and cohesion are particularly evident in studies of citizenship and immigration.

9. Most scholars agree that the issue of whether citizenship regimes must of necessity define boundaries that function to include some people and exclude others is a crucial question.

10. See, for example, Yuval-Davis et al. (2006), and Yuval-Davis (2011).

11. There is a broad literature on this, but the effect of racialization has been a particular focus of the works in the LatCrit movement.

12. For example, see Held (1999) for a detailed discussion of these issues.

13. See Baumeister (2003), Orchard (2002), and Thomas (2002) for discussions of belonging in more general theoretical terms; Yuval-Davis et al. (2006) for the importance of belonging in feminist conceptions of citizenship; and Oboler (2006) for an argument that belonging must be a fundamental part of how we understand Latino citizenship.

14. There are a variety of ardent critiques of "identity politics," particularly works on race, considering it as intellectually passé, or arguing that it undermines efforts at coalition building, or that it reinforces and prolongs racial divisions and conflicts. So I should clarify that the introduction of the dimension of identity here does not signal that I intend to engage that debate or defend what are thought of as identity-politics positions. The study of Latinos and other marginalized groups cannot ignore empirical reality: the fact that identity has been at various times the basis of political mobilizations and contestations. Alcoff points out that it was not "identity" groups that formed initially and then applied political pressures, but rather quite the opposite: "But denigrated identity designations have *originated* with and been enforced by the state in U.S. history. Obviously, it is the U.S. state and U.S. courts that initially insisted on the overwhelming salience of some racial and ethnic identities, to the exclusion of rights to suffrage, education, property, marital and custody rights, immigration, and so on. Denigrated groups are trying to *reverse* that process; they are not the initiators of it" (Alcoff 2006, 231).

15. While there are many academic works that make this claim, see Huntington (2004) for a representative sample of the arguments.

16. For an excellent critique of works based on this assumption, see Gupta and Ferguson (1992).

17. For studies of citizenship that attempt to incorporate a more contextual approach, see the essays in Bauböck and Rundell (1998); Statham and Koopmans (1999); Koopmans et al. (2005).

18. For a close analysis of the central role of the processes of "othering" in the functioning of contemporary forms of citizenship, see Castles and Davidson (2000).

19. In chapter 4, I offer an alternative notion of membership that can address these various elements, and that argues that the mode and level of tolerance adhered to by society is reflective of the degree of solidarity that exists between members of a society. This relationship between solidarity and tolerance, as well as how these are incorporated and reflected in the regime of citizenship, are key elements in the reconstructed notion of societal membership I adopt.

20. For a detailed discussion of these theorists, see Baumeister (2000).

21. For a discussion of the relationship between the process of othering and citizenship, see Jelin (2003).

22. For an analysis of the relationship between ethnic and racial categories in the labeling of Latinos, see the work of Oboler (1995, 2002).

23. Similar arguments have been advanced by scholars working within a critical race theory framework. For some of the key relevant works, see Saito (1997), Malavet (2005), Gotanda (1997), Chavez (2008), Johnson (1997), Chang and Aoki (1997).

24. A volume edited by Cobas, Duany, and Feagin (2009), *How the United States Racializes Latinos: White Hegemony and Its Consequences*, presents a series of essays that examine a wide range of dimensions of the processes of racializing Latinos. The introductory chapter presents a brief but very useful overview of how the initial racializing of Mexicans took place, and argues, as I do, that this frames and continues to influence the way that both later-arriving Mexicans and other Latinos are perceived ideologically in the U.S.

25. The reference to "common sense" is meant to draw on Gramsci's formulation of how

hegemonic processes are maintained and reproduced within civil society and serve to justify and legitimize the marginalized status of subaltern (here understood as disempowered) groups.

26. There is a very large literature that documents the fundamental conflict between Latinos and the dominant society, but see the work by Acuña (2000) for one of the first sustained, detailed documentations of the nature and source of these conflicts, one which has had a great influence on Latino studies scholars.

27. See Rocco (2010) for a critique of some of the formulations and projections of "emerging" Latino political power that neglect to frame their analyses within the context of neoliberalism that has dominated politics in the U.S. since the early 1980s.

28. For a provocative and innovative analysis of the political and cultural role that the category of "foreigner" has played throughout the history of the U.S., see Honig (2001). Also see the essay by Behdad (1997) for a discussion of the relationship between immigration policies and beliefs, and the notion of the "foreigner" in the context of the U.S. Also see Behdad (2005) for a more generalized and extended analysis of the role foreignness has played in configuring the conceptions of national identity. For a discussion of the theme of foreignness as related to Mexicanos, see Weber (1973).

29. Although they do not discuss Latinos as a racialized group, Klinkner and Smith (1999) provide a useful discussion of the role of race in each period of U.S. history. And R. Smith (1997) shows in great detail the connection between racial categories and citizenship in the U.S. that provides convincing evidence of how the former has been a fundamental mechanism for controlling the nature and extent of membership for over two hundred years. For a discussion of the contemporary manifestation of this ideological framing, see Chavez (2008).

30. In addition to being a focus of the works on the racialization of Latinos already cited, it is one of the primary foci of the work being done by primarily legal scholars in Latino Critical Race Theory. For a sample of this perspective, see the essays in the symposium "Difference, Solidarity and Law: Building Latina/o Communities Through Latcrit Theory," *Chicano/a–Latino/a Law Review*, vol. 19, 1998.

31. There is an extensive literature that describes in great detail these processes by which Mexicans were marginalized in terms of both political processes and the quotidian sites of the civil sphere. For representative works, see, for example, Acuña (2000) and Montejano (1987, 1999).

32. This initial period of anti-immigrant sentiment and political mobilization is captured in Perea (1997).

CHAPTER 4. ASSOCIATIVE CITIZENSHIP: CIVIL SOCIETY, RIGHTS CLAIMS, AND EXPANDING THE PUBLIC SPHERE

1. Here I am summarizing the way that Gupta and Ferguson (1992) have characterized and delineated the issue.

2. Mutuality in the sense I am using it includes mutual recognition and mutual obligations.

3. There is obviously a difference between rights claims and citizenship. However, my analysis does assume that rights claims are what are incorporated as the basis of citizenship. Of course not all rights claims lead to citizenship status, and in fact, the former are often the basis on which struggles about citizenship status are fought.

4. For discussions tracing the historical development of civil society, see Cohen and Arato

(1992), Seligman (1992), and Chandhoke (1995). And for a critical discussion of some of the central issues raised in these analyses, see Alexander (1997).

5. For example, see the discussions in Hann and Dunn (1996). For an excellent, explicit discussion of the linkage between civil society and citizenship, see chapter 2, "Citizenship and Civil Society: Liberalism, Republicanism, and Deliberative Politics," in Roland Axtmann's analysis of democracy and citizenship in the context of globalization (Axtmann 1996). Because of limitations of space, I do not review the various issues that are contested in the extensive literature on civil society. Instead, I offer a brief grounding for the particular formulation that I have found most useful in the analysis of the new claims to citizenship.

6. I recognize that this formulation of the concept of public sphere deviates fundamentally from the discussions informed by Habermas's original analysis, and that it is subject to a range of objections and criticisms. However, while I believe it can be adequately defended, again, the limitations on the length of this essay lead me to present it simply as an assertion, with the hope that the remainder of the argument provides a general idea of the reasons for my adoption of it. See Habermas (1989a) and the discussion by Cohen and Arato (1992), particularly pages 211–31 and 241–51.

7. See, for example, the essays by Somers (1993) and McClure (1992).

8. For a critical discussion of these traditions, see Axtmann (1996).

9. These challenges have, of course, not been based on the same premises or theoretical positions. There are considerable theoretical as well as political differences between, for example, those who stress an essentialist position and those who draw upon versions of postmodernism as a means of providing alternatives to the universalism of the more traditional discourse of identity.

10. For a discussion of the notion of the public sphere I am using here, see Fraser (1990).

11. While this position is developed in several of Spivak's works, the clearest and most complete articulation is found in her well-known essay "Can the Subaltern Speak?" (Spivak 1988).

12. The relationship between postcolonial thought and subaltern studies has been the subject of much discussion and debate. My approach here does not engage that larger debate because it is not central to my primary concern, which is to see what there is in subaltern studies that can provide a productive refiguring of the theory and practice of rights in pluricultural liberal democracies.

13. For representative arguments in the critical legal studies movement, see Boyle (1992). For recent studies and assessments, see Bauman (2002) and Brown and Halley (2002).

14. A brief discussion of some of the different positions as they relate to the field of rights and law more generally can be found in Kim (1993, 49–55).

15. See Brems (1997) for a short critique and comparison between feminists and cultural relativists on human rights.

16. For an example of the strongest forms of this type of critique, see Pollis and Schwab (1979). For other critiques with variations on the main theme, see Tesón (1985), Cobbah (1987), Donnelly (1984).

17. I am here summarizing detailed discussions of these points elaborated in several different works. See in particular Nedelsky (1996), Villmoare (1991), and Schneider (1986).

CHAPTER 5. GROUNDED RIGHTS CLAIMS: CONTESTING MEMBERSHIP AND TRANSFORMING CITIZENSHIP IN LATINO URBAN COMMUNITIES

1. For a provocative and innovative analysis of the political and cultural role that the category of "foreigner" has played throughout the history of the United States, see the recent study by Honig (2001). See also the essay by Behdad (1997) for a discussion of the relationship between immigration policies and beliefs, and the notion of the "foreigner" in the context of the U.S.

2. Although they do not discuss Latinos as a racialized group, Klinkner and Smith (1999) provide a useful discussion of the role of race in each period of United States history. And R. Smith (1997) shows in great detail the connection between racial categories and citizenship in the U.S. that provides convincing evidence of how the former has been a fundamental mechanism for controlling the nature and extent of membership for over two hundred years.

3. There is also a substantial literature on African Americans that focuses on similar practices in civil society. See, for example, Harris-Lacewell (2004).

4. See Law and Wolch (1993) for an extensive and detailed analysis of the various institutional dimensions of the restructuring process, which they argue includes four major sites: economy, state, community, and household.

5. For the difference and relationship between these two sets of phenomena, see Ribeiro (1998).

6. For very detailed accounts and explanations of these transnational migrations, see Sassen (1988) and Castles and Miller (2003).

7. Please see the appendix for a description of the various studies and materials that I draw from in the rest of this chapter to illustrate the empirical grounding of the analysis I advance regarding the development of claims of associative citizenship.

8. See study 1 in the appendix for more information.

9. The report issued by the Latino Coalition for a New Los Angeles provides a comparative summary of the changing socioeconomic profiles of Anglo, Latino, Asian, and black populations in Los Angeles. See *Latinos and the Future of Los Angeles*, Latino Futures Research Group, 1993.

10. The distinction here refers to the fact that until the late 1960s, almost all of the Latino population in California was of Mexican origin. The term Latino (rather than Hispanic) is used to refer to populations whose origins are from Mexico, Central and South America, and the Spanish-speaking Caribbean. The term is unsatisfactory because of its tendency to treat a group of very different communities as a homogeneous population, but it is nevertheless the term currently used by many Chicano and Latino scholars carrying out research on these communities.

11. Critiques of theoretical formulations and the advancement of alternative framings are part of the work of political and social theorists. In most cases, these alternatives arise primarily from critical engagement with the various texts that are the focus of study. The reformulation of the conception of citizenship that I developed in chapters 3 and 4, however, was initially driven by my effort to interpret the results of a study of the changes in the profile of Latinos in several communities in Los Angeles carried out over a period of eight years. The initial goal was to understand the ongoing transformation of these communities from a primarily white working-class population to a predominantly Latino one, and how Latinos were negotiating those changes. In the course of doing so, I realized that more than demographic changes were involved, and I began to discover the very kinds of rights claims that I have discussed previously. These were not occasional or epiphenomenal practices, but instead came to be

a common theme in the views, beliefs, and experiences of many of the residents in these communities. Thus the need to interpret their significance in terms of the broader questions of membership, citizenship, and rights, and the effort to develop a model or framework for doing so.

12. On the distinction and functioning of thin and thick social networks, see the work of anthropologist Clifford Geertz (1973).

13. For an important study of the process by which immigrants reconstruct identities on a selective basis as a means of maintaining continuity with their past, see Ganguly (1992). Also see Kondo (1990) for an extremely useful analysis of the process of reconstructing identities.

14. See studies 1 and 2 in the appendix for more information.

15. See the appendix for a description of the sources of these materials.

16. See studies 1 and 2 in the appendix for more information.

17. Based on the data in *Latinos and the Future of Los Angeles* (1993).

18. My brief summary of the historical trajectory of Mexican immigration to the United States draws from several sources, but especially Marc Rosenblum (2011), Rosenblum and Brick (2011), and Glenn (2002).

19. "Demographics of Immigrants in the US Illegally: Countries of Origin, States of Residence, and Employment Data, 2000–2008," available at Immigration.ProCon.org.

20. For a sense of the range of topics and issues regarding the 2006 marches that have been studied, see the December 2008 issue of *American Behavioral Scientist*, which was devoted entirely to studies of the 2006 marches. The recent edited volume by Voss and Bloemraad (2011) includes a broader range of methodological approaches and provides excellent coverage of the significance of relational ties among the protesters. The articles in the volume by Pallares and Flores-González (2010) are organized around a different format, and while focused on the marches in Chicago, these nevertheless offer more general, valuable insights about the role that subjectivity and agency played in the mobilizations.

21. See study 3 in the appendix for more information.

22. I am using the notion of referential trust to indicate relationships where one individual relies on other individuals whom they trust to have a view regarding a situation or action based on interests similar to their own.

CHAPTER 6. CRITICAL THEORY AND THE POLITICS OF SOLIDARITY: CONTRADICTIONS, TENSIONS, AND POTENTIALITY

1. Oboler (1995). See also the critique and alternative proposed in Moya (2002).

2. One of the few efforts to address the lack of attention to this dimension can be found in the broad-ranging essays in Bayertz (1999).

3. The best known of these types of approaches can be found in several of Arendt's works, but see in particular Arendt (1958).

4. The framing of the issue of solidarity along similar lines but in the context of feminist theory can be found in Dean (1996).

5. While Hooker focuses on the case of several racialized groups in Nicaragua to illustrate the process of how these defining parameters are contested, a similar form of contestation of the prevailing conception of the "we" in the U.S. was reflected in one of the dominant themes defining the type of claims of inclusion made by many of the participants in the

immigration mobilizations that took place in 2006. Both in the marches and in the effort to construct a particular image for the larger media, the dominant theme of "Somos America" (We are America) was clearly a contestation of the defining parameters that determine the meaning of being an "American." What was being contested was the criteria that defines the "we" in "we the people," a key ideological construction in the political history of the U.S. See Walzer's argument in *What It Means to Be an American* (1996) for a sustained discussion of this theme of the political meaning and significance of the "we," but one that advances a conception of the criteria for determining political membership completely different from, and at odds with, Hooker's argument.

6. I should make clear that I am not attempting to reduce the breadth, depth, and variety of the sources, nor the range of analysis offered by Beltrán, Hooker, or Shelby, to the specific aspects I am focusing on here. Each in its own right is an innovative intervention in the field of political theory that seeks to open up and claim a space largely ignored within the works framed by the assumptions of the canonical parameters that have "defined" the field for decades. But I believe that none of the many components of their arguments and analysis are inconsistent with the positions and interpretations of them that I focus on. As I indicated earlier, I am focusing on the particular differences in the way that each analysis of the issue of solidarity is framed based on the quite different theoretical, conceptual, and discursive terrain advanced by different approaches, and how these simultaneously enable and restrict the development of their positions.

7. See Baker (2006), Cronin (2006), Muñoz et al. (2008), Muñoz and Buesa-Gómez (2010), Wolf and Fukari (2007).

8. In his analysis of the relation between borders, foreignness, and democracy, Balibar (2010) is concerned with similar issues dealing with commensurability, and suggests that the notion of "translation" more accurately gets at what is involved in the challenge of finding forms of conveying meaning structures that can effectively bridge the kinds of differences in question.

9. Cohen focuses on this emphasis on formal associations as one of the shortcomings of Putnam, Leonardi, and Nanetti's conception of "social capital."

10. The positions articulated by Touraine and Addis are clearly advancing a similar notion of the kind of qualitative bonds necessary for a viable democracy. I suggest that their positions imply a different concept of subjectivity. If by subjectivity we mean how we construe our sense of self and relation to others and to the world—then it would appear that these formulations rest on a notion of subjectivity that develops and is formed through integrating structures of narrativity, rather than free-standing notions of self, reason, or cognitive and/or affective dimensions. Instead, this narrative subjectivity consists of the process that weaves these elements together in both a diachronic and synchronic configuration that provides simultaneously for the continuity and adaptation of the subject. See Somers and Gibson (1994) for a defense of a narrative-based notion of the subject.

References

Abraham, David. 2008. "Constitutional Patriotism, Citizenship, and Belonging." *International Journal of Constitutional Law* 6: 137–52.

Ackerman, Bruce. 1994. "Political Liberalisms." *Journal of Philosophy* 91: 364–86.

Acuña, Rodolfo. 1984. *A Community under Siege: A Chronicle of Chicanos East of the Los Angeles River, 1945–1975*. Los Angeles: Chicano Studies Research Center, UCLA.

———. 2000. *Occupied America: A History of Chicanos*. New York: Longman.

Adamson, Walter L. 1980. *Hegemony and Revolution: A Study of Antonio Gramsci's Political and Cultural Theory*. Berkeley: University of California Press.

Addis, Adeno. 1997. "On Human Diversity and the Limits of Toleration." In *Ethnicity and Group Rights*, ed. Ian Shapiro and Will Kymlicka, 112–53. New York: New York University Press.

Alba, Richard. 2006. "Mexican Americans and the American Dream." *Perspectives on Politics* 4: 289–96.

Alcoff, Linda Martín. 2000. "Is Latina/o Identity a Racial Identity?" In *Hispanics/Latinos in the U.S.: Ethnicity, Race and Rights*, ed. Jorge Gracia and Pablo DeGreiff, 23–44. New York: Routledge.

———. 2003. "Latino/as, Asian Americans, and the Black-White Binary." *Journal of Ethics* 7: 5–27.

———. 2006. *Visible Identities: Race, Gender, and the Self*. New York: Oxford University Press.

———. 2007. "Comparative Race, Comparative Racisms." In *Race or Ethnicity? On Black and Latino Identity*, ed. Jorge Gracia, 170–88. New York: Cornell University Press.

———. 2008. "Mapping the Boundaries of Race, Ethnicity, and Nationality." *International Philosophical Quarterly* 48: 231–38.

———. 2009. "Latinos beyond the Binary." *Southern Journal of Philosophy* 47: 112–28.

———. 2012. "Anti-Latino Racism." In *Decolonizing Epistemologies: Latina/o Theology and Philosophy*, ed. Ada María Isasi-Díaz and Eduardo Mendieta, 107–26. New York: Fordham University Press.

Aleinikoff, T. Alexander. 1998. "Terms of Belonging: Are Models of Membership Self-Fulfilling Prophecies?" *Georgetown Immigration Law Journal* 13: 1–24.

Aleinikoff, T. Alexander, and Douglas Klusmeyer, eds. 2000. *From Migrants to Citizens: Membership in a Changing World*. Washington, DC: Carnegie Endowment for International Peace.

Aleinikoff, Thomas Alexander, and Douglas B. Klusmeyer. 2001. *Citizenship Today: Global Perspectives and Practices*. Washington, DC: Carnegie Endowment for International Peace.

Alexander, Jeffrey C. 1997. "The Paradoxes of Civil Society." *International Sociology* 12: 115–33.

———. 2006. *The Civil Sphere*. New York: Oxford University Press.

Alexander, Jeffrey C., and Philip Smith. 1993. "The Discourse of American Civil Society: A New Proposal for Cultural Studies." *Theory and Society* 22: 151–207.

Allen, James P., and Eugene Turner. 1997. *The Ethnic Quilt: Population Diversity in Southern California*. Northridge, CA: Center for Geographical Studies, California State University.

Almaguer, Tomás. 1994. *Racial Fault Lines: The Historical Origins of White Supremacy in California*. Berkeley: University of California Press.

Alvarez, Sonia E., Evelina Dagnino, and Arturo Escobar. 1998. "Introduction: The Cultural and the Political in Latin American Social Movements." In *Culture of Politics–Politics of Culture: Revisioning Latin American Social Movements*, ed. Sonia E. Alvarez, Evelina Dagnino, and Arturo Escobar, 1–29. Boulder, CO: Westview Press.

Anderson, Benedict. 1991. *Imagined Communities: Reflections on the Origin and Spread of Nationalism*. New York: Verso.

Anderson, Kay, and Affrica Taylor. 2005. "Exclusionary Politics and the Question of National Belonging: Australian Ethnicities in 'Multiscalar' Focus." *Ethnicities* 5: 460–85.

Anthias, Floya. 2002. "Where Do I Belong? Narrating Collective Identity and Translocational Positionality." *Ethnicities* 2: 491–514.

Apostolidis, Paul. 2010. *Breaks in the Chain: What Immigrant Workers Can Teach America about Democracy*. Minneapolis: University of Minnesota Press.

Arendt, Hannah. 1958. *The Human Condition*. Charles R. Walgreen Foundation Lectures. Chicago: University of Chicago Press.

Axtmann, Roland. 1996. *Liberal Democracy into the Twenty-First Century: Globalization, Integration, and the Nation-State*. Manchester, UK: Manchester University Press.

Bada, Xóchitl, Jonathan Fox, and Andrew Selee, eds. 2006. *Invisible No More: Mexican Migrant Civic Participation in the United States*. Washington, DC: Mexico Institute, Woodrow Wilson International Center for Scholars.

Baker, Mona. 2006. *Translation and Conflict: A Narrative Account*. New York: Routledge.

Balibar, Etienne. 2004. *We, the People of Europe? Reflections on Transnational Citizenship*. Princeton, NJ: Princeton University Press.

———. 2005. "Difference, Otherness, Exclusion." *Parallax* 11: 19–34.

———. 2010. "At the Borders of Citizenship: A Democracy in Translation." *European Journal of*

Social Theory 13: 315–22.

Barbalet, J. M. 1988. *Citizenship: Rights, Struggle, and Class Inequality*. Minneapolis: University of Minnesota Press.

Barber, Bernard. 1983. *The Logic and Limits of Trust*. New Brunswick, NJ: Rutgers University Press.

Barreto et al. 2009. "Mobilization, Participation, and Solidaridad: Latino Participation in the 2006 Immigration Protest Rallies." *Urban Affairs Review* 44: 736–64.

Bannerji, Himani. 2000. *The Dark Side of the Nation: Essays on Multiculturalism, Nationalism, and Gender*. Toronto: Canadian Scholars' Press.

Barrera, Mario. 1979. *Race and Class in the Southwest: A Theory of Racial Inequality*. Notre Dame, IN: University of Notre Dame Press.

Barvosa, Edwina. 2008. *Wealth of Selves: Multiple Identities, Mestiza Consciousness, and the Subject of Politics*. College Station: Texas A&M University Press.

Bauböck, Rainer, and John F. Rundell, eds. 1998. *Blurred Boundaries: Migration, Ethnicity, Citizenship*. Aldershot, UK: Ashgate.

Baum, Bruce. "The Whiteness Problem in 'Colorblind' and Multicultural Policy: A Response to Joel Olson." *Stanford Agora: an Online Journal of Legal Perspectives* 2: 29–37.

Bauman, Richard W. 2002. *Ideology and Community in the First Wave of Critical Legal Studies*. Toronto: University of Toronto Press.

Baumeister, Andrea. 2000. *Liberalism and the 'Politics of Difference'*. Edinburgh: Edinburgh University Press.

———. 2003. "Ways of Belonging: Ethnonational Minorities and Models of Differentiated Citizenship." *Ethnicities* 3: 393–416.

Bayertz, Kurt, ed. 1999. *Solidarity*. Dordrecht: Kluwer Academic Publishers.

Behdad, Ali. 1997. "Nationalism and Immigration to the United States." *Diaspora: A Journal of Transnational Studies* 6 (2): 155–78.

———. 2005. *A Forgetful Nation: On Immigration and Cultural Identity in the United States*. Durham, NC: Duke University Press.

Beiner, Ronald. 1995a. "Introduction: Why Citizenship Constitutes a Theoretical Problem in the Last Decade of the Twentieth Century." In *Theorizing Citizenship*, ed. Ronald Beiner, 1–28. Albany: State University of New York Press.

———. 1995b. *Theorizing Citizenship*. Albany: State University of New York Press.

Bellamy, Richard. 2008. "Evaluating Union Citizenship: Belonging, Rights and Participation within the EU." *Citizenship Studies* 12: 597–611.

Beltrán, Cristina. 2010. *The Trouble with Unity: Latino Politics and the Creation of Identity*. Oxford; New York: Oxford University Press.

Benhabib, Seyla. 1992. "The Generalized and the Concrete Other: The Kohlberg-Gilligan Controversy and Moral Theory." In *Situating the Self: Gender, Community, and Postmodernism in Contemporary Ethics*, ed. Seyla Benhabib, 148–77. New York: Routledge.

———. 1994. "Deliberative Rationality and Models of Democratic Legitimacy." *Constellations* 1: 26–52.

———. 1996a. "Models of Public Space: Hannah Arendt, the Liberal Tradition and Jurgen Habermas." In *Situating the Self: Gender, Community, and Postmodernism in Contemporary Ethics*, ed. Seyla Benhabib, 89–120. New York: Routledge.

———. 1996b. *Democracy and Difference: Contesting the Boundaries of the Political*. Princeton, NJ:

Princeton University Press.

Beverly, John. 1999. *Subalternity and Representation: Arguments in Cultural Theory*. Durham, NC: Duke University Press.

Bhabha, Homi K., ed. 1994. *The Location of Culture*. New York: Routledge.

———. 1995. "Cultural Diversity and Cultural Differences." In *The Post-Colonial Studies Reader*, eds. Bill Ashcroft, Gareth Griffiths and Helen Tiffin. New York: Routledge. 206–9.

Bielefeldt, Heiner. 2000. "'Western' versus 'Islamic' Human Rights Conceptions? A Critique of Cultural Essentialism in the Discussion of Human Rights." *Political Theory* 28: 90–121.

Birch, Kean, and Vlad Mykhnenko. 2010. *The Rise and Fall of Neoliberalism: The Collapse of an Economic Order*. London: Zed Books.

Bloemraad, Irene. 2006. *Becoming a Citizen: Incorporating Immigrants and Refugees in the United States and Canada*. Berkeley: University of California Press.

Bloemraad, Irene, Anna Korteweg, and Gökçe Yurdakul. 2008. "Citizenship and Immigration: Multiculturalism, Assimilation, and Challenges to the Nation-State." *Annual Review of Sociology* 34: 153–79.

Bloemraad, Irene, and Christine Trost. 2011. "It's a Family Affair: Intergenerational Mobilization in the Spring 2006 Protests." In *Rallying for Immigrant Rights: The Fight for Inclusion in 21st Century America*, eds. Kim Voss and Irene Bloemraad. Berkeley, CA: University of California Press. 180–97.

Blum, Lawrence. 1994. "Multiculturalism, Racial Justice, and Community: Reflections on Charles Taylor's 'Politics of Recognition.'" In *Defending Diversity: Contemporary Philosophical Perspectives on Pluralism and Multiculturalism*, ed. Lawrence Foster and Patricia Herzog, 175–205. Amherst: University of Massachusetts Press.

———. 1998. "Recognition, Value, and Equality: A Critique of Charles Taylor's and Nancy Fraser's Accounts of Multiculturalism." *Constellations* 5: 51–68.

———. 2007. "Three Kinds of Race-Related Solidarity." *Journal of Social Philosophy* 38: 53–72.

Bohman, James. 1995. "Public Reason and Cultural Pluralism: Political Liberalism and the Problem of Moral Conflict." *Political Theory* 23: 253–79.

———, ed. 1996. *Public Deliberation: Pluralism, Complexity and Democracy*. Cambridge, MA: MIT Press.

Booth, William James. 1997. "Foreigners, Insiders, Outsiders and the Ethics of Membership." *Review of Politics* 59: 259–92.

Boyle, James, ed. 1992. *Critical Legal Studies*. New York: New York University Press.

Brah, Avtar, and Annie E. Coombes. 2000. *Hybridity and Its Discontents: Politics, Science, Culture*. New York: Routledge.

Braithwaite, Valerie, and Margaret Levi, eds. 1998. *Trust and Governance*. New York: Russell Sage Foundation. Brems, Eva. 1997. "Enemies or Allies? Feminism and Cultural Relativism as Dissident Voices in Human Rights Discourse." *Human Rights Quarterly* 19: 136–64.

Brenner, Neil, and Nik Theodore. 2002, eds. *Spaces of Neoliberalism: Urban Restructuring in North America and Western Europe*. Malden, MA: Blackwell.

Brimelow, Peter. 1995. *Alien Nation: Common Sense about America's Immigration Disaster*. New York: Random House.

Brown, Wendy, and Janet Halley, eds. 2002. *Left Legalism/Left Critique*. Durham, NC: Duke University Press.

Brunkhorst, Hauke. 2005. *Solidarity: From Civic Friendship to a Global Legal Community*. Studies in Contemporary German Social Thought. Cambridge, MA: MIT Press.

Cabranes, José A. 1978. "Citizenship and the American Empire: Notes on the Legislative History of the United States Citizenship of Puerto Ricans." *University of Pennsylvania Law Review* 127: 391–492.

Calhoun, Cheshire. 1994. "Review of *Situating the Self: Gender, Community, and Postmodernism in Contemporary Ethics* by Seyla Benhabib." *Journal of Philosophy* 91: 426–30.

Calhoun, Craig. 1993. "Civil Society and the Public Sphere." *Public Culture* 5: 267–80.

———. 1999. "Nationalism, Political Community, and the Representation of Society: Or, Why Feeling at Home Is Not a Substitute for Public Space." *European Journal of Social Theory* 2: 217–31.

———. 2003. "'Belonging' in the Cosmopolitan Imaginary." *Ethnicities* 3: 531–68.

———, ed. 1992. *Habermas and the Public Sphere*. Cambridge, MA: MIT Press.

Carens, Joseph H. 2000. *Culture, Citizenship, and Community: A Contextual Exploration of Justice as Evenhandedness*. Oxford; New York: Oxford University Press.

Castles, Stephen, and Alastair Davidson. 2000. *Citizenship and Migration: Globalization and the Politics of Belonging*. New York: Routledge.

Castles, Stephen, and Mark J. Miller. 2003. *The Age of Migration*. New York: Guilford Press.

Chambers, Iain. 1994. *Migrancy, Culture, Identity*. New York: Routledge.

Chambers, Simone, and Jeffrey Kopstein. 2001. "Bad Civil Society." *Political Theory* 29: 837–65.

Chandhoke, Neera. 1995. *State and Civil Society: Explorations in Political Theory*. New Delhi; Thousand Oaks, CA: Sage Publications.

Chang, Robert S., and Keith Aoki. 1997. "Centering the Immigrant in the Inter/National Imagination." *California Law Review* 85: 1395–447.

Chang, Robert S., and Neil Gotanda. 2007. "Afterword: The Race Question in LatCrit Theory and Asian American Jurisprudence." *Nevada Law Journal* 7: 1012–29.

Charney, Evan. 1998. "Political Liberalism, Deliberative Democracy, and the Public Sphere." *American Political Science Review* 92: 97–110.

Chavez, Leo R. 2008. *The Latino Threat: Constructing Immigrants, Citizens, and the Nation*. Stanford, CA: Stanford University Press.

"China Trade: Deficits, Jobs, Investment and Exploitation." 2009. AFL-CIO. http://www.afl-cio/issues/jobseconomy/globaleconomy/upload/china_learnfacts.pdf.

Clarke, Susan E. 2008. "Community and Problematic Citizenship." *Political Geography* 27: 22–28.

Cobas, José A., Jorge Duany, and Joe R. Feagin. 2009. *How the United States Racializes Latinos: White Hegemony and Its Consequences*. Boulder, CO: Paradigm.

Cobbah, Josiah A. M. 1987. "African Values and the Human Rights Debate: An African Perspective." *Human Rights Quarterly* 9: 309–31.

Cohen, James. 2005. "Sociopolitical Logics and Conflicting Interpretations of 'Latinization' in the United States." In *Latinos in the World-System: Decolonization Struggles in the Twenty-First Century U.S. Empire*, ed. Ramón Grosfoguel, Nelson Maldonado-Torres, and José David Saldívar, 165–82. Boulder, CO: Paradigm.

Cohen, Jean. 1988. "Discourse Ethics and Civil Society." *Philosophy and Social Criticism* 14: 315–37.

———. 1999a. "Trust, Voluntary Association and Workable Democracy: The Contemporary American Discourse of Civil Society." In *Democracy and Trust*, ed. Mark E. Warren, 208–48.

Cambridge: Cambridge University Press.

———. 1999b. "American Civil Society Talk." In *Civil Society, Democracy, and Civic Renewal*, ed. Robert K. Fullinwider, 55–85. Lanham, MD: Rowman and Littlefield Publishers.

Cohen, Jean L., and Andrew Arato. 1992. *Civil Society and Political Theory*. Cambridge, MA: MIT Press.

Cohen, Joshua. 1989. "Deliberation and Democratic Legitimacy." In *The Good Polity: Normative Analysis of the State*, ed. Alan Hamlin and Philip Pettit, 17–34. London: Blackwell.

Cohen, Joshua, and Joel Rogers, eds. 1995. *Associations and Democracy*. New York: Verso.

Cole, Phillip. 2000. *Philosophies of Exclusion: Liberal Political Theory and Immigration*. Edinburgh: Edinburgh University Press.

Coll, Kathleen M. 2010. *Remaking Citizenship: Latina Immigrants and New American Politics*. Stanford, CA: Stanford University Press.

Collins, Jane Lou, Micaela Di Leonardo, and Brett Williams. 2008. *New Landscapes of Inequality: Neoliberalism and the Erosion of Democracy in America*. Santa Fe, NM: School for Advanced Research Press.

Cook, Karen S. 2001. *Trust in Society*. New York: Russell Sage Foundation.

Cook, Karen S., Margaret Levi, and Russell Hardin. 2009. *Whom Can We Trust? How Groups, Networks, and Institutions Make Trust Possible*. New York: Russell Sage Foundation.

Coutin, Susan Bibler. 2003. *Legalizing Moves: Salvadoran Immigrants' Struggle for U.S. Residency*. Ann Arbor: University of Michigan Press.

Cox, Kevin R., ed. 1997. *Spaces of Globalization: Reasserting the Power of the Local*. Perspectives on Economic Change. New York: Guilford Press.

Cronin, Michael. 2006. *Translation and Identity*. New York: Routledge.

Dahl, Robert Alan. 1956. *A Preface to Democratic Theory*. Chicago: University of Chicago Press.

Daly, Mary, and Hilary Silver. 2008. "Social Exclusion and Social Capital: A Comparison and Critique." *Theory and Society* 37: 537–66.

Dávila, Arlene M. 2001. *Latinos, Inc.: The Marketing and Making of a People*. Berkeley: University of California Press.

Davis, Mike. 1990. *City of Quartz*. New York: Verso.

———. 1992. "Realities of the Rebellion." *Against the Current* (July/August): 14–18.

De Genova, Nicholas, and Ana Y. Ramos-Zayas. 2003. *Latino Crossings: Mexicans, Puerto Ricans, and the Politics of Race and Citizenship*. New York: Routledge.

De León, Arnoldo. 2002. *Racial Frontiers: Africans, Chinese, and Mexicans in Western America, 1848–1890*. Albuquerque: University of New Mexico Press.

Dean, Jodi. 1996. *Solidarity of Strangers: Feminism after Identity Politics*. Berkeley: University of California Press.

Dear, Michael, ed. 1996. *Atlas of Southern California*. Vol. 1. Los Angeles: Southern California Studies Center, University of Southern California.

———, ed. 1998. *Atlas of Southern California*. Vol. 2. Los Angeles: Southern California Studies Center, University of Southern California.

Dear, Michael J., H. Eric Schokman, and Greg Hise, eds. 1996. *Rethinking Los Angeles*. Thousand Oaks, CA: Sage Publications.

de la Garza, Rodolfo O., Louis DeSipio, and David L. Leal, eds. 2010. *Beyond the Barrio: Latinos in the 2004 Election.* Notre Dame, IN: University of Notre Dame Press.

Delanty, Gerard. 2000. *Citizenship in a Global Age: Society, Culture, Politics.* Buckingham, Eng.: Open University Press.

Dhamoon, Rita. 2009. *Identity/Difference Politics: How Difference Is Produced and Why It Matters.* Vancouver: University of British Columbia Press.

"Difference, Solidarity and Law: Building Latina/o Communities Through Latcrit Theory." 1998. *Chicano/a–Latino/a Law Review* 19.

Dirlik, Arif. 1994. "The Postcolonial Aura: Third World Criticism in the Age of Global Capitalism." *Critical Inquiry* 20 (Winter): 328–56.

Donnelly, Jack. 1984. "Cultural Relativism and Universal Human Rights." *Human Rights Quarterly* 6: 400–419.

Douglass, R. Bruce. 2012. "John Rawls and the Revival of Political Philosophy: Where Does He Leave Us?" *Theoria* 59 (133): 81–97

Duany, Jorge. 2002. *The Puerto Rican Nation on the Move: Identities on the Island and in the United States.* Chapel Hill: University of North Carolina Press.

———. 2003. "Nation, Migration, Identity: The Case of Puerto Ricans." *Latino Studies* 1: 424–44.

Echeverría, Darius V. 2008. "Beyond the Black-White Binary Construction of Race: Mexican Americans, Identity Formation, and the Pursuit of Public Citizenship." *Journal of American Ethnic History* 28: 104–11.

Edwards, Bob, Michael W. Foley, and Mario Diani. 2001. *Beyond Tocqueville: Civil Society and the Social Capital Debate in Comparative Perspective.* Hanover, NH: University Press of New England.

Edwards, Michael. 2009. *Civil Society.* Malden, MA: Polity Press.

———. 2011. *The Oxford Handbook of Civil Society.* New York: Oxford University Press.

Ehrenberg, John. 1999. *Civil Society: The Critical History of an Idea.* New York: New York University Press.

Ennis, Sharon R., Merarys Ríos-Vargas, and Nora G. Albert. 2011. *The Hispanic Population: 2010.* 2010 Census Briefs. http://www.census.gov/prod/cen2010/briefs/c2010br-04.pdf.

Faist, Thomas. 2009. "Diversity—a New Mode of Incorporation?" *Ethnic and Racial Studies* 32: 171–90.

Farley, Reynolds. 1996. *The New American Reality: Who We Are, How We Got Here, Where We Are Going.* New York: Russell Sage Foundation.

Faulks, Keith. 2000. *Citizenship.* New York: Routledge.

Featherstone, Mike, Scott Lash, and Roland Robertson, ed. 1995. *Global Modernities.* Thousand Oaks, CA: Sage Publications.

Flores, Bill, and Rina Benmayor, eds. 1997. *Latino Cultural Citizenship: Claiming Identity, Space, and Rights.* Boston: Beacon Press.

Fogg-Davis, Hawley. 2003. "The Racial Retreat of Contemporary Political Theory." *Perspectives on Politics* 1: 555–64.

Foley, Douglas E. 1990. *Learning Capitalist Culture: Deep in the Heart of Tejas.* Philadelphia: University of Pennsylvania Press.

Foley, Michael W., and Bob Edwards. 1996. "The Paradox of Civil Society." *Journal of Democracy* 7: 38–52.

Foster, Lawrence, and Patricia Susan Herzog, eds. 1994. *Defending Diversity: Contemporary Philosophical Perspectives on Pluralism and Multiculturalism*. Amherst: University of Massachusetts Press.

Fox, Jonathan, and Xóchitl Bada. 2011. "Migrant Civic Engagement." In *Rallying for Immigrant Rights: The Fight for Inclusion in 21st Century America*, eds. Kim Voss and Irene Bloemraad. Berkeley, CA: University of California Press. 142–60.

Frankenberg, Ruth, and Lati Mani. 1993. "Crosscurrents, Crosstalk: Race, 'Postcoloniality' and the Politics of Location." *Cultural Studies* 7 (2): 292-310.

Fraser, Nancy. 1986. "Toward a Discourse Ethic of Solidarity." *Praxis International* 25: 425–29.

——. 1990. "Rethinking the Public Sphere." *Social Text* 25/26: 56–80.

——. 2009a. *Scales of Justice: Reimagining Political Space in a Globalizing World*. New York: Columbia University Press.

——. 2009b. "Transnationalizing the Public Sphere: On the Legitimacy and Efficacy of Public Opinion in a Post-Westphalian World." In *Scales of Justice: Reimagining Political Space in a Globalizing World*, ed. Nancy Fraser, 76–99. New York: Columbia University Press.

Friedmann, John. 1992. *Empowerment: The Politics of Alternative Development*. Cambridge, MA: Blackwell.

Fullinwider, Robert K. 1999. *Civil Society, Democracy, and Civic Renewal*. Lanham, MD: Rowman & Littlefield Publishers.

Fulton, William B. 1997. *The Reluctant Metropolis: The Politics of Urban Growth in Los Angeles*. Point Arena, CA: Solano Press Books.

Gambetta, Diego. 1988. *Trust: Making and Breaking Cooperative Relations*. New York: Basil Blackwell.

Ganguly, Keya. 1992. "Migrant Identities: Personal Memory and the Construction of Selfhood." *Cultural Studies* 6: 51–72.

Garbutt, Rob. 2009. "Social Inclusion and Local Practices of Belonging." *Cosmopolitan Civil Societies Journal* 1: 84–108.

Garcia, Soledad. 1996. "Cities and Citizenship." *International Journal of Urban and Regional Research* 20: 7–21.

García Bedolla, Lisa. 2006. "Rethinking Citizenship: Noncitizen Voting and Immigrant Political Engagement in the United States." In *Transforming Politics, Transforming America: The Political and Civic Incorporation of Immigrants in the United States*, eds. Taeku Lee, S. Karthick Ramakrishnan and Ricardo Ramírez, 51–70. Charlottesville: University of Virginia Press.

——. 2007. "Race, Social Relations, and the Study of Social Capital." In *Race, Neighborhoods, and the Misuse of Social Capital*, ed. James Jennings, 7–20. New York: Palgrave Macmillan.

Geertz, Clifford. 1973. *The Interpretation of Cultures: Selected Essays*. New York: Basic Books.

Glenn, Evelyn Nakano. 2002. *Unequal Freedom: How Race and Gender Shaped American Citizenship and Labor*. Cambridge, MA: Harvard University Press.

Goldberg, David Theo. 2002. *The Racial State*. Malden, MA: Blackwell Publishers.

Gómez, Laura E. 2007. *Manifest Destinies: The Making of the Mexican American Race*. New York: New York University.

Gooding-Williams, Robert. 1998. "Race, Multiculturalism and Democracy." *Constellations* 5: 18–41.

Gotanda, Neil. 1997. "Race, Citizenship, and the Search for Political Community among 'We the People.'" *Oregon Law Review* 76: 233–59.

Gramsci, Antonio. 1971. *Selections from the Prison Notebooks of Antonio Gramsci.* Edited and translated by Quentin Hoare and Geoffrey Nowell Smith. London: Lawrence & Wishart.

Grosfoguel, Ramon. 2003. *Colonial Subjects: Puerto Ricans in a Global Perspective.* Berkeley: University of California Press.

———. 2004. "Race and Ethnicity or Racialized Ethnicities? Identities within Global Coloniality." *Ethnicities* 4: 315–66.

Gupta, Akhil, and James Ferguson. 1992. "Beyond 'Culture': Space, Identity, and the Politics of Difference." *Cultural Anthropology* 7: 6–23.

Gutierrez, David G. 2004. "Demography and the Shifting Boundaries of 'Community': Reflections on 'U.S Latinos' and the Evolution of Latino Studies." In *The Columbia History of Latinos in the United States since 1960*, ed. David G. Gutierrez, 1–42. New York: Columbia University Press.

Habermas, Jürgen. 1989a. *The Structural Transformation of the Public Sphere: An Inquiry into a Category of Bourgeois Society.* Cambridge, MA: MIT Press.

———. 1989b. "Justice and Solidarity: On the Discussion Concerning 'Stage 6.'" *Philosophical Forum* 21: 32–52.

———. 1991. "Ethnicity: Identity and Difference." *Radical America* 23: 9–20.

———. 1995a. "Citizenship and National Identity: Some Reflections on the Future of Europe." In *Theorizing Citizenship*, ed. Ronald Beiner. Albany: State University of New York Press.

———. 1995b. "Multiculturalism and the Liberal State." *Stanford Law Review* 47: 849–53.

———. 1996. "Three Normative Models of Democracy." In *Democracy and Difference: Contesting the Boundaries of the Political*, ed. Seyla Benhabib, 21–30. Princeton, NJ: Princeton University Press.

———. 1998. *Between Facts and Norms: Contributions to a Discourse Theory of Law and Democracy.* Cambridge, MA: MIT Press.

Hall, Stuart. 1996. "When Was 'the Post-Colonial'? Thinking at the Limit." In *The Post-Colonial Question: Common Skies, Divided Horizons*, ed. Iain Chambers and Lidia Curti, 242–60. New York: Routledge.

Hamilton, Nora, and Norma Stoltz Chinchilla. 2001. *Seeking Community in a Global City: Guatemalans and Salvadorans in Los Angeles.* Philadelphia: Temple University Press.

Haney-López, Ian. 1996. *White by Law: The Legal Construction of Race.* New York: New York University Press.

Hann, Chris, and Elizabeth Dunn, eds. 1996. *Civil Society: Challenging Western Models.* New York: Routledge.

Hansen, Randall. 1999. "Migration, Citizenship and Race in Europe: Between Incorporation and Exclusion." *European Journal of Political Research* 35: 415–44.

Hardy-Fanta, Carol. 1993. *Latina Politics, Latino Politics: Gender, Culture, and Political Participation in Boston.* Philadelphia: Temple University Press.

Harris-Lacewell, Melissa Victoria. 2004. *Barbershops, Bibles, and BET: Everyday Talk and Black Political Thought.* Princeton, NJ: Princeton University Press.

Harman, Lesley D. 1988. *The Modern Stranger: On Language and Membership.* Contributions to the Sociology of Language. New York: Mouton de Gruyter.

Harvey, David. 1989. *The Condition of Postmodernity: An Enquiry into the Origins of Cultural Change.* Cambridge, MA: Blackwell.

———. 2005. *A Brief History of Neoliberalism.* New York: Oxford University Press.

Hayes-Bautista, David E. 2004. *La Nueva California: Latinos in the Golden State*. Berkeley: University of California Press.

Heater, Derek Benjamin. 1990. *Citizenship: The Civic Ideal in World History, Politics, and Education*. London: Longman.

———. 1999. *What Is Citizenship?* Cambridge, UK: Polity Press

Held, David. 1991. "Between State and Civil Society: Citizenship." In *Citizenship*, ed. Geoff Andrews, 19–25. *Citizenship*. London: Lawrence & Wishart.

———. 1999. *The Transformation of Political Community: Rethinking Democracy in the Context of Globalization*. Cambridge: Cambridge University Press.

Heredia, Luisa. 2011. "From Prayer to Protest: The Immigrant Rights Movement and the Catholic Church." In *Rallying for Immigrant Rights: The Fight for Inclusion in 21st Century America*, eds. Kim Voss and Irene Bloemraad. Berkeley, CA: University of California Press. 101–22.

Hing, Bill Ong. 2004. *Defining America through Immigration Policy*. Philadelphia: Temple University Press.

Hirschmann, Nancy J. 1992. *Rethinking Obligation: A Feminist Method for Political Theory*. Ithaca, NY: Cornell University Press.

Hirst, Paul Q. 1994. *Associative Democracy: New Forms of Economic and Social Governance*. Amherst: University of Massachusetts Press.

———. 1997. *From Statism to Pluralism: Democracy, Civil Society, and Global Politics*. London; Bristol, PA: UCL Press.

Holston, James, and Arjun Appadurai. 1996. "Cities and Citizenship." *Public Culture* 8: 187–204.

Hondagneu-Sotelo, Pierrette. 2001. *Doméstica: Immigrant Workers Cleaning and Caring in the Shadows of Affluence*. Berkeley: University of California Press.

Honig, Bonnie. 2001. *Democracy and the Foreigner*. Princeton, NJ: Princeton University Press.

Hooker, Juliet. 2009. *Race and the Politics of Solidarity*. Transgressing Boundaries. Oxford; New York: Oxford University Press.

Huntington, Samuel P. 2004. *Who Are We? The Challenges to America's National Identity*. New York: Simon & Schuster.

Hutchings, Kimberly, and Roland Dannreuther. 1999. *Cosmopolitan Citizenship*. New York: St. Martin's Press.

Isin, Engin F. 2000. *Democracy, Citizenship, and the Global City*. London; New York: Routledge.

———. 2002. *Being Political: Genealogies of Citizenship*. Minneapolis: University of Minnesota Press.

Isin, Engin F., and Bryan S. Turner. 2002. *Handbook of Citizenship Studies*. Thousand Oaks, CA: Sage Publications.

Isin, Engin F., and Patricia K. Wood. 1999. *Citizenship and Identity*. Thousand Oaks, CA: Sage Publications.

Ivekovic, Rada. 2005. "Transborder Translating." *Eurozine* 18: 1–10.

Jameson, Fredric. 1981. *The Political Unconscious: Narrative as a Socially Symbolic Act*. Ithaca, NY: Cornell University Press.

Janoski, Thomas. 1998. *Citizenship and Civil Society: A Framework of Rights and Obligations in Liberal, Traditional, and Social Democratic Regimes*. Cambridge: Cambridge University Press.

Jelin, Elizabeth. 2003. "Citizenship and Alterity: Tensions and Dilemmas." *Latin American Perspectives* 30: 309–25.

Johnson, Kevin R. 1997. "Racial Hierarchy, Asian Americans and Latinos as 'Foreigners,' and Social Change: Is Law the Way to Go?" *Oregon Law Review* 76: 347–68.

Jones-Correa, Michael. 1998. *Between Two Nations: The Political Predicament of Latinos in New York City*. Ithaca, NY: Cornell University Press.

Katz, Michael B. 2001. *The Price of Citizenship: Redefining the American Welfare State*. New York: Metropolitan Books.

Kearney, Michael. 1995. "The Local and the Global: The Anthropology of Globalization and Transnationalism." *Annual Review of Anthropology* 24: 547–65.

———. 1996. *Reconceptualizing the Peasantry: Anthropology in Global Perspective*. Critical Essays in Anthropology. Boulder, CO: Westview Press.

Kennedy, Duncan. 2002. "The Critique of Rights in Critical Legal Studies." In *Left Legalism/Left Critique*, eds. Wendy Brown and Janet Halley, 178–228. Durham, NC: Duke University Press.

Kim, Nancy. 1993. "Toward a Feminist Theory of Human Rights: Straddling the Fence between Western Imperialism and Uncritical Absolutism." *Columbia Human Rights Law Review* 36: 49–105.

King, Anthony D., ed. 1996. *Re-Presenting the City: Ethnicity, Capital, and Culture in the 21st-Century Metropolis*. New York: New York University Press.

Kingfisher, Catherine, and Jeff Maskovsky. 2008. "Introduction: The Limits of Neoliberalism." *Critique of Anthropology* 28: 115–26.

Klinkner, Philip A., and Rogers M. Smith. 1999. *The Unsteady March: The Rise and Decline of Racial Equality in America*. Chicago: University of Chicago Press.

Knox, Paul L., and Peter J. Taylor. 1995. *World Cities in a World-System*. Cambridge: Cambridge University Press.

Kondo, Dorinne K. 1990. *Crafting Selves: Power, Gender, and Discourses of Identity in a Japanese Workplace*. Chicago: University of Chicago Press.

Koopmans, Ruud, Paul Statham, Marco Giugni, and Florence Passy. 2005. *Contested Citizenship: Immigration and Cultural Diversity in Europe*. Minneapolis: University of Minnesota Press.

Kraidy, Marwan M. 2005. *Hybridity, or the Cultural Logic of Globalization*. Philadelphia: Temple University Press.

Krugman, Paul R. 2009. *The Return of Depression Economics and the Crisis of 2008*. New York: W.W. Norton.

Kuisma, Mikko. 2008. "Rights or Privileges? The Challenge of Globalization to the Values of Citizenship." *Citizenship Studies* 12: 613–27.

Ku, Agnes S. 2002. "Beyond the Paradoxical Conception of 'Civil Society without Citizenship.'" *International Sociology* 17: 529–48.

Kymlicka, Will. 1995a. *The Rights of Minority Cultures*. New York: Oxford University Press.

———. 1995b. *Multicultural Citizenship: A Liberal Theory of Minority Rights*. New York: Oxford University Press.

Kymlicka, Will, and Wayne Norman. 1995. "Return of the Citizen: A Survey of Recent Work on Citizenship Theory." In *Theorizing Citizenship*, ed. Ronald Beiner, 283–322. Albany: State University of New York Press.

Kymlicka, Will, and Wayne Norman, eds. 2000. *Citizenship in Diverse Societies*. New York: Oxford University Press.

Lamphere, Louise. 1992. *Structuring Diversity: Ethnographic Perspectives on the New Immigration*.

Chicago: University of Chicago Press.

Lavie, Smader, and Ted Swedenburg. 1996. "Between and among the Boundaries of Culture: Bridging Text and Lived Experience in the Third Timespace." *Cultural Studies* 10: 154–79.

Law, Robin M., and Jennifer R. Wolch. 1993. "Social Reproduction in the City: Restructuring in Time and Space." In *The Restless Urban Landscape*, ed. Paul L. Knox, 165–206. Englewood Cliffs, NJ: Prentice Hall.

"Latinos and the Future of Los Angeles: A Guide to the Twenty-First Century." 1993. Los Angeles: Latino Coalition for a New Los Angeles: Latino Futures Research Group.

Leacock, Eleanor Burke, ed. 1971. *The Culture of Poverty: A Critique*. New York: Simon and Schuster.

Lecours, André. 2000. "Theorizing Cultural Identities: Historical Institutionalism as a Challenge to the Culturalists." *Canadian Journal of Political Science* 33: 499–522.

Lee, Jennifer. 2005. "Who We Are: America Becoming and Becoming American." *Du Bois Review* 2: 287–302.

Leitner, Helga, Jamie Peck, and Eric S. Sheppard, eds. 2007. *Contesting Neoliberalism: Urban Frontiers*. New York: Guilford Press.

Lewis, Oscar. 1966. *La Vida: A Puerto Rican Family in the Culture of Poverty—San Juan and New York*. New York: Random House.

Lippard, Cameron D., and Charles A. Gallagher, eds. 2011. *Being Brown in Dixie: Race, Ethnicity, and Latino Immigration in the New South*. Boulder: First Forum Press.

Lister, Ruth. 1997. *Citizenship: Feminist Perspectives*. New York: New York University Press.

Lomnitz, Larissa Adler de. 1977. *Networks and Marginality: Life in a Mexican Shantytown*. New York: Academic Press.

Lowndes, Vivien. 1995. "Citizenship and Urban Politics." In *Theories of Urban Politics*, ed. David Judge, Gerry Stroker, and Harold Wolman, 160–80. Thousand Oaks, CA: Sage Publications.

MacKinnon, Catharine. 1983. "Feminism, Marxism, Method, and the State: Toward Feminist Jurisprudence." *Signs: Journal of Women, Culture, and Society* 8.

Macpherson, C. B. 1962. *The Political Theory of Possessive Individualism: Hobbes to Locke*. Oxford: Clarendon Press.

Mahler, Sarah J., and Dusan Ugrina. 2006. "Central America: Crossroads of the Americas." In *Migration Information Source*. Washington, DC: Migration Policy Institute.

Malavet, Pedro. 2005. "Afterword: Outsider Citizenships and Multidimensional Borders: The Power and Danger of Not Belonging." *Cleveland State Law Review* 52: 321ff.

Mann, Michael. 1987. "Ruling Class Strategies and Citizenship." *Sociology* 21: 339–54.

Marotta, Vince. 2000. "The Stranger and Social Theory." *Thesis Eleven* 62: 121–34.

Marshall, T. H. 1950. *Citizenship and Social Class*. Cambridge: Cambridge University Press.

Marston, S. A., and L. A. Staeheli. 1994. "Citizenship, Struggle, and Political and Economic Restructuring." *Environment and Planning A* 26: 840–48.

Martinez, George A. 1997. "The Legal Construction of Race: Mexican Americans and Whiteness." *Harvard Latino Law Review* 2: 321–47.

———. 1998. "African-Americans, Latinos, and the Construction of Race: Toward an Epistemic Coalition." *Chicano-Latino Law Review* 19: 213–22.

———. 2007. "Immigration and the Meaning of United States Citizenship: Whiteness and Assimilation." *Washburn Law Journal* 46: 335–44.

Martinez, Lisa M. 2008. "'Flowers from the Same Soil': Latino Solidarity in the Wake of the 2006 Immigrant Mobilizations." *American Behavioral Scientist* 52: 557–79.

Martinez, Rubén O., ed. 2011. *Latinos in the Midwest*. East Lansing: Michigan State University Press.

Marx, Karl. [1848] 1978. "On the Jewish Question." In *The Marx-Engels Reader*, ed. Robert Tucker, 26–46. New York: Norton and Co.

Matos Rodríguez, Félix V., and Linda C. Delgado. 1998. *Puerto Rican Women's History: New Perspectives*. Perspectives on Latin America and the Caribbean. Armonk, NY: M.E. Sharpe.

McCarthy, Thomas. 2009. *Race, Empire, and the Idea of Human Development*. New York: Cambridge University Press.

McClure, Kirstie. 1992. "On the Subject of Rights: Pluralism, Plurality and Political Identity." In *Dimensions of Radical Democracy: Pluralism, Citizenship, Community*, ed. Chantal Mouffe, 108–27. London: Verso Press.

McGrew, Anthony G. 1997. "Globalization and Territorial Democracy: An Introduction." In *The Transformation of Democracy? Globalization and Territorial Democracy*, ed. Anthony G. McGrew, 1–24. Cambridge, MA: Polity Press.

Meléndez, Edwin, and Edgardo Meléndez. 1993. "Introduction." In *Colonial Dilemma: Critical Perspectives on Contemporary Puerto Rico*, ed. Edwin Meléndez and Edgardo Meléndez, 1–16. Boston: South End Press.

Melucci, Alberto. 1989. *Nomads of the Present: Social Movements and Individual Needs in Contemporary Society*. Eds. John Keane and Paul Mier. Philadelphia: Temple University Press.

Menchaca, Martha. 2001. *Recovering History, Constructing Race: The Indian, Black, and White Roots of Mexican Americans*. Austin: University of Texas Press.

Menjívar, Cecilia. 2000. *Fragmented Ties: Salvadoran Immigrant Networks in America*. Berkeley: University of California Press.

——. 2006. "Liminal Legality: Salvadoran and Guatemalan Immigrants' Lives in the United States." *American Journal of Sociology* 111: 999–1037.

Millard, Ann V., and Jorge Chapa. 2004. *Apple Pie & Enchiladas: Latino Newcomers in the Rural Midwest*. Austin: University of Texas Press.

Mills, Charles W. 1997. *The Racial Contract*. Ithaca, NY: Cornell University Press.

Minow, Martha. 1987. "Interpreting Rights: An Essay for Robert Cover." *Yale Law Journal* 96: 1860–915.

Misztal, Barbara A. 1996. *Trust in Modern Societies: The Search for the Bases of Social Order*. Cambridge, MA: Blackwell Publishers, Inc.

Mollenkopf, John H., and Manuel Castells, eds. 1991. *Dual City: Restructuring New York*. New York: Russell Sage Foundation.

Montejano, David. 1987. *Anglos and Mexicans in the Making of Texas, 1836–1986*. Austin: University of Texas Press.

——. 1999. *Chicano Politics and Society in the Late Twentieth Century*. Austin: University of Texas Press.

Morín, José Luis. 2005. *Latino/a Rights and Justice in the United States: Perspectives and Approaches*. Durham, NC: Carolina Academic Press.

Motel, Seth, and Eileen Patten. 2013. *Statistical Portrait of Hispanics in the United States, 2011*. Washington, D.C.: Pew Hispanic Center.

Mouffe, Chantal. 1992a. "Feminism, Citizenship, and Radical Politics." In *Feminists Theorize the*

Political, ed. Judith Butler and Joan Scott, 369–84. New York: Routledge.

———. 1992b. "Democratic Citizenship and the Political Community." In *Dimensions of Radical Democracy: Pluralism, Citizenship, Community*, ed. Chantal Mouffe, 225–39. London: Verso Press.

Moya, Paula M. L. 2002. *Learning from Experience: Minority Identities, Multicultural Struggles.* Berkeley: University of California Press.

Muñoz, Micaela, and Carmen Buesa-Gómez, eds. 2010. *Translation and Cultural Identity: Selected Essays on Translation and Cross-Cultural Communication.* New Castle upon Tyne, UK: Cambridge Scholars.

Muñoz, Micaela, Carmen Buesa-Gómez, and M. Ángeles Ruiz-Moneva. 2008. *New Trends in Translation and Cultural Identity.* Newcastle upon Tyne: Cambridge Scholars Pub.

Munoz-Dardé, Véronique. 1999. "Fraternity and Justice." In *Solidarity*, ed. Kurt Bayertz, 81–97. Vol. 5. Dordrecht: Kluwer Academic Publishers.

Murguia, Edward, and Edward Telles. 1996. "Phenotype and Schooling among Mexican Americans." *Sociology of Education* 69: 276–89.

Murguia, Edward, and Tyrone Forman. 2003. "Shades of Whiteness: The Mexican American Experience in Relation to Blacks and Anglos." In *White Out: The Continuing Significance of Racism*, ed. Ashley Doane and Eduardo Bonilla-Silva, 63–80. New York: Routledge.

National Urban League. 2010. *State of Black America Report.* New York: National Urban League.

Nedelsky, Jennifer. 1996. "Reconceiving Rights as Relationship." In *Explorations in Difference: Law, Culture, and Politics*, ed. Jonathan Locke Hart and Richard W. Bauman, 67–88. Toronto: University of Toronto Press.

———. 2011. *Law's Relations: A Relational Theory of Self, Autonomy, and Law.* New York: Oxford University Press.

Nederveen Pieterse, Jan. 1995. Globalization as Hybridization." In *Global Modernities*, eds. Mike Featherston, Scott Lash, and Roland Robertson, 45–68. Thousand Oaks, CA: Sage Publications.

Nieguth, Tim. 1999. "Beyond Dichotomy: Concepts of Nation and the Distribution of Membership." *Nations and Nationalism* 5: 155–73.

Oboler, Suzanne. 1995. *Ethnic Labels, Latino Lives: Identity and the Politics of (Re)Presentation in the United States.* Minneapolis: University of Minnesota Press.

———. 2002. "The Politics of Labeling: Latino/a Cultural Identities of Self and Others." In *Transitional Latina/o Communities: Politics, Processes, and Cultures*, ed. Carlos G. Vélez-Ibañez and Anna Sampaio, 73–89. New York: Rowman and Littlefield.

———. 2006. *Latinos and Citizenship: The Dilemma of Belonging.* New York: Palgrave Macmillan.

Odem, Mary E., and Elaine Lacy. 2009. *Latino Immigrants and the Transformation of the U.S. South.* Athens: University of Georgia Press.

Omi, Michael, and Howard Winant. 1994. *Racial Formation in the United States: From the 1960s to the 1990s.* New York: Routledge.

Ong, Aihwa. 1996. "Cultural Citizenship as Subject-Making: Immigrants Negotiate Racial and Cultural Boundaries in the United States." *Current Anthropology* 37: 737–62.

———. 1999. *Flexible Citizenship: The Cultural Logics of Transnationality.* Durham, NC: Duke University Press.

Orchard, Vivienne. 2002. "Culture as Opposed to What? Cultural Belonging in the Context of

National and European Identity." *European Journal of Social Theory* 5: 419–33.

Ortega, Mariana, and Linda Alcoff. 2009. *Constructing the Nation: A Race and Nationalism Reader.* Albany: SUNY Press.

Pallares, Amalia, and Nilda Flores-González. 2010. *¡Marcha! Latino Chicago and the Immigrant Rights Movement.* Urbana: University of Illinois Press.

Parekh, Bhikhu C. 2000. *Rethinking Multiculturalism: Cultural Diversity and Political Theory.* Cambridge, MA: Harvard University Press.

Parry, Benita. 1995. "Problems in Current Theories of Colonial Discourse." In *The Post-Colonial Studies Reader*, eds. Bill Ashcroft, Gareth Griffiths, and Helen Tiffin, 36–44. New York: Routledge.

Passel, Jeffrey S., and D'Vera Cohn. 2008. *U.S. Population Projections: 2005–2050.* Washington, DC: Pew Hispanic Center.

Passel, Jeffrey S., D'Vera Cohn, and Ana Gonzalez-Barrera. 2013. *Population Decline of Unauthorized Immigrants Stalls, May Have Reversed—New Estimate: 11.7 Million in 2012.* Washington, D.C.: Pew Hispanic Center.

Passel, Jeffrey S., D'Vera Cohn, and Mark Hugo Lopez. 2011. *Hispanics Account for More than Half of Nation's Growth in Past Decade: Census 2010: 50 Million Latinos.* Washington, DC: Pew Hispanic Center.

Perea, Juan F. 1995. "Los Olvidados: On the Making of Invisible People." *New York University Law Review* 70: 965–92.

———. 1997. *Immigrants Out!: The New Nativism and the Anti-Immigrant Impulse in the United States.* Critical America. New York: New York University Press.

Pettit, Philip, ed. 1989. *The Good Polity.* London: Blackwell.

Pew Hispanic Center. 2009. "Between Two Worlds: How Young Latinos Come of Age in America." Washington, DC, December 11.

Phillips, Kevin. 2002. *Wealth and Democracy: A Political History of the American Rich.* New York: Broadway Books.

Pincetl, S. 1994. "Challenges to Citizenship: Latino Immigrants and Political Organizing in the Los Angeles Area." *Environment and Planning A* 26: 895–914.

Plascencia, Luis F. B. 2012. *Disenchanting Citizenship: Mexican Migrants and the Boundaries of Belonging.* New Brunswick, NJ: Rutgers University Press.

Pollis, A., and P. Schwab. 1979. "Human Rights: A Western Construct with Limited Applicability." In *Human Rights: Cultural and Ideological Perspectives*, ed. A. Pollis and P. Schwab, 1–18. New York: Praeger.

Putnam, Robert D. 1995. "Bowling Alone: America's Declining Social Capital." *Journal of Democracy* 6: 65–78.

———. 2000. *Bowling Alone: The Collapse and Revival of American Community.* New York: Simon & Schuster.

Putnam, Robert D., Robert Leonardi, and Raffaella Nanetti. 1993. *Making Democracy Work: Civic Traditions in Modern Italy.* Princeton, NJ: Princeton University Press.

Rawls, John. 1971. *A Theory of Justice.* Cambridge, MA: Belknap Press of Harvard University Press.

———. 1996. *Political Liberalism.* The John Dewey Essays in Philosophy. New York: Columbia University Press.

Raz, Joseph. 1990. "Facing Diversity: The Case of Epistemic Abstinence." *Philosophy and Public Affairs* 19: 3–46.

———. 1994. "Multiculturalism: A Liberal Perspective." In *Ethics in the Public Domain: Essays in the Morality of Law and Politics*, ed. Joseph Raz, 155–76. Oxford: Oxford University Press.

Rehg, William. 2007. "Solidarity and the Common Good: An Analytic Framework." *Journal of Social Philosophy* 38: 7–21.

Ribeiro, Gustavo. 1998. "Cybercultural Politics: Political Activism at a Distance in a Transnational World." In *Culture of Politics/Politics of Culture: Re-Visioning Latin American Social Movements*, ed. Sonia E. Alvarez, Evelina Dagnino, and Arturo Escobar, 325–52. Boulder, CO: Westview Press.

Roberts, Bryan R. 1995. *The Making of Citizens: Cities of Peasants Revisited*. London: Arnold Publishing.

———. 1996. "The Social Context of Citizenship in Latin America." *International Journal of Urban and Regional Research* 20: 38–65.

Robertson, Roland. 1994. "Globalisation or Glocalization?" *Journal of International Communication* 18 (2): 191–208.

Robertson, Roland. 1995. "Glocalization: Time-Space and Homogeneity-Heterogeneity." In *Global Modernities*, ed. Mike Featherstone, Scott Lash, and Roland Robertson, 25–44. London: Sage.

Rocco, Raymond A. 1990. "The Theoretical Construction of the 'Other' in Postmodernist Thought: Latinos in the New Urban Economy." *Cultural Studies* 4: 321–30.

———. 1996. "Latino Los Angeles: Reframing Boundaries/Borders." In *The City: Los Angeles and Urban Theory at the End of the Twentieth Century*, ed. Allen J. Scott and Edward W. Soja, 365–89. Berkeley: University of California Press.

———. 1997. "Citizenship, Culture, and Community: Restructuring in Southeast Los Angeles." In *Latino Cultural Citizenship: Claiming Identity, Space, and Rights*, ed. Bill Flores and Rina Benmayor, 97–123. Boston: Beacon Press.

———. 1999. "The Formation of Latino Citizenship in Southeast Los Angeles." *Citizenship Studies* 3: 253–66.

———. 2000. "Associational Rights-Claims, Civil Society and Place." In *Democracy, Citizenship, and the Global City*, ed. Engin F. Isin, 218–39. New York: Routledge.

———. 2002a. "Reframing Postmodernist Constructions of Difference: Subaltern Spaces, Power and Citizenship." In *Transnational Latina/o Communities: Politics, Processes, and Cultures*, ed. Carlos Vélez-Ibañez, Anna Sampaio, and Manolo González-Estay, 91–113. Boulder, CO: Rowland and Littlefield.

———. 2002b. "Citizenship, Civil Society, and the Latino City: Claiming Subaltern Spaces, Reframing the Public Sphere." In *Transnational Latina/o Communities: Politics, Processes, and Cultures*, ed. Carlos Vélez-Ibañez, Anna Sampaio, and Manolo González-Estay, 273–92. Boulder, CO: Rowland and Littlefield.

———. 2004. "Transforming Citizenship: Membership, Strategies of Containment, and the Public Sphere in Latino Communities." *Latino Studies* 2: 4–25.

———. 2005. "Democracy, Education, and Human Rights in the U.S. Strategies of Latino Empowerment." In *Latino Education: An Agenda for Community Action Research*, ed. Pedro Pedraza and Melissa Rivera, 425–56. Mahwah, NJ: Lawrence Erlbaum Associates.

———. 2010. "Neoliberalism and the Structuring of Latino Politics: Membership, Incorporation, and Citizenship." *NACLA: Report on the Americas* 43: 40–45.

Rodriguez, Clara E. 2000. *Changing Race: Latinos, the Census, and the History of Ethnicity in the United States*. New York: New York University Press.

Rodríguez, Havidán, Rogelio Saenz, and Cecilia Menjívar. 2008. *Latino/as in the United States Changing the Face of America*. New York; London: Springer.

Rodríguez, Néstor, and Cecilia Menjívar. 2009. "Central American Immigrants and Racialization in a Post–Civil Rights Era." In *How the United States Racializes Latinos: White Hegemony and Its Consequences*, ed. José A. Cobas, Jorge Duany, and Joe R. Feagin, 183–99. Boulder, CO: Paradigm Publishers.

Román, Ediberto. 2000–2001. "Members and Outsiders: An Examination of the Models of United States Citizenship as Well as Questions Concerning European Citizenship." *University of Miami International and Comparative Law Review* 9: 81–113.

———. 2010. *Citizenship and Its Exclusions: A Classical, Constitutional, and Critical Race Critique*. Critical America. New York: New York University Press.

Romo, Ricardo. 1983. *East Los Angeles: History of a Barrio*. Austin: University of Texas Press.

Roniger, Luis. 1994. "The Comparative Study of Clientelism and the Changing Nature of Civil Society in the Contemporary World." In *Democracy, Clientelism, and Civil Society*, ed. Luis Roniger and Ayse Gunes-Ayata, 1–18. Boulder, CO: Lynne Rienner Publishers.

Rosenblum, Nancy L. 1998. *Membership and Morals: The Personal Uses of Pluralism in America*. Princeton, NJ: Princeton University Press.

Rosenblum, Marc R. 2011. *US Immigration Policy since 9/11: Understanding the Stalemate over Comprehensive Immigration Reform*. Washington, DC: Migration Policy Institute.

Rosenblum, Marc R., and Kate Brick. 2011. *US Immigration Policy and Mexican/Central American Migration Flows: Then and Now*. Washington, DC: Migration Policy Institute.

Rosenfeld, Michel. 1994. *Constitutionalism, Identity, Difference, and Legitimacy: Theoretical Perspectives*. Durham, NC: Duke University Press.

———. 2010. *The Identity of the Constitutional Subject: Selfhood, Citizenship, Culture, and Community*. New York: Routledge.

Rowe, William, and Vivian Schelling. 1991. *Memory and Modernity: Popular Culture in Latin America*. Critical Studies in Latin American Culture. London; New York: Verso.

Roy, Ananya. 2009. "Strangely Familiar: Planning and the Worlds of Insurgence and Informality." *Planning Theory* 8: 7–11.

Rubin, Jeffrey. 1998. "The Cultural Politics of Ethnicity, Race, and Gender." In *Cultures of Politics—Politics of Culture: Re-Visioning Latin American Social Movements*, ed. Sonia E. Alvarez, Evelina Dagnino, and Arturo Escobar, 141–64. Boulder, CO: Westview Press.

Rundell, John. 2004. "Strangers, Citizens and Outsiders: Otherness, Multiculturalism and the Cosmopolitan Imaginary in Mobile Societies." *Thesis Eleven* 78: 85–101.

Sabagh, Georges, and Mehdi Bozorgmehr. 1996. "Population Change: Immigration and Ethnic Transformation." In *Ethnic Los Angeles*, ed. Roger Waldinger and Mehdi Bozorgmehr, 79–107. New York: Russell Sage Foundation.

Said, Edward W. 1978. *Orientalism*. New York: Pantheon Books.

Saito, Natsu Taylor. 1997. "Alien and Non-Alien Alike: Citizenship, 'Foreignness,' and Racial Hierarchy in American Law." *Oregon Law Review* 76: 261–345.

Saldívar, José David. 1997. *Border Matters: Remapping American Cultural Studies*. Berkeley: University of California Press.

Sampaio, Anna. 2004. "Theorizing Women of Color in a New Global Matrix." *International Feminist Journal of Politics* 6.

Sanchez, George J. 1993. *Becoming Mexican American: Ethnicity, Culture, and Identity in Chicano Los Angeles, 1900–1945*. New York: Oxford University Press.

Sassen, Saskia. 1988. *The Mobility of Labor and Capital: A Study in International Investment and Labor Flow*. Cambridge: Cambridge University Press.

———. 1992. "Why Migration?" *Report on the Americas* 26: 14–19.

———. 1994. *Cities in a World Economy*. Thousand Oaks, CA: Pine Forge Press.

———. 1996a. "Rebuilding the City: Economy, Ethnicity, and Space." In *Re-Presenting the City: Ethnicity, Capital, and Culture in the 21st Century Metropolis*, ed. Anthony King, 183–202. New York: New York University Press.

———. 1996b. "Whose City Is It? Globalization and the Formation of New Claims." *Public Culture* 8: 205–23.

———. 1996c. *Losing Control? Sovereignty in an Age of Globalization*. New York: Columbia University Press.

———. 1998. *Globalization and Its Discontents*. New York: New Press.

———. 2000. *Cities in a World Economy*. Thousand Oaks, CA: Pine Forge Press.

———. 2001. *The Global City: New York, London, Tokyo*. Princeton, NJ: Princeton University Press.

Schlesinger, Arthur M. 1998. *The Disuniting of America: Reflections on a Multicultural Society*. New York: W.W. Norton.

Schneider, E. 1986. "The Dialectic of Rights and Politics: Perspectives from the Women's Movement." *New York University Law Review* 61: 589–652.

Scholz, Sally J. 2008. *Political Solidarity*. University Park: Pennsylvania State University Press.

Scott, Allen J. 1996. "The Manufacturing Economy: Ethnic and Gender Divisions of Labor." In *Ethnic Los Angeles*, ed. Roger Waldinger and Mehdi Bozorgmehr, 215–44. New York: Russell Sage Foundation.

Scott, Allen J., and Edward W. Soja. 1996. *The City: Los Angeles and Urban Theory at the End of the Twentieth Century*. Berkeley: University of California Press.

Scott, David. 1999. *Refashioning Futures: Criticism after Postcoloniality*. Princeton, NJ: Princeton University Press.

Seligman, Adam B. 1992. *The Idea of Civil Society*. Princeton, NJ: Princeton University Press.

———. 1997. *The Problem of Trust*. Princeton, NJ: Princeton University Press.

Seshadri-Crooks, Kalpana. 2000. "At the Margins of Postcolonial Studies: Part 1." In *The Pre-Occupation of Postcolonial Studies*, ed. Fawzia Afzal-Khan and Kalpana Seshadri-Crooks, 3–23. Durham, NC: Duke University Press.

Shachar, Ayelet. 2001. *Multicultural Jurisdictions: Cultural Differences and Women's Rights*. New York: Cambridge University Press.

Shafir, Gershon. 1998. *The Citizenship Debates: A Reader*. Minneapolis: University of Minnesota Press.

Shelby, Tommie. 2005. *We Who Are Dark: The Philosophical Foundations of Black Solidarity*. Cambridge, MA: Belknap Press of Harvard University Press.

Sibley, Mulford Q. 1970. *Political Ideas and Ideologies: A History of Political Thought*. New York: Harper & Row.

Simmel, Georg. 1950. "The Stranger." In *The Sociology of Georg Simmel*, ed. Kurt H. Wolff, 404–408. Glencoe, IL: The Free Press.

———. 2009. "Racism, Identity, and Latinos: A Comment on Alcoff." *Southern Journal of Philosophy* 47: 129–36.

Shklar, Judith N. 1991. *American Citizenship: The Quest for Inclusion*. Cambridge, MA: Harvard University Press.

Singley, Catherine. 2009. "Fractures in the Foundation: The Latino Worker's Experience in an Era of Declining Job Quality." Washington, DC: National Council of La Raza.

Smith, Michael P., and Joe R. Feagin. 1987. *The Capitalist City: Global Restructuring and Community Politics*. New York: Basil Blackwell.

Smith, Rogers M. 1997. *Civic Ideals: Conflicting Visions of Citizenship in U.S. History*. New Haven, CT: Yale University Press.

Smith, Michael Peter, and Matt Bakker. 2008. *Citizenship across Borders: The Political Transnationalism of* El Migrante. Ithaca, NY: Cornell University Press.

Smith, Heather A., and Owen J. Furuseth. 2006. *Latinos in the New South: Transformations of Place*. Burlington, VT: Ashgate.

———. 2003. *Stories of Peoplehood: The Politics and Morals of Political Membership*. Cambridge; New York: Cambridge University Press.

———. 2011. *Citizenship, Borders, and Human Needs*. Philadelphia: University of Pennsylvania Press.

Soja, Edward W. 1987. "Economic Restructuring and the Internationalization of the Los Angeles Region." In *The Capitalist City: Global Restructuring and Community Politics*, ed. Michael Peter Smith and Joe R. Feagin, 178–89. New York: Basil Blackwell.

———. 1989a. *Postmodern Geographies: The Reassertion of Space in Critical Social Theory*. London; New York: Verso.

———. 1989b. "It All Comes Together in Los Angeles." In *Postmodern Geographies: The Reassertion of Space in Critical Social Theory*, ed. Edward W. Soja, 190–221. New York: Verso.

———. 1989c. "Taking Los Angeles Apart: Towards a Postmodern Geography." In *Postmodern Geographies: The Reassertion of Space in Critical Social Theory*, ed. Edward W. Soja, 222–48. New York: Verso.

———. 1996. *Thirdspace: Journeys to Los Angeles and Other Real-and-Imagined Places*. Cambridge, MA: Blackwell.

———. 2000. *Postmetropolis: Critical Studies of Cities and Regions*. Malden, MA: Blackwell.

Somers, Margaret R. 1992. "Narrativity, Narrative Identity, and Social Action: Rethinking English Working Class Formation." *Social Science History* 16: 591–630.

———. 1993. "Citizenship and the Place of Public Sphere: Law, Community, and Political Culture in the Transition to Democracy." *American Sociological Review* 58: 587–620.

———. 1995. "What's Political or Cultural about Political Culture and the Public Sphere? Toward an Historical Sociology of Concept Formation." *Sociological Theory* 13: 113–44.

———. 2008. *Genealogies of Citizenship: Markets, Statelessness, and the Right to Have Rights*. Cambridge: Cambridge University Press.

Somers, Margaret R., and Gloria D. Gibson. 1994. "Reclaiming the Epistemological 'Other': Narrative and the Social Constitution of Identity." In *Social Theory and the Politics of Identity*, ed. Craig Calhoun, 37–99. Cambridge, MA: Blackwell.

Sorkin, Michael. 1992. *Variations on a Theme Park: The New American City and the End of Public Space*. New York: Hill and Wang.

Soutphommasane, Tim. "Grounding Multicultural Citizenship: From Minority Rights to Civic

Pluralism." *Journal of Intercultural Studies* 26: 401–16.

Spinner-Halev, Jeff. 1994. *The Boundaries of Citizenship: Race, Ethnicity, and Nationality in the Liberal State*. Baltimore: Johns Hopkins University Press.

Spivak, Gayatri Chakravorty. 1988a. "Can the Subaltern Speak?" In *Marxism and the Interpretation of Culture*, ed. Cary Nelson and Larry Grossberg, 271–313. Urbana: University of Illinois Press.

———. 1988b. "Subaltern Studies: Deconstructing Historiography." In *Selected Subaltern Studies*, eds. Ranajit Guha and Gayatri Chakravorty Spivak, 3–34. New York: Oxford University Press.

Staeheli, Lynn A. 1994. "Restructuring Citizenship in Pueblo, Colorado." *Environment and Planning A* 26: 849–71.

———. 2008. "Citizenship and the Problem of Community." *Political Geography* 27: 5–21.

Statham, Paul, and Ruud Koopmans. 1999. "Challenging the Liberal Nation-State: Postnationalism, Multiculturalism, and the Collective Claims Making of Migrants and Ethnic Minorities in Britain and Germany." *American Journal of Sociology* 105: 652–96.

Stiglitz, Joseph E. 2010. *Freefall: America, Free Markets, and the Sinking of the World Economy*. New York: W.W. Norton & Co.

Suárez-Orozco, Marcelo M., and Mariela M. Páez. 2002. "Introduction: The Research Agenda." In *Latinos: Remaking America*, ed. Marcelo M. and Mariela M. Páez Suárez-Orozco, 1–37. Berkeley: University of California Press.

Swyngedouw, Erik. 1997. "Neither Global nor Local: 'Glocalization' and the Politics of Scale." In *Spaces of Globalization: Reasserting the Power of the Local*, ed. Kevin R. Cox, 137–66. New York: Guilford.

Taylor, Charles. 1994. "The Politics of Recognition." In *Multiculturalism: Examining the Politics of Recognition*, ed. Charles Taylor and Amy Gutmann, 25–73. Princeton, NJ: Princeton University Press.

Taylor, Charles, Amy Gutmann, and Charles Taylor. 1994. *Multiculturalism: Examining the Politics of Recognition*. Princeton, NJ: Princeton University Press.

Tesón, F. R. 1985. "International Human Rights and Cultural Relativism." *Virginia Journal of International Law* 25: 896ff.

Thomas, Elaine R. 2002. "Who Belongs? Competing Conceptions of Political Membership." *European Journal of Social Theory* 5: 323–49.

Torres-Saillant, Silvio. 1998. "The Tribulations of Blackness: Stages in Dominican Racial Identity." *Latin American Perspectives* 25: 126–46.

———. 2000. *Diasporic Disquisitions: Dominicanists, Transnationalism, and the Community*. New York: CUNY Dominican Studies Institute, City College of New York.

———. 2003. "Inventing the Race: Latinos and the Ethnoracial Pentagon." *Latino Studies* 1: 123–51.

Touraine, Alain. 1981. *The Voice and the Eye: An Analysis of Social Movements*. New York: Cambridge University Press.

———. 1997. *What Is Democracy?* Boulder, CO: Westview Press.

Tully, James. 1995. *Strange Multiplicity: Constitutionalism in an Age of Diversity*. Cambridge; New York: Cambridge University Press.

———. 2000. "The Challenge of Reimagining Citizenship and Belonging in Multicultural and Multinational Societies." In *The Demands of Citizenship*, ed. Catriona McKinnon and Iain Hampshere-Monk, 212–35. New York: Continuum.

Valdez, Inés. 2012. "Perpetual What? Injury, Sovereignty, and a Cosmopolitan View of Immigration."

Political Studies 60: 93–114.

Varsanyi, Monica W. 2008. "Rescaling the 'Alien,' Rescaling Personhood: Neoliberalism, Immigration, and the State." *Annals of the Association of American Geographers* 98: 877–96.

———. 2010. *Taking Local Control: Immigration Policy Activism in U.S. Cities and States.* Stanford, CA: Stanford University Press.

Vélez-Ibañez, Carlos G. 1983a. *Bonds of Mutual Trust: The Cultural Systems of Rotating Credit Associations among Urban Mexicans and Chicanos.* New Brunswick, NJ: Rutgers University Press.

———. 1983b. *Rituals of Marginality: Politics, Process, and Culture Change in Urban Central Mexico, 1969–1974.* Berkeley: University of California Press.

Villmoare, A. H. 1991. "Women, Differences, and Rights as Practices: An Interpretative Essay and Proposal." *Law and Society* 25: 385–410.

Von Vacano, Diego A. 2007. "Race and Political Theory: Lessons from Latin America." In *Race or Ethnicity? On Black and Latino Identity*, ed. Jorge Gracia, 248–66. New York: Cornell University Press.

———. 2012. *The Color of Citizenship: Race, Modernity and Latin American/Hispanic Political Thought.* New York: Oxford University Press.

Voss, Kim, and Irene Bloemraad. 2011. *Rallying for Immigrant Rights: The Fight for Inclusion in 21st Century America.* Berkeley: University of California Press.

Walker, R. B. J. 1999. "Citizenship after the Modern Subject." In *Cosmopolitan Citizenship*, ed. Kimberly Hutchings and Roland Dannreuther, 171–200. London: Macmillan Press.

Walzer, Michael. 1983. *Spheres of Justice: A Defense of Pluralism and Equality.* Oxford: M. Robertson.

———. 1994. *Thick and Thin: Moral Argument at Home and Abroad.* Notre Dame, IN: University of Notre Dame Press.

———. 1995. "The Civil Society Argument." In *Theorizing Citizenship*, ed. Ronald Beiner, 153–74. Albany: SUNY Press.

———. 1996. *What It Means to Be an American.* New York: Marsilio.

———. 1997. *On Toleration.* Castle Lectures in Ethics, Politics, and Economics. New Haven, CT: Yale University Press.

Wang, Ted, and Robert C. Winn. 2006. "Groundswell Meets Groundwork." New York and Sebastopol, CA: Four Freedoms Fund and Grantmakers Concerned with Immigrants and Refugees.

Warren, Mark. 2001. *Democracy and Association.* Princeton, NJ: Princeton University Press.

Waterston, Alisse. 2006. "Are Latinos Becoming 'White' Folk? And What That Still Says about Race in America." *Transforming Anthropology* 14: 133–50.

Weber, David J. 1973. *Foreigners in Their Native Land: Historical Roots of the Mexican Americans.* Albuquerque: University of New Mexico Press.

Welch, Susan. 1997. "An Ethic of Solidarity and Difference." In *Postmodernism, Feminism, and Cultural Politics: Redrawing Educational Boundaries*, ed. Henry A. Giroux, 83–99. Albany: State University of New York.

Werbner, Pnina, and Nira Yuval-Davis. 1999. *Women, Citizenship and Difference.* London: Zed Books.

Williams, Patricia J. 1992. *The Alchemy of Race and Rights.* Cambridge, MA: Harvard University Press.

Williams, Robert A. 1987–1988. "Taking Rights Aggressively: The Perils and Promise of Critical Legal Theory for Peoples of Color." *Law and Inequality* 5: 103–34.

Williams, Melissa S., and Stephen Macedo, eds. 2005. *Political Exclusion and Domination.* New

York: New York University Press.

Wolf, Michaela, and Alexandra Fukari. 2007. *Constructing a Sociology of Translation*. Benjamins Translation Library. Amsterdam; Philadelphia: J. Benjamins Pub. Co.

Young, Iris Marion. 1990. *Justice and the Politics of Difference*. Princeton, NJ: Princeton University Press.

———. 1999. "State, Civil Society, and Social Justice." In *Democracy's Value*, ed. Ian Shapiro and Casiano Hacker-Calderon, 141–62. Cambridge: Cambridge University Press.

———. 2000a. *Inclusion and Democracy*. New York: Oxford University Press.

———. 2000b. "Structure, Difference, and Hispanic/Latino Claims of Justice." In *Hispanics/Latinos in the United States: Ethnicity, Race, and Rights*, ed. Jorge J. E. Garcia and Pablo De Greiff. New York: Routledge.

Yuval-Davis, Nira. 2011. *The Politics of Belonging: Intersectional Contestations*. London: Sage.

Yuval-Davis, Nira, Kalpana Kannabiran, and Ulrike Vieten. 2006. *The Situated Politics of Belonging*. Sage Studies in International Sociology 55. Thousand Oaks, CA: Sage.

Index